WOMEN AND AGING

This multidisciplinary book expands our understanding of women as they age by assuming continuity and interdependence, rather than opposition and contradiction, between biological and environmental forces. The author documents and interprets evidence that challenges traditional assumptions that aging is necessarily associated with intellectual deterioration, depression, physical disability, and social disengagement. Physical competence, social skills and economic independence are highlighted as determinants of well-being and life satisfaction in aging women. The combined effects of sexism and ageism are viewed as impeding the development of women through middle and old age.

The author argues that the variety of factors in Western societies create lifestyles, expectations, and roles that place women at risk. And menopause, as one of eight chapters, is "put in its place" as a salient but not terribly important process in the lives of women.

This unique and accessible book serves as a useful and provocative summary of the scholarly work on women for students of aging and suggests new manners of conceptualizing and facilitating new lives for aging women.

Linda R. Gannon is Professor in the Department of Psychology and the School of Medicine at Southern Illinois University and has contributed numerous research articles in the areas of behavioral medicine, women's health and the psychology of women.

WOMEN AND PSYCHOLOGY
Series editor: Jane Ussher
Department of Psychology, University College London

This series brings together current theory and research on women and psychology. Drawing on scholarship from a number of different areas of psychology, it bridges the gap between abstract research and the reality of women's lives by integrating theory and practice, research and policy.

Each book addresses a "cutting edge" issue of research, covering such topics as postnatal depression, eating disorders, theories and methodologies.

The series provides accessible and concise accounts of key issues in the study of women and psychology, and clearly demonstrates the centrality of psychology to debates within women's studies or feminism.

The Series Editor would be pleased to discuss proposals for new books in the series.

Other titles in this series:

THIN WOMAN
Helen Malson

THE MENSTRUAL CYCLE
Anne E. Walker

POST-NATAL DEPRESSION
Paula Nicolson

RE-THINKING ABORTION
Mary Boyle

BEING MARRIED, DOING GENDER
Caroline Dryden

WOMEN AND AGING

Transcending the myths

Linda R. Gannon

London and New York

First published 1999
by Routledge
11 New Fetter Lane, London EC4P 4EE

Simultaneously published in the USA and Canada
by Routledge
29 West 35th Street, New York, NY 10001

Typeset in Baskerville by Routledge
Printed and bound in Great Britain by MPG Books Ltd, Bodmin

British Library Cataloguing in Publication Data
A catalogue record for this book is available from the British Library

Library of Congress Cataloging in Publication Data
Gannon, Linda.
Women and aging: transcending the myths / Linda R. Gannon
(Women and psychology)
Includes bibliographical references and index.
1. Aged women – United States – Psychology. 2. Aged women – United States –
Physiology. 3. Sexism – United States. 4. Ageism – United States.
I. Title. II. Series.
HQ1064.U5G35   1999
305.26–dc21   98–35617

ISBN 0–415–16909–7 (hbk)
ISBN 0–415–16910–0 (pbk)

This book is dedicated to the memory of
IVANELLE ORR ZEUNERT
1907–94

CONTENTS

PREFACE

What determines health and happiness for an 80-year old woman? With unprecedented numbers of people approaching old age in Western societies, many have provided answers to this question: the quality of her medical care, how much she exercises, the nutritional value of the food she eats, her genetic make-up, her medication regimen. These responses can be roughly categorized as biological versus environmental or, more traditionally, as nature versus nurture. Most individuals are acquainted with the "nature–nurture" controversy: are behaviors, personalities, intelligence, emotions, professions, performance, and health a consequence of "nature" (genes, hormones, biology) or a consequence of "nurture" (learning, socialization, culture, physical environment, trauma, nutrition, material resources)? Feminists have addressed this question because the dominant viewpoint in Western cultures is that men are determined by nurture, whereas women are determined by nature – a theory of convenience which acts to perpetuate the oppression of women. Thus, men create their lives through study and effort, whereas women reproduce "as nature intended"; men's job performance is dependent on wisdom and motivation, whereas women's job performance is influenced by the raging hormones associated with their menstrual cycle, pregnancy, or menopause. Not surprisingly, nature–nurture solutions tend to parallel political trends so that conservatism tends to be associated with an emphasis on "nature" (e.g., the biological differences among races preclude true equality), whereas liberalism tends to be associated with an emphasis on "nurture" (e.g., persons of all races may succeed equally if their environment is comparable).

Evolutionary theory of the nineteenth century forged the beginnings of the current nature–nurture controversy. Darwin viewed the organism and the environment as independent – as completely separate spheres of influence – and, in this way, created a dualism in which nature and nurture are incompatible and opposing forces. Among scholars who have crossed disciplinary boundaries and whose thinking is minimally constrained by ideology, there no longer seems a rational escape from the conclusion that nature and nurture are interdependent. Yet, the dualism persists and is a continuing point of contention. Scientists have attempted to resolve this issue by examining organisms prior to exposure to the environment in order to get a "pure" assessment of the nature component but, even at birth, tests of intelligence and performance are influenced by the fetal environment and the fetal environment is influenced by the maternal environment and so forth. The relative balance of nature and nurture forces most likely varies with culture, species, and age. One could speculate that as humans age in Western cultures, biology and genes become relatively less important as the combined influences of pollution, diet, activity level, substance abuse, and access to quality health care accumulate over time. My perspective, and that of this book, is that nurture and nature are essentially interdependent, interactive, synergistic, and inseparable – progress lies in understanding their combined forces.

The nature–nurture conflict is but one example of the uneasy and troubled alliance between feminism and science. Feminists have sought various ways of resolving the inherent contradictions: some have dismissed science as fatally misogynistic, others have limited their view to science by feminists. Both are productive solutions. Yet, there is no one answer to this dilemma and, in this book, I have chosen a third path – to analyze, integrate, and discuss scientific methodologies and outcomes within an overtly feminist context while recognizing and making explicit the considerable limitations and potential for harm to women. Ideally, the problem of reconciling feminism and science will resolve as both scientists and the public recognize and acknowledge the subjective nature of the scientific endeavor and incorporate this knowledge into the doing and using of science.

Although trained in psychology and physiology, the more I studied, wrote, taught, and listened, the more convinced I became that the boundaries between disciplines are arbitrary, artificial, and unnecessarily restrictive. This is nowhere more obvious than at the intersection of women, aging, and well-being. To illustrate, depression is assumed to be the purview of psychologists. None the less, a truly adequate study of depression in mid- and old-age women requires cooperation among psychologists, sociologists, anthropologists, and biologists: the best predictor of depression in elderly women is physical health and functional capacity; the depth of depression is influenced by the quality of the social environment; lifelong habits and environmental stimuli determine the pattern of mood-related neurotransmitters; and the culture-specific socialization of women shapes the skills required to navigate the challenges of aging. A single individual cannot have expertise in all disciplines, rendering all attempts, including this one, necessarily limited. None the less, a partial, if incomplete, synthesis of diverse paradigms offers greater potential for growth and development than a resolution of conflicts and contradictions through reductionism.

Readers will no doubt wonder why I have selected certain topics, neglected others and why I have chosen to explore some in depth and others more superficially. To a large extent, the specific topics and extent of detail grew from the available information. My initial intention was to place more-or-less equal emphasis on physical and psychological well-being but, as the book took shape, these distinctions blurred. The strong interdependence that emerged between physical and psychological well-being is, perhaps, particularly evident in Western cultures where life expectancy has been greatly extended and in which independence and control are revered. In this context, disability and deterioration prior to death are probable and, as these conditions threaten independence, they are likely to create psychological distress. Of the many physical afflictions common in elderly women, I have focused on osteoporosis and cardiovascular disorders because risk factors for these disorders exacerbate with natural aging. Misogyny may partially inform the conceptualization and treatment of these disorders in women, and many cultural, social, political, and psychological factors in Western cultures create lifelong lifestyles that place women at risk. Breast, ovarian, and uterine cancers are obvious omissions but this information is widely available at all levels of readership – from popular to scholarly.

In the last several decades, the medical profession has "medicalized menopause." As a consequence of the medical obsession, as well as the subsequent attention by the mass media, menopause has become almost synonymous with aging in women: today, women are referred to as "postmenopausal" rather than as "75 years old." One of my goals in writing this book is to "put menopause in its place" by presenting it as one of many biological, psychological, social, and cultural changes that accompany middle and old age. In spite of this plan, I have devoted more space and energy to menopause than its importance warrants since I felt obligated to not only address what menopause is, but also to explain what menopause isn't. In this book, menopause refers, unless otherwise stated, to natural menopause. I have not specifically addressed, described, or discussed in detail surgical or early menopause since both are essentially atypical experiences.

A few comments on language are in order. I have used the term "patriarchy" rather loosely. Lorber (1994) defines patriarchy as "simultaneously the process, structure, and ideology of women's subordination" (p. 3). I have used the term to mean "simultaneously the process, structure, and ideology of subordination." It is, I believe, various manifestations of the same ideology that oppress women, lesbians and gays, racial and ethnic minorities, other species, and the environment. The outcomes, consequences, and tragedies of oppression take different forms but the motivation of those who oppress is similar. Patriarchy is a way of life dictated by deriving self-esteem and self-confidence through control and dominance over other people, other species, and material resources.

The medical terms commonly used to describe the surgical removal of the ovaries are oophorectomy and surgical menopause, whereas the term used to describe the surgical removal of the testicles is castration. Yet, the actual definition of castration is the removal of the ovaries or the testicles. I believe that the motivation behind the use of euphemisms when referring to castration in women is to desensitize women to the seriousness of the procedure and, therefore, to render women more likely to acquiesce to a medical recommendation for the procedure. Since women's reproductive systems are (often incorrectly) assumed to be the cause of numerous physical and psychological problems, women are frequently encouraged by physicians, particularly in the United States, to have healthy ovaries removed. This has resulted in a large number of women who have been deprived of healthy, functioning organs because the patriarchal medical establishment considers the ovaries of middle-aged women to be "useless." A similar argument is not applied to the removal of testicles in men. In fact, castration in both women and men is associated with adverse health consequences. In spite of tradition, I have used the term "castration" to refer to removal of the ovaries. I have done this with considerable hesitation since I fear further stigmatizing those women who have been victimized; yet, I have done so intentionally in order to emphasize the grave and vital consequences of this procedure that has been sold to the public as trivial and inconsequential.

Hormone replacement therapy or HRT has been advertised as sort of a miracle drug to combat all the ill-effects of aging. The use of the term "replacement" implies that the drug is replacing an essential substance that has been lost. Only within the theoretical context of menopause being a deficiency disease is the concept of replacement a logical one. I do not believe that natural menopause constitutes any sort of disease or illness; I do believe that the diminished levels of estrogen and progesterone that accompany natural menopause are endocrinologically appropriate and healthy in a woman's reproductive development. In this context, the term "replacement" is a misnomer and, instead, I have used the term "hormone therapy."

A limitation of this book is that it is, as are all endeavors, culture-bound – my perspective and vision are limited by my education and experiences and by the scholarly information available to me. Although I have utilized information, publications, and research from other cultures when possible, the United States and the United Kingdom are the primary sources. The role of women and the experience of aging vary dramatically around the world, and the information presented here will not necessarily generalize to other cultures. Yet, some experiences are universally shared: oppression based on sexism, ageism, racism, homophobia, and/or classism compromise the physical and psychological well-being of people in every country and culture. However, the targets, expressions, and consequences of oppression vary as does the most effective resistance.

The purpose of this book, then, is to bring a feminist analysis to the documentation of current knowledge and to the synthesis of scholarship grounded in diverse but related disciplines in the physical and social sciences on the psychological and physical well-being of middle-aged and elderly women.

This book has taken several years to research and write but is truly the outcome of a lifetime. I became a feminist and a psychologist at about the same time, in the early 1970s, and, since then, have tried to live and work as both. As a feminist, I readily admit the impossibility of an individual producing anything of value in isolation. Thus, this book is the product of a lifetime of formal and informal learning as a student, teacher, supervisor, friend, and colleague.

I would like to thank the following individuals – some for reading and commenting on early drafts of various chapters, some for providing that rare combination of intellectual stimulation and emotional support, others for being wonderful friends and family: Vicki Andersen, Precilla Choi, Blair Gannon, Stephen Haynes, Tracy Luchetta, Kim Zeunert Mattison, George Moskos, Lynn Otterson, Lynn Pardie, JoAnn Pitz, Elizabeth Reichert, Kelly Rhodes, Lana Starnes, Jill Stevens, Marie Sweeney, Kim Herron Titus, Jane Ussher, Alan Vaux, Barbara Yanico, and Dennis Zeunert. And, for the pure pleasure of their company, I thank Andy, Emma, Sadie, Clementine, Hester, Thoby, Merlin, and Jackson.

1

INTRODUCTION

One is not born, but rather becomes, a woman;…it is civilization as a whole that produces this creature…which is described as feminine.

(de Beauvoir, 1953, p. 267)

Women's biological, psychological, and social development across the life span is compromised by cultural, political, and economic factors creating long-long lifestyles, habits, expectations, and roles that place women at risk. The first step in reducing the risk is to understand it. My goal is to promote understanding of the physical and psychological well-being of women as they age. Many of the common concerns in middle-aged and elderly women (e.g., cardiovascular disorders, sexuality) are at the nexus of scholarly tensions between explanatory models emphasizing normal aging versus disease and nature versus nurture. These concerns also continue to be targets of scientific sexism in research and treatment. In a feminist context, the traditional assumptions that aging is necessarily associated with intellectual deterioration, depression, physical disability, and social disengagement are challenged. Social skills and support, control over one's life, and social and economic roles are emphasized as major determinants of psychological well-being. Physical well-being is discussed in the context of diet, exercise, substance abuse, and obesity. Even the common separation of psychological and physical well-being, while convenient, is restrictive in that the strongest predictor of psychological well-being in aged women is physical health. While many seek solutions and answers within a medical paradigm, feminist scholarship invalidates this route by elaborating the essential synergism of nurture and nature. Appreciating the complexities of women as they age in Western society and facilitating healthy development requires assuming continuity and interdependence, rather than opposition and contradiction, between biological and environmental forces. Indeed, with age, biology becomes relatively less important as the combined influences of pollution, trauma, sexism, ageism, poverty and access to quality health care accumulate over a lifetime.

In the last several decades, science has been inundated with criticisms aimed at questioning the legitimacy of the essential underlying principles of the

1

endeavor. Critics from a wide variety of disciplines and professing an even wider variety of ideologies have challenged priorities, funding sources, assumptions, methodologies, interpretations, goals, applications, and ethics of scientific research. Postmodernists, social constructionists, and deconstructionists have created an atmosphere of intellectual challenge as well as considerable professional insecurity and defensiveness. A dominant force in this search for valid, useful and humane theory and practice has been and continues to be feminism. A crucial contribution of feminism to the revolution in the physical and social sciences has been to provide critique based on an examination of the ideological underpinnings of theory, methodology, and interpretation – to demand acknowledgment of the fact and the meaning of the social, political, financial, and personal context within which research is embedded. In all respects, the ideology and practice of feminism is the basic context and motivation of this book.

In the following chapters, I have attempted to gather together information from a variety of sources and disciplines and to offer interpretation, synthesis and resolution of contradictions from a feminist perspective. There were several themes that repeatedly emerged from the integration of feminism and science in the study of aging women. The first is androcentrism: an ideology in which males are recognized as the "standard" or "norm" of a species and females are acknowledged only as "different" or "other." The second is biological reductionism. This is the conversion of biology to ideology – the goal being the legitimization of ideology by appealing to biology. And the third is the dualism that has traditionally guided scientific thought and has transformed our conception of nature from one of continuity to one of antagonistic opposites. These themes are basic and salient to the discussions in the following chapters and are elaborated here.

ANDROCENTRISM: WOMEN AS OTHER

Charlotte Perkins Gilman may have been the first feminist to write of androcentrism. In her book, *The Man Made World or Our Androcentric Culture* (1911 [1970]), Gilman provides various descriptions of androcentrism:

> The man was accepted as the race type without one dissentient voice: and the woman – a strange, diverse creature, quite disharmonious in the accepted scheme of things – was excused and explained only as a female. (p. 18)

> She has held always the place of a preposition in relation to man. She has been considered above him or below him, before him, behind him, beside him, a wholly relative existence. (p. 20)

That one sex should have monopolized all human activities, called them "man's work," and managed them as such, is what is meant by the phrase "Androcentric Culture." (p. 25)

While Gilman provides a definition of androcentrism, MacKinnon (1987) describes the everyday implications of an androcentric culture:

Men's physiology defines most sports, their needs define auto and health insurance coverage, their socially designed biographies define workplace expectations and successful career patterns, their perspectives and concerns define quality in scholarship, their experiences and obsessions define merit, their objectification of their life defines art, their military service defines citizenship, their presence defines family, their inability to get along with each other – their wars and rulerships – defines history, their image defines god, and their genitals define sex.

(MacKinnon, 1987, p. 36)

And Bem (1993) describes the political implications:

although males and females differ from one another in many biological and historical characteristics, what is ultimately responsible for every aspect of female inequality, from the wage gap to the rape rate, is not male–female difference but a social world so organized from a male perspective that men's special needs are automatically taken care of while women's special needs are either treated as special cases or left unmet. (p. 183)

Thus, the ideology of androcentrism is the basis for a culture in which men's bodies, feelings, activities, behaviors, interests, desires, and occupations are taken as "the point of reference"; women are ignored or characterized as deviant. In some cultures, the "standard" human is further limited to those men who are White, heterosexual, and middle- or upper-class.

Not surprisingly, those who are the "standard" human are those with the power and authority to define what is normal for others, and those who are powerless are "normal" when they comply with their second-class citizenship. Women, ethnic and racial minorities, and gays and lesbians are normal only if they behave in a manner that reinforces the primacy of those in power. Thus, subservient roles and biologically defined roles are deemed "normal" for women and minorities; striving to become heterosexual or acknowledging their "illness" is judged "normal" for gays and lesbians. Essentially, those who lack power are "normal" when their physical, psychological, biological, and sociological natures are such that they support and reinforce the supremacy of the physical, psychological, biological, and sociological natures of those in power. Ideologies, practices, and laws are constructed to maintain this structure by defining as "normal," standard, or healthy that which either defines or serves androcentric culture. An obvious consequence is inequality, and this inequality provides the basic ingredient for patriarchy.

Androcentric ideology has provided the basic, underlying structure for medical and social science research. Historically and to some extent currently, across academic disciplines, "normality" is defined as that which men are, do, and desire: medical schools teach anatomy and physiology of men with women as a variant; men's professional career paths are standard while women tag along with "mommy tracks" and "biological clocks"; personality characteristics more common in men are normal while those more common in women are pathologized (Kaplan, 1983); men have rational responses to a stressful environment, women have irrational responses during the premenstrual period; aging men are wise, charming, and sexy, whereas aging women have a hormone deficiency.

"BIOLOGY AS IDEOLOGY"

This title is borrowed from the title of an incisive and brilliant book by R. C. Lewontin (1992). Biological determinism is a philosophical, scientific, and political theory within which the social and economic differences between women and men (or among racial and ethnic minorities or among persons of various sexual orientations) are attributed to natural, biological differences – the goal being to legitimize inequality, to make inequality a natural and inevitable consequence of human culture. The outcome is that the politically disenfranchised are told, "that their position is the inevitable outcome of their own innate deficiencies and that, therefore, nothing can be done about it" (Lewontin, 1992, p. 20).

Cultural institutions and structures have been created for this purpose. According to Lewontin (1992):

> For an institution to explain the world so as to make the world legitimate, it must possess several features. First, the institution as a whole must appear to derive from sources outside of ordinary human social struggle. It must not seem to be the creation of political, economic, or social forces, but to descend into society from a supra-human source. Second, the ideas, pronouncement, rules, and results of the institution's activities must have a validity and a transcendent truth that goes beyond any possibility of human compromise or human error. Its explanations and pronouncements must seem to be true in an absolute sense and to derive somehow from an absolute source. They must be true for all time and all place. And finally, the institution must have a certain mystical and veiled quality so that its innermost operation is not completely transparent to everyone. It must have an esoteric language, which needs to be explained to the ordinary person by those who are especially

knowledgeable and who can intervene between everyday life and myste-
rious sources of understanding and knowledge. (p. 7)

In the past, these institutions have been religious; today, they are scientific ones.

As the reader might anticipate, biology is assumed to determine destiny only
when this assumption reinforces the prevailing ideology. Albee (1982) comments:

people, and especially social scientists, select theories that are consistent
with their personal values, attitudes, and prejudices and then go out
into the world, or into the laboratory, to seek facts that validate their
beliefs about the world and about human nature, neglecting or denying
observations that contradict their personal prejudices. (p. 5)

Thus, the discourse surrounding biological determinism focuses on information
that supports the theory and ignores that which contradicts it. To illustrate, a
recent scholarly focus is the relatively high rate of osteoporosis among aging
women in Western society. This has been incorporated into scientific dogma as
evidence for women's innate biological inferiority. That osteoporosis is
uncommon among mid- and old-age African American women is conveniently
ignored. Why has no one suggested that African American women are biologically superior to European American women? Why has no one suggested that
we study the lifestyle of African American women in order to determine the
cause of their superior bones? This racial difference has not been emphasized
because it is not consistent with Western beliefs in the superiority of the
Caucasian race. Similarly, until recently, insurance companies claimed that
women's longer life spans justified the practice of awarding women monthly
retirement dividends that were lower than those given to men; a logical extension
of this policy – one that is not mentioned or followed – would be to award high
dividends to ethnic and racial minorities – persons whose life span is considerably shorter than that of Caucasians (Lorber, 1994). Contradictions such as these
are the consequence of a science done in order to be consistent with a specific
ideology rather than one driven by common logic or common benefit. The
dilemma is not that all scholarship is shaped by the beliefs and values of its
creators; the dilemma is that this influence is unacknowledged and denied – the
consequence being that the beliefs and values of those in power are sold as
universal truths. Scholarly rhetoric claims that the "facts" emerging from
Western scientific tradition will enhance freedom and equality; yet, it seems to be
the status quo that is enhanced.

Historically and currently, the theory of biological determinism has been
utilized, not only to support gender inequality, but also to pathologize women.
The medical paradigm of development and aging in women has redefined
women's normal developmental transitions and experiences as medical problems
that require medical interventions. Not only does the medical community benefit
by increased profits and status, but defining an experience that is common or

universal to all women as a disease supports women's inferior status. In this way, biological gender differences may be invoked to justify inequality: economic, political, and social differences between women and men are dismissed as the natural consequences of biological differences. But attributing difference to biology is highly selective – the selection being consistent with ideology and self-interest. In order to maintain the inferior status of women in Western society and to limit the options, power, and control of women, certain biological states are labeled as healthy and normal, whereas others are branded as abnormal and indicative of illness: although the hormonal profile of childhood and that of postmenopause are similar, the former is normal, the latter is abnormal; although pregnancy is associated with far greater hormonal fluctuations than is the menstrual cycle, the former is normal, the latter is abnormal; while both the reproductive years and the postmenopause are characterized by some health benefits and some health risks, the former is normal, the latter is abnormal; while puberty and perimenopause are both characterized by hormonal, physical, and psychological changes, the former is normal, the latter is abnormal. Those biological states associated with or preparing for fertility and reproduction are good, healthy, and, above all, feminine, whereas menstruation – *prima facie* evidence that a woman is not pregnant – and menopause – the absence of potential pregnancy – are pathological. In other words, those biological phases in which women are free from reproductive concerns are designated illnesses.

DUALISM

Dualism is a philosophical doctrine that organizes constructs into two radically different and opposing elements. Classic dualistic notions include Descartes' mind–body dichotomy and Darwin's separation of nurture and nature. Many philosophers and scientists have criticized this manner of thinking as being motivated by a desire to dominate and control nature by imposing ill-fitting order, hierarchy, and dichotomy rather than being inspired by a longing to understand and comprehend. Feminist scientist, Ruth Blier (1984) proposes that the majority of our cultural dualisms reflect the basic female–male dichotomy: thus, we have private–public, body–mind, subject–object, subordination–domination, feeling–thought, and passive–active – all are gendered. According to Blier (1984):

> The problems with a dualistic mode of thought are several. It structures our approach to knowledge of the world, it structures the world itself in an *a priori* fashion and imposes, as premises, dualisms and dichotomies onto the organization of the natural world that do not exist. Most basically, it obscures a fundamental characteristic of life and matter, perhaps first enunciated by Heraclitus over 2000 years ago: everything is in a constant state of flux, change, interaction. With such a view of reality, we cannot separate genes from environment, culture from

nature, subject from object. We cannot view science as an act of domination and objectivity, but rather as one of mutuality and interaction with nature. (p. 201)

In spite of brilliant, creative, and varied criticism, dualistic thinking continues to dominate discourse in health, medicine, and psychology and to obscure continuity and interdependence because doing so serves the interests of those in power.

A basic dualism of Western medicine is "sick" versus "well." The underlying medical assumption is that the ill are not quantitatively different, but qualitatively different, from the well – an assumption requiring the imposition of the discrete categories of "sick" and "well" on essentially continuous functions. To illustrate, in a study in the UK (Cohen *et al.*, 1993), research participants were intentionally exposed to a virus; 6 days later, the researchers measured the degree of viral replication in the blood and the extent of clinical symptoms. On both measures, participants showed a wide range of responses; and clinical symptoms were not necessarily related to the degree of viral replication. At what point on either dimension do we label an individual "sick"? One could specify a particular criterion for "sick" but, without cause, the criterion would be necessarily arbitrary. A better question is why do we need to make the distinction? By forcing both risk factors and disease processes into poorly fitting dualistic paradigms, both diagnosis and treatment are compromised.

The essential dualism underlying traditional medicine and health creates a context in which it is believed to be both possible and desirable to distinguish normal aging from disease. This creates an artificial dichotomy since the deterioration associated with normal aging is unrecognizable from illness. Charcot, in the nineteenth century, stated the problem as "the textural changes which old age induces in the organism sometimes attain such a point that the physiological and pathological states seem to mingle by an imperceptible transition, and to be no longer sharply distinguishable" (cited in Katz, 1996, p. 81). The criterion is, thus, both arbitrary and temporary and depends, to some extent, on medical advances. As soon as a medical procedure is devised to modify a particular age progression, the previously "normal aging deterioration" is labeled a disease: menopause was first labeled an illness when estrogen therapy became available and inexpensive. Katz (1996) proposes, "The object of treatment in senescence should be to restore the diseased organ or tissue to the state *normal to senescence* and not a restoration to the condition normal in maturity" (p. 88, emphasis added). Yet, the goal of hormone therapy is to achieve a hormonal profile typical of a woman 20 years younger.

A dread and fear of aging is, perhaps, "natural" since aging culminates in death. None the less, an even greater source of fear is the illness, pain, disability, loss of independence, and loss of control that often precede death, particularly death in old age and particularly in Western societies where many survive to old age. As more and more individuals live to an old age, our understanding of the aging process has increased. Age-related changes are, by definition, universal and inevitable, illness is not. At what point does the deterioration associated with normal aging end and illness begin? What purpose is served by distinguishing the two? The traditional scientific discourse favors dualistic concepts and, as such, has assumed the reality of discrete categories – chronic and acute diseases, normal and abnormal aging. But the contents of these categories are often determined by ideology, self-interest and historical precedent rather than scholarship. Defining normal aging (or acknowledging the impossibility of defining normal aging) is an issue of particular relevance to women since women live longer and suffer from more chronic diseases and disabilities than do men (Cantor, 1989).

AGING WOMEN

Androcentrism, biological determinism, and dualism merge in forming the ideological background for the study of aging in women. The most salient consequence of biological determinism for aging women is the labeling of menopause as a disease. This advances patriarchal ideology by rendering all women over 50 sick and in need of help – reinforcing their inferior status throughout life. Casting age-related disorders, such as cardiovascular disease, as a consequence of menopause diverts attention from the economic, political, and cultural causes of these disorders and supports the "menopause as disease" perspective. Even the language of menopause has been infused with illness terminology: "during the climacteric transition, a woman progresses from *normal* levels of steroids to significantly decreased levels" (Hammond, 1996, p. 5S, emphasis added). Or, in more popular jargon "women need to know that estrogen is 'natural' and that living 30 years or more without it may be less so (Ettinger, 1988, p. 34S). Estrogen "deficiency" and hormone "replacement" therapy imply that estrogen levels typical of women between the ages of 15 and 45 are normal or natural, when, in fact, women who live to age 75 spend more years in a state of "estrogen deficiency" than they do in a state of "estrogen abundance." Fertility aside, a high estrogen environment (fertile) and a low estrogen environment (menopause) are both associated with significant health benefits and risks. There are no obvious health or medical reasons or justifications for labeling one life stage as normal, another as abnormal. There are, however, political reasons for designating fertile or pregnant women as normal: as long as women are defined biologically, that is, according to their reproductive status, their biology can be used to render them different from men and, therefore, inferior to men.

Biological determinism has long been recognized by feminists as a paradigm that ill-serves women. However, biological determinism alone is not sufficient to maintain the traditional gender differences in status, power, and influence. This has required the application of biological determinism to women, and not to

men, in the context of patriarchal and androcentric ideologies. Biological determinism ensures that women's primary roles are reproductive, patriarchy ensures
that these roles carry an inferior status, and androcentrism ensures that these
roles are superficial and extraneous. Although women and women's roles are
considered of little importance, they are recognized as necessary because of
their reproductive value. However, when no longer fertile, women no longer
serve a purpose in a patriarchal, androcentric world. Thus, in this context,
menopause is not a change in life, a life transition, a mildly irritating event, but
a definitive and all-consuming disease – a deficiency disease – one that is said
to be the cause of any and all changes that are designated as age-related when
occurring in men. Not only does this interpretation effectively put and keep
women in their place, but it also puts men at their ease. They need not worry
about age-related deterioration because they are not women; their experience
of aging is determined by their life experience and their accumulated wisdom,
not by their biology.

Dualistic thinking and constructs pervade and limit scholarly work on aging
women. A recent and relevant example is the current practice, begun in
medicine, but adopted by the media, of labeling adult women as
"premenopausal" or "postmenopausal." Since actual menopausal status is relatively meaningless, this dichotomy is usually invoked as a convenient proxy for
age or hormonal status. If the purpose is to convey age, then "premenopausal"
typically includes women from 20 to 50 years of age and "postmenopausal"
women from 50 years of age and older. Reducing the continuity of age to the
dichotomy of menopausal status results in less information and less precision –
generally not the goal of science. Similarly, sex hormones typically begin to
decline when a woman is in her thirties and continue to do so throughout life;
there is not an abrupt and dramatic drop in hormone levels with natural
menopause. Again, replacing the natural continuity of hormonal variation with
"man"-made, discrete categories is inconsistent with our understanding of the
goals of science. Perhaps, most significantly, labeling women as pre- or postmenopausal in a context devoid of menopausal meaning is yet one more way to
essentialize women as reproductive beings. Selecting a biological, reproductive
event as the only event of importance to aging in women not only serves the
medical community by enhancing their status and profits but also diverts attention away from the economic and political oppression of women – both of
which intensify with age. Recognizing the inherent misogyny of this paradigm,
feminists have worked to develop a paradigm within which a comprehensive and
holistic view of aging in women is possible.

Scientists, however, continue to deny the role of ideology and justify their
position through claims of "objective empiricism." According to Sherwin (1993):

> The ideological dispute as to whether menopause is a normal reproduc-
> tive event or whether it is an endocrine deficiency disease or an
> endocrinopathy requiring medical intervention continues to rage.

Indeed, it is unlikely that it will ever be resolved, simply because this is a conceptual and not an empirical issue. (p. 235)

Yet, separating conceptual from empirical issues is not possible since one's conceptual framework determines the planning, doing, and interpreting of empirical research – if one did not conceive of menopause as an illness, one would not do research on ways to *treat* menopause. Indeed, Sherwin's own language reveals her underlying conceptual system – one that clearly impacts her own empirical research: she uses "deprivation" to describe menopause, "degenerative" to describe changes of the reproductive tract associated with menopause, "normal" to refer to blood levels of estrogen resulting from hormone therapy, hormone levels as being "diagnostic" of menopause, and "untreated" to identify postmenopausal women who are not taking hormone therapy. According to Lock (1993), ideology is most powerful when ideology is renamed as science and ideological assumptions are referred to as facts.

The ultimate dualism, and one that guides others, is the artificially created split between normality and abnormality. Normality is, in an absolute sense, indefinable. The definition of normality is relative to a particular time, place, individual, and circumstance and is motivated by social, political, and economic agenda. Normality is routinely invoked in order to pathologize certain people who fail to conform to the dominant ideology. Women are not normal because they are not men, elderly women are not normal because they are not fertile, women who are not mothers or not heterosexual are not normal because they have failed to follow the normal life course dictated by a patriarchal culture, and normal aging for women is dismissed as unimportant or uninteresting, exploited and pathologized in order to make a profit, or assumed to be similar to that of men. Aging women necessarily face considerable difficulty in maintaining psychological health, self-esteem, energy, and enthusiasm for the future when their cultural identity renders them abnormal and obsolete.

This is the context in which the psychological and physical well-being of mid- and old-age women has been studied. The physical and social sciences have operated "as if" the goal were an apolitical search for the truth when, in fact, a primary driving force has been to provide a justification and rationale for the political, social, and economic status quo. Consequently, information emerging within this context must be approached with caution and skepticism and the limitations recognized and articulated while paradigms, methodologies, and solutions consistent with the goals of health and equality are created and developed.

2

PSYCHOLOGICAL WELL-BEING

Girls...are stuffed with certain stereotyped sentiments from their infancy, and when that painful process is completed, intelligent philosophers come and smile upon the victims, and point to them as proofs of the intentions of Nature regarding our sex, admirable examples of the unvarying instincts of the feminine creature. In fact...it's as if the trainer of that troop of performing poodles...were to assure the spectators that the amiable animals were inspired, from birth, by a heaven-implanted yearning to jump through hoops, and walk about on their hind legs.

(Caird, 1989 [1894], p. 23)

Are not women of the harem more happy than women voters? Is not the housekeeper happier than the working women? It is not too clear just what the word *happy* really means and still less what true values it may mask. There is no possibility of measuring the happiness of others, and it is always easy to describe as happy the situation in which one wishes to place them.

(de Beauvoir, 1953, p. xxxiii)

Psychological well-being has different meanings for different people and contexts: happiness, peace, satisfaction, euphoria, tranquillity, pleasure, serenity, comfort, gratification, delight, joy – all contribute to well-being. The salience of a particular definition is dependent upon individual factors, such as gender, race, financial status, and age, as well as social, political, and biological factors. Persons of all ages experience emotional disturbance, psychological distress, and cognitive difficulties. Yet, these and related phenomena are studied almost exclusively in young adults and, until quite recently, young adult men. This may be acceptable to those who attribute psychological problems to genetic factors or childhood trauma since paradigms that locate causality within the individual would predict minimal change in psychological dysfunction over the lifetime. On the other hand, those scholars who believe psychological distress and cognitive function to be essentially due to stressful contextual factors – poor working conditions, sexual and racial discrimination and oppression, poor health, hostile family environment, poverty, inadequate social support – find the scholarship to fall far short of the goal of understanding psychological well-being in mid- and old-age women. As a feminist social scientist, I endorse this view: the sources of emotional disturbance, psychological distress, and cognitive difficulties are largely contextual and are largely dependent upon the current and past life circumstances of the individual.

The research literature on psychological well-being in mid- and old-age women is rapidly growing but currently quite limited. For the purposes of this discussion, the available information is organized into several areas: control, social activity, roles, life span norms, depression, and cognitive function. (1) The construct of control pervades the theoretical and empirical literature on both depression and cognitive function, as well as that of aging. Links to depression are explicit in the literature of learned helplessness (Seligman, 1975), locus of control (Rotter, 1966), and self-efficacy (Bandura, 1977). And the belief that one has control – that one can impact the environment through her/his behavior – underlies the motivation for action, performance, and achievement (Seligman, 1975; Weiner, 1972). (2) Social activity and social roles have considerable salience in psychological well-being and serve as a source of both distress and strength. (3) Developmental psychologists have recently expanded their sphere from childhood and adolescence to the full life span; this has spurred an interest in studying the psychological consequences of events and activities occurring at an age different than that dictated by the normative developmental sequence. (4) Depression and cognitive function are two of many ways of operationalizing psychological well-being and the two primary outcome measures in the research on aging.

CONTROL

The salience of control over important life events and experiences relative to an individual's physical and psychological well-being has repeatedly captured the interests of researchers in diverse disciplines. Issues of control have been central in research in animal and human models of learning (Maier and Seligman, 1976; Wiener, 1972) and in human models of psychological well-being such as learned helplessness (Seligman, 1975), locus of control (Rotter, 1966), and self-efficacy (Bandura, 1977), as well as in categories of psychological diagnoses including depression (Seligman, 1975), post-traumatic stress disorder (Foa et al., 1992), and neuroses (Mineka and Kihlstrom, 1978). As persons age, they are increasingly likely to experience a loss of control due to disability, chronic disease, poverty, and threats to personal safety. Perceiving important events to be beyond one's control tends to reduce motivation and increase depression – both of which, in turn, may result in acquiescing to lifestyles that further reduce the opportunity for control.

The learned helplessness model, emerging from conceptual innovations and empirical research by Seligman (1975) is, perhaps, the impetus for the current generation of scholarly work on the association between control and psychological well-being. According to Seligman, persons who are exposed to situations in which their behavior does not impact their environment, their responses do not affect outcomes, and/or the environment appears to be not contingent upon their activity will feel useless and helpless; two of the components of helplessness are depression and diminished motivation. The basic concept advanced by Seligman is conveyed by the label: persons *learn* to be *helpless* if they are exposed to repeated evidence that they have little control over their environment. If severe or continuous, the helplessness results in depression. In traditional Western societies, gender is a strong predictor of control. Most of the governing, financial, and commercial aspects of society are controlled by men; men are viewed as "head" of their families. The masculine sex role (decisive, self-confident) implies control while the feminine sex role (unassertive, dependent) implies helplessness. Since women tend to have less control throughout life than do men, women might be expected to respond with helplessness and depression when faced with the prospect of aging and the loss of what little control they did have.

Interestingly, women do not get more depressed with age, aged women have considerably lower suicide rates than do aged men, and, importantly, women live longer. Schlossberg (1980) suggested that women do not miss that which they never had:

> Generally speaking, women are more likely than men to experience changes whose source is external and thus to develop a pervasive feeling of powerlessness (and, consequent to that, of depression). By the same token, however, she may fare better when faced with changes over which she has no control. The man, unused to the feeling of powerlessness, may suffer greater negative affect when, for instance, he is forced to retire from his job or to slow down his pace because of ill health. (p. 13)

An alternative explanation is that the changes in control that occur after middle age are somewhat different for women and men, particularly among those who have led relatively traditional lives. In this context, men's lives were essentially their work lives, characterized by paid employment and much influence in the social, political, and family spheres – roles typified by considerable control. In this same tradition, women's lives were essentially nurturance of their children and dependence on their husbands – roles with little opportunity for control. With age, men tend to lose control when they retire and their children leave home but, I would argue, the changes accompanying middle age in women are often associated with *increased* control. A rather basic and essential form of control is to determine one's own schedule for eating, sleeping, working, and leisure – a goal precluded by being responsible for the care and feeding of others. For women, control over their everyday schedule increases when the children grow up and leave home. Indeed, many researchers have found that women report an increased sense of well-being at the "empty nest" (Neugarten, 1979). If a woman is newly divorced or widowed, although the loss is distressing, the ultimate result is likely to be an increase in control. For some women, this is the first time in their lives they have lived alone and been responsible for their own personal care. They may, of necessity, learn about finances and how to fix the plumbing and, while these experiences may be approached with fear and foreboding, meeting the challenges increases self-esteem, self-efficacy, and feelings of being in control. This interpretation applies primarily to women who are sufficiently wealthy and healthy to meet the challenge successfully; my intention is not to diminish the stress, trauma, and helplessness experienced by the many elderly women who live with poverty and poor health.

More recent formulations of control have argued convincingly that "perceived control" rather than "actual control" is the key to psychological well-being (Abramson et al., 1978; Bandura, 1977). Rodin (1989) has proposed that the importance of perceived control becomes greater as one ages because, increasingly, one has more experiences in which control is lacking – mandatory retirement, chronic illness, death of friends – and because one's actual control diminishes with age-related disability and illness. Davis-Berman (1988) studied the manner in which perceived control in various domains and depression were related in the elderly. She reported that perceived control in the physical domain accounted for 30% of the variance in depression, whereas perceived control in the social domain was not predictive. Clearly, health becomes a greater source of concern as one ages, perhaps because in order to participate in any activities, including social ones, good health is a requirement.

Rotter's (1966) theory of "locus of control" is yet another theory that emphasizes perceived control as salient to health. He distinguishes internal and external sources of control. Internal people believe that they have volition over their own behavior and, in this way, determine the environmental consequences of their behavior; they perceive themselves to have control. External people believe other forces or people determine their lives, and they perceive little control. Emerging from Rotter's theory, the "health locus of control" concept refers to persons' beliefs concerning the control they have over their health. Framers of the health locus of control theory (Wallston and Wallston, 1978) proposed that those expressing internal beliefs regarding health would be those who took charge of their health behaviors (e.g., diet, exercise) and who were actively involved in treatment decisions when they required medical care. Wallhagen et al. (1994) followed a large sample (n = 356) of older adults for six years in a longitudinal study. For women, those who were judged to be internal at the beginning of the study had better physical functioning six years later than those judged to be external. Furthermore, internal women engaged in more self-care behaviors and health-promoting activities.

In more recent developments, scholars have attempted to categorize or classify various types of control in order to develop and test emerging theoretical frameworks of control. Heckhausen and Schulz (1995) proposed a dichotomous schema consisting of primary and secondary control:

> Primary control involves behavior aimed at achieving effects in the immediate environment external to the individual. Secondary control targets the self in attempts to achieve changes directly within the individual....Primary control is usually characterized in terms of active behavior engaging the external world, whereas secondary control is predominantly characterized in terms of cognitive processes localized within the individual. (p. 297)

Primary and secondary controls are linked in the sense that secondary control acts to develop and facilitate primary control. When primary control fails, secondary control may act to modify the importance of the failure by restructuring priorities or may serve to minimize the impact on self-esteem by cognitively reframing the failure. These authors interpret the research literature to indicate that the use of primary control remains stable or decreases with age while the use of secondary control strategies increases with age. The elderly are commonly faced with age-related health decline that precludes primary control. In this context, they may depend on secondary control strategies including adherence to religious beliefs, adjusting downward their concepts of ideal self, contrasting their own situation with that of others who have less control, and increasing the value of available activities while decreasing the value of activities no longer possible. According to these authors, it is only when both primary control and subsequent secondary control strategies fail that individuals become helpless and depressed.

Primary and secondary controls roughly parallel distinctions in the coping literature. Blanchard-Fields (1989) discusses problem-focused coping – direct action aimed at solving the problem or eliminating the stress – and emotion-focused coping – indirect action with the goal of minimizing the impact of the stressor on the individual. A simple example might be dealing with an automobile breakdown: problem-focused coping might be to fix the problem or find someone to fix it while emotion-focused coping might involve having a whiskey. A "healthy" coping style is defined as relying on emotion-focused coping in uncontrollable situations and problem-focused coping in controllable situations. Blanchard-Fields found that, as persons traverse mid- and old-age, they more closely approach this ideal. The author notes that this allows the elderly to maintain a sense of internal control while acknowledging the lack of external control, when necessary. The appropriate use of these forms of coping requires the individual accurately to assess the situation and her/his own competencies. The ability to make accurate assessments may increase with age and life experience – perhaps, we should call this wisdom:

> As the person grows older not only do mental operations become more complex but learning also takes place. This culminates in a greater

comprehension of the complexity of the world. The result is that people learn that they have more influence on some aspects of their world than on other aspects. People also learn to recognize situations where they cannot have an influence. This latter recognition is very critical, for then the individual can know when not to respond, which is itself an action. In other words, when recognizing the dominance of external over internal forces, they now can act upon this reality and doing so gives them considerable control.

(Blanchard-Fields, 1989, pp. 238–9)

Situations that are particularly characteristic of the elderly include residence in a nursing home or other similar institutions, disability, and chronic pain – all of which are associated with diminished control (Logue, 1991). Nursing homes severely restrict individual choice in most life activities, resulting in extremely low levels of control. Residents are often not free to choose their diet, their bed time, or their leisure activities. In the poorer of such institutions, care is inadequate, malnutrition is common, and drugs are overused in order to ease the burdens of the staff (Logue, 1991). Hospitals and nursing homes often implicitly or explicitly reinforce dependency and obedience and/or punish independence and individualism (Rodin, 1989). Such treatment often results in a downward spiral of health, since lack of control is associated with diminished competency of the immune system, rendering the individual vulnerable to illness; illness, in turn, acts to decrease control further which, in turn, increases vulnerability to illness (Rodin, 1989). According to Fry (1989), passivity in the elderly is often an iatrogenic disease brought about by the deprivation, rigidity, and lack of control that characterize the environments where the elderly live.

Indeed, the level of personal control in institutions designed to provide residential care for the elderly is so low that enhancements of control which, in other contexts would be considered trivial, act to improve mood, alertness, and sociability. Langer and Rodin (1976) assigned one of two floors of a nursing home as the intervention group, the other as the reference group. (Most research on the elderly, particularly studies of institutionalized elderly, do not report the sex of the residents; however, the overwhelming majority are women.) Residents on both floors received a plant and a lecture: individuals in the enhanced-control group were given the responsibility for caring for their plants and, in addition, were encouraged to exercise personal choice concerning their friends and leisure activities; individuals in the reference group were told that the staff would look after their plant and stressed the staff's responsibility for taking care of the residents. Although the enhanced-control group did not improve on a measure of perceived control, they were found to be more happy, active, alert, and social compared to the reference group. At an 18-month follow-up (Rodin and Langer, 1977), 30% of the reference group had died while 15% of the enhanced-control group had died. One must wonder about the deprivation of such institutional environments that would allow such an inconsequential (to most of us) responsibility, as caring for a plant, to effect significant change. When introducing their study, Langer and Rodin (1976) noted that survival in the Nazi concentration camps depended on keeping control of some, even a minute, aspect of one's life. Recognizing similarities between the modern method of caring for dependent elderly and concentration camps is comment on our society's attitudes toward the elderly.

Fry (1989) notes that encouraging individuals to believe they have control when they clearly do not is likely to lead to anger, loss of self-esteem and depression. A false sense of control is often precisely what nursing home staff offer the residents. Residents are rarely asked their opinion, but rather told their opinion. "Isn't this food good?" Or, as the resident is unexpectedly wheeled outside, a staff member might say, "Wouldn't you enjoy a bit of time outdoors?" Schulz and Hanusa (1978) studied the effects of control and predictability in the schedule of volunteers visiting nursing homes; they compared the differences in outcomes among those residents who decided the frequency and duration of the visits (control and predictability), those whose visits were announced but determined by the staff (predictability, no control), and those who received visits on a random schedule (neither predictability nor control). The authors measured health status and "zest for life" – both were significantly higher in those persons who had either or both predictability or control compared to those without either. An interesting, and perhaps not unexpected, finding of this study was that at 30- and 42-month follow-ups, those who had benefited from the control and/or predictability had fallen below their initial baseline levels and exhibited a higher rate of mortality than those who had never been provided with control or predictability. The authors noted, with dismay, that providing control, and then removing it, was worse than never providing it at all. Many communities encourage citizens to volunteer at nursing homes, some high school and college courses require that students volunteer in nursing homes, and social service fraternities and sororities often volunteer. In these instances, there is no guarantee of continuity, indeed, the probability is high that student volunteers will be temporary with the result of not only negating, but perhaps even reversing, the benefits for the residents.

As in other areas relevant to physical and psychological health, "nature versus nurture" is a source of controversy in theories related to control. Heckhausen and Schulz (1995) commented: "primary control is invariant across cultures and historical time" (p. 286). These authors have failed to acknowledge their own cultural beliefs and values in claiming the high salience of personal control to have a universal nature. Most of the theory and research on control has originated in the United States – a society in which control, influence, and power are essential components of the culture. The high value placed on control in determining physical and psychological well-being may well be unique to the US and, perhaps, other Western cultures, limiting the generalizability of the scholarly literature. As with other behaviors, beliefs, and feelings, the need and desire for control are, to some extent, culturally determined. Cultures in which the values of cooperation and nonviolence, rather than achievement and competition, form the basis of beliefs and values are common in history and continue successfully today; such cultures have "internalized their...values so that their psychological structures accord with their beliefs" (Bonta, 1997, p. 299). Indeed, one could argue that the research literature on personal control does not apply, even within the Western cultures, to those who are politically and economically oppressed for reasons of race, ethnicity, gender or age. More importantly, the perpetuation of the high value placed on control by those in power acts to maintain the inequalities. Gergen (1989) comments:

> the value placed on personal control allows those who are in control to maintain it. When researchers verify that powerful positions are the just rewards for a life well-planned and well-executed they provide a rationale for the power inequities of the "late capitalist period." (p. 282)

Not only does the importance of control vary with cultural values, but the definition of personal or perceived control varies among cultures and sub-cultures. Heckhausen and Schulz (1995) define control as changing the environment to fit one's own needs, implying that control over others is desirable. In contrast, Gergen (1989) states the essence of control to be the freedom to act, the ability to plan and pursue one's own goals, and a recognition of the consequences of one's actions, implying that control over oneself is key. Gergen's definition of control suggests that personal control results from the wise incorporation of experience into one's life schemas; through learning and development – rather than through human nature – individuals achieve personal agency. These two conceptions of control may be reconcilable in the context of life-span theory. Children and adolescents may experience their first lessons of gaining control by environmental manipulation – infants learn their crying brings nurturance; a major developmental task of childhood is the instrumental manipulation of the environment. After childhood, cultures diverge: in highly competitive, capitalistic societies, late childhood and adolescence may be marked by adherence to Heckhausen and Schulz's concept of control in the pursuit of power over others through the gaining of money and other material possessions whereas, in cooperative societies, beginning in late childhood, individuals follow a different path and adhere to Gergen's concept of control by placing high value on personal and interpersonal control with the goal of contributing to the welfare of all (Bonta, 1997). In capitalistic societies, individuals who adapt well to the culmination of their wage-earning years and to aging may be those who successfully transform their goal from that of controlling others to that of controlling themselves.

In Western societies, men who adhere to traditional values seek power over others. Women, on the other hand, are not encouraged to dominate or control others. If socialized to place great value on reproduction and nurturing roles, they are, perhaps, more likely to follow the "cooperative" path and achieve psychological and physical well-being through self-awareness, social under-standing, and control over their own lives. If this is the case, then the transition into old age for women may be an easier course than for men. Old age for women might be viewed as a continuation of their earlier years; their accumulated wisdom and experience may provide considerable benefit and ever greater development. In contrast, expertise and comprehension of the corporate world are relatively useless in old age, and, after retirement, men may find that they are ineffective in their new world with their old skills. Their own and others' expectations that they maintain high levels of primary control may serve to diminish self-esteem: "Moral pressures on older persons to stay active and in control under most situations are more demoralizing and behaviorally self-debilitating than are external impediments in the physical environment" (Fry, 1989, p. 8).

Control issues are often central to satisfaction (and dissatisfaction) with medical care. The typical medical interaction of expert male doctor and sick female patient parallels and reinforces the sex-role socialization of most Western cultures and provides the woman patient little chance of self-determination. When the baby boomers reached young adulthood, the women were informed that pregnancy required medical care and treatment, that a physician would be "supervising the care of her pregnancies and the regulation of her fertility" (Cutler and Garcia, 1992, p. 26), and that she would have a pain-free birth while rendered unconscious by drugs. But these women refused the, perhaps well-intentioned, paternalism and have transformed the manner in which the medical profession participates in pregnancy and birth. Although the aged may not command the physical resources to perform a similar miracle for their medical care, perhaps their wisdom and experience will guide them toward increased participation in their health and health care.

The ultimate control is control over one's death. As technology permits the saving and supporting of life to greater and greater extents, this issue becomes increasingly important. In addition to deliberate suicide, methods of exerting a degree of control over death include active and passive euthanasia, decisions to forego or terminate life-saving or life-supporting treatment, and, in the event of incapacity, selecting individuals who will carry out the individual's wishes (Logue, 1991). In a rather unique study on gender and "the right to die in the US," Miles and August (1990) examined judicial decisions arising when a family member or health care provider of a medical patient requested legal sanction for terminating life-sustaining treatment. The outcome was that 2 of the 14 women and none of the 8 men were ordered to be continued on life-sustaining treatment. While this gender difference was not dramatic, the author highlighted several important gender differences with regard to the court proceedings: (a) the opinions of men patients were accepted as rational, sound, intelligent, and mature while those of women were seen as remote, emotional, and wish-fulfilling; (b) men's emotions were portrayed as "passionate conviction" while women's emotions were taken as indicative of a disturbed mind; (c) the state of being dependent on life-support technology was described as degrading, helpless, and infantile when the patient was a man, but as an indication of needing medical and judicial protection when the patient was a woman. Apparently, our cultural imperatives afford more control to men than to women even when utterly help-less.

SOCIAL LIFE

Since the industrial revolution, scholars concerned with individual well-being have studied the changing social relationships associated with the massive indus-trialization and urbanization of the twentieth century. Historically, social life was focused in the family and community. Throughout the twentieth century, forces associated with industrialization and urbanization, such as increased mobility, divorce, and, more recently, dual-career partnerships, have impacted the tradi-tional concepts of family and community. While bemoaning the loss of these social resources, scholars and politicians have typically emphasized "band-aid" solutions by advocating ways and means of facilitating a return to traditional values which emphasize family coherence and involvement in community life rather than by recognizing, accepting, and studying the emerging social customs within the social, economic, and political structures of the twentieth century. The lack of forethought and social planning to deal effectively with the ensuing threats to psychological and physical well-being is nowhere more apparent than in matters of concern to the aged.

The social environment is believed to exert a strong and remarkable influence on both physical and psychological well-being. Carroll *et al.* (1993) noted that there is considerable documentation on the benefits of social support: low social support has been found to be related to increased morbidity and mortality and slower recovery from illness and injury. Specifically in elderly women, Mutran *et al.* (1995) reported that recovery from hip fracture was quicker and was associ-ated with less depression among those women who had strong social support. On the other hand, social activity is not always beneficial. Seeman and McEwen (1996) reviewed the evidence relating social characteristics to neuroendocrine indices of stress. The most important aspect of the social environment was found to be the quality of social relationships: supportive social relationships tended to attenuate neuroendocrine responses to stress while unsupportive or hostile rela-tionships were associated with enhanced reactivity. Carroll *et al.* (1993) suggest that one way in which social support is beneficial is in promoting health behav-iors. In support of this, O'Brien and Vertinsky (1991) noted that social support and social interaction are among the most important factors in adherence with exercise programs.

"Social support" is the term adopted by psychologists to refer to:

> Instrumental functions...served through the provision of goods or money (material aid or financial assistance) and through providing

information, making suggestions, and clarifying issues (advice and guidance). This latter mode of supportive behavior...may also serve functions related to esteem and identity. Affective functions include meeting needs for love and affection, esteem and identity, and belonging and companionship. These needs are met respectively through emotional support, feedback and social reinforcement, and socializing.

(Vaux, 1988, p. 21)

Up until the late nineteenth century, the expectation was that these needs would be met by the family, the community, and, perhaps, religious organizations – all of which tended to remain constant throughout one's life. Today, mobility demanded by employment has increased dramatically as has the divorce rate, interrupting and diminishing community and family sources of social support. As a consequence, instrumental functions are increasingly met by employers and professionals, such as counselors, stock brokers, and social workers, while the affective functions continue to be met through personal relationships, although the form of the personal relationships has changed. Today's adults may go to singles bars, adjust to "blended families," create a social network through their place of employment, or become involved in religious or community organizations. Regardless of the source, today's social network is one that is of shorter duration and less intensity than the traditional extended family.

For the elderly, instrumental needs are increasingly met by government, retirement plans, social agencies, and insurance plans. In the US, aid from these sources is dependent upon previous employment. Elderly women who had been financially dependent upon a partner who has died may find themselves with no financial, housing, or health security. As lifetime employment for women becomes the rule, rather than the exception, this problem will lessen. None the less, needs previously met by family have transferred to impersonal sources and the elderly, particularly those with vision, hearing, and/or cognitive deficits, often encounter difficulties with the procedural demands of governmental, medical, and social agencies.

In contrast, the affective needs of the elderly continue to be met by friends, neighbors, and family. Although the latter is often long-distance, Hogan and Eggebeen (1995) found in a US survey that most (93%) of the elderly report having someone, typically adult children, who is available in emergencies. Men, more than women, rely on their spouses for support and are more likely to lack sources of advice and intimacy in old age. Hatch (1991) examined informal sources of support among elderly African–American and Caucasian women. African–Americans, compared to Whites, were more likely to be single, have more children, be heads of households, live in extended family settings, and, in general, have larger and more complex support networks.

A major life transition and significant loss of social support for married women is widowhood. According to Howie (1992–3), the women's extended longevity, the tendency for women to marry men older than themselves, and the low rates of remarriage among elderly widows necessarily result in a high number of elderly women who are widows. In Canada, 82% of the widowed are women; in Britain, 45% of women over the age of 65 live alone; and, in the US, over half of the widows live alone. The social consequences of living alone do not appear to be highly stressful for women. In the US, 31% of elders live alone and wish to do so as long as they can. Consistent with these statistics are those of Davis *et al.* (1997) who studied the impact of living alone on survival. These authors reported that, while living alone or with someone other than a spouse was associated with a higher mortality risk for men, there was no detrimental influence on survival in women. A partial explanation for these data may be that the death of a spouse is a greater loss of social support for men than for women: Depner and Ingersoll-Dayton (1985) noted that, compared to men, elderly women reported that they provided more social support to their spouses than they received. Furthermore, McKinlay *et al.* (1990) studied 2000 middle-aged women and reported that one-third of the married women did not include their husbands as members of their support network. Lesbians are less likely to lose their partners since women are less vulnerable than are men to premature death, but, when this does occur, the loss may be more stressful than it is for hetero-sexual women if there has not been a public or legal acknowledgment of the relationship.

In Western societies, women are socialized to a gender-specific role character-ized by nurturing, compassion, caring, concern, and empathy. Consequently, women of all ages are consistently found to have more close friends, to be on more intimate terms with close friends, and to have a wider and more complex network of friends compared to men (Grambs, 1989; Lewittes, 1988). The skills required to develop and maintain close relationships with both family and friends serve women well in societies that are highly mobile and in which family members often do not live in close geographic proximity. In a study of elderly widows (Arling, 1976), contact with adult children was unrelated to psychological well-being while maintaining closeness with friends and neighbors was associated with fewer feelings of loneliness and greater self-esteem. Even when limited by institutionalization, women continue to develop and maintain social networks. Powers (1996) studied the social activities of institutionalized men and women – most of whom had some functional disability. Social relationships developing among men tended to be low intensity and the primary goal seemed to be to "pass the time" while women had more balanced and active networks consisting of other residents, staff, kin and outside friends.

Social support and social interaction have obvious benefits through the conveyance of pleasure, empowerment, and self-esteem as well as serving as a buffer for stress and traumatic life events. There is, however, danger in promoting the overly simplistic view of "the more, the better." In some cultures, solitude and introspection are seen as indicative of depression and to be avoided; persons suffering from a recent loss or trauma or from recurrent depressed mood are often encouraged by friends and family to "get out and meet people." Institutionalized elderly are often forced to engage in social recreational activities "for their own good," and engaging others in conversation is taken as evidence of contentment and satisfaction with their surroundings. Despite the absence of evidence indicating that any type of social behavior – irrespective of personal meaning – is beneficial to individuals, this is one of the criteria often employed when evaluating psychological well-being. The underlying assumption that any and all social activity enhances well-being has little empirical support. Indeed, individuals vary considerably in their need for, their desire for, and the benefits or costs they derive from social relationships. Reeves and Darville (1994) studied the frequency of and satisfaction with social networks in retired women. Contrary to hypotheses, the authors did not find frequency of social contact or variety of contact to influence life satisfaction. On the other hand, the *disparity* between preferred and actual social contact did affect satisfaction. Interestingly, both more or less social activity than desired was associated with low satisfaction.

There is some evidence that the social responsibilities placed on women may be excessive: both men and women rely on women for most of their intimate and emotional support needs (Carroll *et al.*, 1993). In spite of the recent women's movement, women continue in most instances to be responsible for child care and elder care in the family. Women's compassion, caring and nurturance are compelling forces to get emotionally involved in the lives of others. Trauma to friends and family is highly stressful to the empathic individual and meeting felt obligations for coming to the aid of friends and family offers considerable challenge in terms of time and effort. Thus, while there is a considerable body of literature documenting the benefits of the availability of social support for psychological and physical well-being – both directly and as a way of coping with stress – gender differences must be acknowledged: the data tend to be strong and consistent for men but not for women. More is not always better for those women who have large and complex social networks and/or who perceive themselves to be giving far more than they are receiving.

A balance between giving and receiving in social relationships is referred to as reciprocity. While most comfort and pleasure is gained in social relationships that are characterized by a more-or-less equal exchange of giving and receiving, elderly persons are often in the situation of being the recipient of help; because of illness or disability or frailty, they may be unable to return instrumental, financial, or emotional help. Being either the donor or the receiver in an unbalanced relationship has been found to be associated with poor mental health, less satisfaction with the relationship, and negative affect (Albert and Cattell, 1994). In explaining why friends seem to be more important than family to elderly women, Unger and Crawford (1992) implicate the desire for reciprocity: "old women may feel that their families give them support out of a sense of duty, while friends do so in the expectation that each can contribute to the other's welfare by 'helping out' on an equal basis" (p. 526). The likelihood of achieving reciprocity is increased with the duration of the relationship. Given sufficient time, trauma and life transitions – events that place demands on intimate social relationships for emotional support – the exchange may become more-or-less equal. Indeed, this may be an essential reason for the high satisfaction expressed with friendships of long duration.

In summary, I refer the interested reader to a delightful novel by Vita Sackville-West (1931 [1984]) titled *All Passion Spent*. The story is of the widow of an Earl, recently deceased, and the mother of six adult children. At their father's death, the children discuss the disposition of their mother – with which child should she live and in which charitable activities she should become involved so that she may "keep busy." The children then announce their plan to their mother, only to find to their shock and dismay, that she has already made other plans. She wishes to live alone with her maid in a cottage she has already selected. She rejects their offers of assistance and help and carries out the renovations and move on her own. The transformation from a dependent and frail wife and mother to an independent and decisive widow, despite a nagging and pompous family, is extraordinary and touching. Although the story focuses on the British upper class, I believe the message is universal.

ROLES

Roles may be defined as expected, socially encouraged patterns of behaviors for individuals within a particular social context. Although roles are often accepted and acted out, they are, theoretically, thought to be superimposed on the individual rather than to be part of the individual. This distinction, however, becomes blurred when the individual internalizes social-role expectations, transforming cultural expectations to "natural" behaviors. The salience of roles is roughly parallel to the time and/or effort devoted to involvement in the role and to the strength of the influence of the role in dictating behavior, goals, and values. Thus, for example, occupational roles are salient to those who work full time and family roles are important to the woman who has adhered to the female gender role as the guide for major decisions of her life.

Mid- and old-age are characterized by role transitions and redefinitions. A woman's life may change dramatically when her last child leaves home, when she receives a major promotion, when she obtains a divorce, when she becomes a grandmother, or when she retires. The research focus on roles has differed in women and men – a difference that reflects traditional gender roles. For men, the interest has been work roles whereas, for women, the interest has been relational roles. There have not, for example, been any studies devoted to the "empty-nest syndrome" in men. Since the mid-1970s, women have increasingly entered the paid labor force, and researchers have studied the effects of adding the role of worker to women's physical and psychological well-being.

Haertel *et al.* (1992) found beneficial changes in cardiovascular risk to be associated with employment. Women were evaluated for three years: those employed had healthier cholesterol profiles than those not employed; those who became employed during this time, exhibited no change in cholesterol while those who became unemployed during this time experienced a significant decrease in healthy cholesterol. Consistent with these findings, Hibbard and Pope (1992) noted that "Women not in the workforce in 1970–1 were at a 70% greater risk of dying in the following 15 years than employed women" (p. 809). Studies such as these support the conclusion that "paid employment is crucial for both financial and physical/mental well-being, and that…employment and childcare policies which do not facilitate the economic independence of women may have disadvantageous health consequences" (Arber and Lahelma, 1993, p. 1965). However, both this study and one by Bromberger and Matthews (1994) found that the benefits of employment for women depended upon the type of employment; as one might predict, those women who became employed in low-status, low-pay jobs, and who had little education benefited little or not at all. Aber (1992) found that women, aged 55 to 75 years, who were employed (or had been and retired) and who had a positive attitude toward their work, were healthier during the bereavement period following their husband's death than unemployed women.

An assumption underlying the interpretation of these studies is that all women are homemakers. In this context, working increases the number of roles in which a woman is engaged. Interestingly, the opposite is not applied to men – benefits accrued when becoming a husband or a father are not interpreted as "another role" but as increased social support or stability. Thus, the research literature on women and paid employment has been consistently interpreted to mean that multiple roles, as opposed to paid employment *per se*, are beneficial to women's health. However, these studies did not actually assess roles other than work – the homemaker role was assumed. In one exception, Adelmann (1993) compared life satisfaction, depression, and self-esteem in older women who considered themselves retired only, homemakers only, or both: "Retired women and homemakers did not differ in well-being; women who called themselves both had higher self-esteem and lower depression than single-role women" (p. 195). The benefits of multiple roles have been explained by the expanded reinforcement potential: if a woman's partner relationship deteriorates and becomes stressful and her only source of reinforcement is her role as homemaker, she will experience more distress than if she has other sources of reinforcement, such as paid employment. McKinlay *et al.* (1990) suggest an alternative explanation. They studied a large sample of middle-aged women over a 5-year period and concluded that, not only are women who work healthier, but work may actually serve to buffer the effects of stressful family roles: "Work, with its clear expectations may provide a sense of satisfaction and self worth not equalled by the familial nurturing roles, for which expectations are implicit and more ambiguous" (McKinlay *et al.*, 1990, p. 133).

While the assumption that all women are homemakers may have reflected reality 30 years ago, it is no longer true today. Today, many women have chosen not to be wives, mothers, or homemakers. While roles associated with reproduction have been emphasized in women's lives in the past, considerable changes in the last several decades have occurred, resulting in unprecedented educational and career opportunities for women. Assumptions and theories regarding women's roles, however, have not kept pace as is evidenced by the continued cultural importance of biological motherhood – the "mommy track," the "biological clock," and the development of dramatic, expensive, and potentially dangerous methods of achieving biological motherhood for essentially infertile women. A further assumption, one more insidious, that underlies much of the research in this area, is that employment is a choice or an indulgence for women. Consider the title of a chapter: "Women's behavior: Do mothers harm their children when they work outside the home?" (Walsh, 1997) or "The effect of wives' employment on the mental health of married men and women" (Kessler and McRae, 1982). To reveal the underlying sexism, the reader might note the absurdity when changing genders: "Men's behavior: Do fathers harm their children when they work outside the home?" and "The effect of husbands' employment on the mental health of married women and men." Most women today work for the same reasons men do: to survive, to earn a living, and, for the fortunate ones, to gain a sense of achievement, fulfillment, and independence. Women and men may well differ in their choice of occupation, their enjoyment of work, or the benefits they derive but to design and conduct research in the context that men work because they have to and women work for fun is to demean and degrade women's work and women's professions.

In recent years, another role has been added to the lives of an increasing number of mid- and old-age women – that of caretaker for an infirm parent or partner. According to Moen *et al.* (1994), 45% of the women born between 1905 and 1917 had been caregivers while 64% of those born in 1927 to 1934 had done so. The presence of other roles, such as employment and motherhood did not seem to impact the probability of becoming a caretaker. Franklin *et al.* (1994) studied the conflicts encountered by employed, middle-aged women who became caretakers. At the inception of the caretaking responsibilities, the percentage of those employed full time dropped from 68 to 43.2%. Similar changes were found for other indicators of conflict such as arriving at work late and refusing a promotion. On the other hand, within three months of assuming this added responsibility, women had managed to reprioritize their activities and responsibilities, and the work indicators of conflict had lessened. In a recent study, Lawrence *et al.* (1998) studied factors influencing the psychological consequences of caregiving in 118 family caregivers (spouse, children) of whom 69% were women. The authors found, as they expected, an association between problem behaviors (hitting, cursing, wandering) of the care recipient and subjective feelings of overload, captivity (loss of freedom), and depression reported by the caregiver. Surprisingly, cognitive impairment and disability did not predict these outcomes. However, the quality and closeness of the relationship between the caregiver and the care recipient were strongly correlated with these psychological consequences.

In reviewing the literature in this area, Doress-Worters (1994) assumes the common view that caregiving is socially isolating, oppressive, time consuming, freedom limiting and lacking in rewards; in this context, she concludes that "adding" employment may improve women's mental health but "adding" caregiving reduces it. Although women are assumed to find psychological fulfillment in the role of caretaking for their children and although research on women in work roles is conducted in the context of the benefits of multiple roles, most of the research on caregiving is designed with the expectation that caregiving creates "role conflict" and is stressful. Consequently, primarily distress, alienation, and conflict have been studied in association with the role of caretaker while satisfaction, serenity, intimacy, and comfort have been mostly ignored as potential benefits.

In one of the few studies to acknowledge the possibility that pleasure and satisfaction may be gained by caregiving, McGrew (1998) explored the decision-making process of caregiving daughters in a qualitative study. The author discusses the interview data in terms of the feeling and motivations associated with the assumption, sharing, and relinquishing of care with considerable appreciation for both the complexities and the conflicts; the possibilities of reward and benefit for the caregiver are acknowledged and causes of negative caregiving experiences are explored. This is a beginning. As this role becomes increasingly frequent in the lives of aging women, the study of caregiving deserves the attention of feminist researchers. In the context of patriarchal ideology, caring for elderly parents or disabled spouses is too often construed as a "natural" role for women. Consequently, if accepting this role causes distress or conflict, the cause is assumed to be a failing of the individual rather than a result of acquiescing to socialized gender roles. Conversely, Western society places such considerable emphasis on individual freedom and material wealth that the potential benefits of caregiving, such as intimacy and emotional expression, are ignored.

A major role transition for men in mid-age is retirement, and men have typically found this to be a stressful time. One could argue that the stress is exacerbated in those men who have only one major role in adulthood – that of worker – and that when this ends, they are left with few resources and few sources of pleasure and reward. Haber (1983) in discussing nineteenth-century roles of aging men and women comments: "By retiring from their principal calling, they were acknowledging an end to their primary role in society" (p. 19) whereas "The female could slowly adjust to her new state of life, while her domestic duties remained the same" (p. 70). This view has prevailed during most of the twentieth century as a partial explanation for the high suicide rate among older men and their shorter life expectancy compared to women. Since women have entered the labor force in large numbers only in the last few decades, there are insufficient numbers to study the impact of retirement from work on women's physical and psychological well-being. However, if multiple roles are, indeed, beneficial to health, then we might expect women to find retirement less stressful than men do: losing one of several roles may cause less distress than losing one's only role. Furthermore, women tend to have better social skills than do men and to have larger, more complex and diverse social networks – resources that could minimize the impact of the stress of retirement.

Aging past the retirement years tends to be associated with a merging of gender roles. Men may find this distressing due to traditional admonitions to keep roles separate: "Don't take your work home," and "Don't get personal calls at work." Women, on the other hand, have had to deal with the complexities of multiple roles throughout their lives. Since women have entered the labor force in large numbers, there have been steady changes in the structures and policies of the work place in order to encourage and enable the merging of roles, such as day care and elder care at the work site, as well as medical and dental services. Perhaps women, accustomed to juggling their time and switching their focus in response to need, find changes in type and/or number of roles to be "normal" and challenging.

LIFE-SPAN NORMS

Traditional perspectives of aging emphasized growth, development, and change from birth to young adulthood, constancy during adulthood, and deterioration with old age. The more recent life span perspective of aging assumes growth, development and change throughout life. One outcome of this perspective has been the delineation of normative ages for particular activities and events. Thus, puberty is a normative event for persons of a particular age range, menopause is a normative event within a different, but specific, age range. Cultural and historical influences dictate normative ages for events such as marriage, parenthood, and retirement. With the description of age-normative events came an interest in studying the consequences of events that occur out of phase with the normative developmental sequence.

The theoretical and empirical research on the effects of stressful life events on physical and psychological well-being make frequent reference to the effect of timeliness. Although not systematically studied, phrases such as "developmentally appropriate tasks" and "the right task at the right time" are becoming common in the scholarly literature (Harlow and Cantor, 1996). Hays *et al.* (1994) interviewed persons aged 44 to 80 years in order to examine the psychological distress subsequent to the death of a spouse; middle-aged persons reported more distress than did the elderly – perhaps because old age is the appropriate time for death. Similarly, Leahy (1992–3), in a sample of middle-aged women, found that those who lost a daughter to death reported significantly higher depression than those who lost a mother or a spouse to death – the latter reflecting more "normal" life-course events. In a study on menopause as reported by Greek and Mayan women, Beyene (1986) noted that if menopause occurred at the normal time, there were no ill effects while early menopause (less than 40 years old) was associated with ill health.

The idea that "on-time" events are less stressful than "off-time" events is not new. As early as 1979, Neugarten hypothesized that individuals anticipate and expect certain life events to occur at certain ages. Persons are thought to have a "mental clock" keeping them aware of how closely they are adhering to the schedule. There is a correct time to marry, have children, get educated, and die. Neugarten assumed that all life events and transitions demand changes in self-concept and identity but only those that are "off-time" produce a crisis. She suggested that a young adult child not leaving home is more traumatic than one leaving, and that, although death is always tragic, the response only reaches crisis proportions when the young die. "Events that are expected and timely do not precipitate crises...but constitute a significant point in time for a development that allows integration" (Schmid, 1991, p. 363).

Some of the possible explanations for the benefits of experiencing events in a "timely" manner are, perhaps, self-evident. Experiencing stressful events at a time similar to that of one's peers provides a ready source of social support. Certain structures in the culture are designed to facilitate events at a particular age. For example, in many countries, persons over the age considered elderly (65 in the US) are assumed to be retired and living on a fixed income and, consequently, are allowed financial advantages in taxes, film admissions, and the purchase of some consumer products.

An alternative explanation for the heightened distress associated with "off-time" events is one grounded in the scholarship on biological rhythms. In general, biological rhythms are assumed to be the result of adaptation to an external temporal structure: endogenous rhythms develop in response to and in coordination with environmental patterns by entraining to temporally predictable stimuli (Aschoff, 1982). The most well-known examples are circadian rhythms which entrain to the light–dark cycle: "a major function of the circadian timing system is the internal sequencing of physiological events and metabolic processes so that interdependent functions are coordinated and incompatible processes separated in time" (Moore-Ede *et al.*, 1983, p. 469). A biological process, referred to as "predictive homeostasis" maintains an acceptable internal environment by anticipating the rhythm of the entraining stimuli so that the organism is prepared in advance to deal with temporally predictable circumstances (Aschoff, 1980). Thus, for example, the circadian temperature rhythm is characterized by gradually increasing heat production beginning several hours before and reaching optimal day time levels about the time of normal wakening. Desynchronization, or the disruption of biological rhythms, refers to biological rhythms no longer in phase with the environment or to the lack of harmony among various endogenous rhythms. The psychological and behavioral consequences or correlates include lack of energy, lack of interest in family/friends/work, decreased motivation, variable mood, slowing of psychomotor functioning, disorientation, headaches, and disrupted sleep, appetite and libido (Aschoff, 1980, 1982; Graeber, 1982). As Healy and Williams (1988) note, these are also the somatic signs of clinical depression.

The elderly are often disparaged for their rigid schedules for meals and bedtimes. They are pitied for their lack of spontaneity and impulsiveness – the cause of which is frequently assumed to be boredom, disappointment, and pessimism. Yet, with age, persons may come to recognize the threats to well-being from desynchrony, and their inflexibility may be a healthy coping response to the threatened effects of desynchronization on psychological and physical well-being. Monk and colleagues (Monk *et al.*, 1996; Prigerson *et al.*, 1995–6) developed the Social Rhythm Metric (SRM) – a self-report assessment of the degree of routine present in an individual's everyday life; they found routine to increase with age, thus confirming the stereotype. None the less, greater regularity on the SRM predicted less depression one year following the death of a spouse. In the face of biological dysrhythmia consequent to a traumatic event, the maintenance of other routines and structures may minimize discomfort. Others (Aschoff, 1982; Wever, 1982) have noted that the tendency toward spontaneous internal desynchronization increases with age and that the aging circadian system seems to require strong entraining stimuli to maintain synchrony. Perhaps the tendency to increase the rigidity of one's schedule and routine with age is a self-protective and healthy mechanism. As discussed in other chapters of this book, the elderly place high value on their health and independence – both of which could be compromised by the apparent sequelae of desynchronization. It is difficult to feel healthy in the face of sleep, energy, and appetite dysfunction. Yet, the timeliness of an event or life transition is rarely considered, assessed, or acknowledged in research on the physical and psychological well-being of the aged.

Circadian rhythms and life-span rhythms may be similar phenomena but differing in periodicity – 24 hours versus a lifetime. Perhaps, individuals are biologically programmed for the timing of certain events, such as menarche and menopause, while being culturally programmed for the timing of other events, such as marriage, parenthood, and retirement. Obviously, biological and cultural entraining stimuli interact so that one's culture does not encourage parenthood at an age when one is infertile. It seems that when individuals follow the biological and cultural programming, they are less likely to experience extreme stress responses to traumatic events. They are able to predict, and therefore prepare for, stress; social support is available through cohorts with similar experiences; the structures and institutions of the culture facilitate predictable events and transitions. Thus, a middle-aged woman with three young children finds it difficult to return to school full-time since the pace of the classes and the lifestyle is set for the minds and bodies of 20-year-olds, a ready-made social network is lacking, and day-care facilities are often not available to students. The result is desynchronization between the woman's desired life course and the cultural and biological entraining stimuli; the consequence may be somatic and psychological distress.

In the last several decades, cultural changes and technological advancements have necessitated a redefinition of "normal" timing. Marriage, parenthood, attending educational institutions, beginning a new career, and retirement no longer occur at a precise age but have become accepted options of persons within an ever-expanding age range. Although the outcome of these cultural changes may be increased flexibility and a broadening of the definition of "on-time," the potential benefits for women may be constrained by patriarchal ideology. Thus, a request for sterilization by a healthy young woman is likely to elicit medical protest, demands for a psychological assessment, or permission of a husband, whereas a request for a high-technology pregnancy by a post-menopausal woman is welcomed and valued as "natural." Off-time events are more readily accepted when they reinforce the values consistent with the dominant ideology.

DEPRESSION

The most common psychological disturbance among women throughout the adult life span, certainly the one of most interest to scholars and researchers, is and has been depression. Some scholars interested in the relationship between age and depression in women have hypothesized a decrease with age, whereas others have proposed an increase. In support of the former, scholars argue that as women grow older many of the stressors known to be associated with depression tend to diminish, such as changing jobs, moving to a strange city, and becoming a parent; additionally, one would expect that, from their life experiences, persons learn effective methods of coping with or avoiding situations likely to cause distress. In contrast, chronic stressors, such as poverty and racial and sexual discrimination, remain the same or may even increase. Traumatic events that signal loss, such as death of a parent or divorce, tend to become more probable with age; losses are particularly associated with depression.

The empirical data indicate that the incidence of depression in women tends to decrease in mid- and old-age and that women reporting the greatest depression are those with young children at home (Pearlin, 1975; Radloff, 1975). This is not to say that depression is trivial for aging women. Several longitudinal studies have examined the impact of psychological disorders on mortality. Huppert and Whittington (1995) reported that the frequency of psychological symptoms was related to mortality seven years later. Similarly, Bruce *et al.* (1994) assessed psychological dysfunction in a community sample of 3560 women and men over 40 years of age and, nine years later, recorded deaths from all causes. Depression was one of the diagnoses significantly related to mortality. One might expect psychological maladjustment, particularly depression, to be associated with later suicide, but these figures refer to all causes of mortality. Furthermore, although the probability of suicide has been found to increase after age 65, 80% of suicides in the elderly are men (Casey, 1994).

Regardless of whether depression increases or decreases with age in women, many mid- and old-age women do experience depression, and it is likely that the sources of this depression differ from those of younger women. Elderly women are far more likely to be widowed than are older men: women tend to marry men older than they are, they have a longer life expectancy, and they are less likely to remarry than are men. Howie (1992–3) reports that, in Canada, widows outnumber widowers by 5 to 1 and that widowed women are more likely to suffer a decrease in income and material resources than are widowed men. There have been several studies examining the psychological impact of bereavement of a spouse. Thompson *et al.* (1991) followed widows and widowers for 2.5 years following the death of their spouse. Two months after the loss, bereaved persons were more severely depressed than a comparison group but this depression diminished by 12 months. Nolen-Hoeksema *et al.* (1994) examined a specific coping style – rumination, characterized as a chronic, passive focus on negative emotions – in relation to depression following the death of a spouse. High levels of rumination were associated with poor social support and a stressful life and predicted post-loss depression. Thus, in spite of the fact that widowhood is almost an expected life event for elderly women, the death of a spouse is often associated with time-limited depression. For those in whom the loss of a spouse causes additional stress such as social isolation and financial hardship, the recovery from depression appears to be prolonged.

The lack of standard assessment techniques for depression in the aged has created methodological difficulties for researchers. Instruments developed and standardized on young adults may not readily transfer to the aged. One difficulty involves the inclusion of somatic symptoms, such as appetite, sleep, and sexual problems. These symptoms are generally considered to be pathognomic of depression in young adults, while in the elderly, these symptoms may be associated with illness and/or frailty rather than being a manifestation of psychological disturbance. "What seem to be age-related effects on depression are attributable to physical health problems and related disability" (Roberts *et al.*, 1997, p. 1384). The Centre for Epidemiologic Studies Depression Scale (CES-D), a common depression measure utilized by researchers, was evaluated in a study of community-residing older adults. Lewinsohn *et al.* (1997) confirmed that the validity of the CES-D was not compromised with this population. In contrast, Knight *et al.* (1997) used the CES-D to diagnose depression in a group of middle-aged women. The scale was found to have good reliability but the scores tended to be inflated in women with chronic health problems. Thus, the assessment of depression in the elderly is complicated by the likely presence of physical illness or chronic, disabling conditions. The solution to this dilemma is not straightforward since the symptoms of illness (e.g., sleep and appetite problems) may inappropriately inflate the apparent severity of depression; however, ignoring somatic symptoms when diagnosing depression would be likely to underestimate depression because, in the elderly, two of the major determinants of psychological well-being are health and functional capacity.

The importance of physical health

Steiner and Marcopulos (1991) suggest that "depressed elderly patients often present with somatic complaints, anxiety, or hypochondriasis rather than reporting feelings of depression or sadness" (p. 588); the authors refer to this as "masked depression." However, the medical interpretation of physical complaints as due to anxiety or hypochondriasis is often a way to dismiss persons whose physical symptoms do not conform to a known medical entity; while this may allow medicine and insurers cleaner bookkeeping, it does not benefit the patient. These authors also discuss medical illnesses that are often associated with depressed mood, such as congestive heart failure, Parkinson's disease, and hypothyroidism, and medications that cause depression as a common side-effect, such as antihypertensives and barbiturates. They emphasize the importance of distinguishing true depression from symptoms caused by medical illnesses or medications. Although theoretically important, this distinction may have little practical importance. One assumes that medical patients are taking only those medications that are necessary; if a co-occurring depression is present, the person's medical condition and medications would be considered in developing an overall treatment plan. If depression co-occurs with a medical illness, there is no particular reason to assume that the person requires treatment other than that typically employed to treat depression – psychotherapy and/or antidepressants.

Many clinicians have expressed the belief that depression is far more common in the elderly than is currently recognized and that by applying the same "standards" for diagnosis that are used for young people, many depressed elderly go undetected and untreated. According to Cohen (1994), only 2 to 4% of older persons are diagnosed as depressed using traditional criteria, whereas, the "true" incidence is 13 to 15%. Blazer *et al.* (1991) noted that, when assessing depression in the elderly, the use of traditional diagnostic criteria may fail to detect many depressed persons – that elderly persons may not satisfy all of the traditional criteria for clinical depression but may exhibit a high frequency of the symptoms. Although a valid criticism and one that is consistent with the idea that depression varies among persons and times in a quantitative, rather than qualitative, manner, depressed persons of any age or gender may be undetected if assessment is limited to measurement instruments designed for young, heterosexual, middle-class men. Medical professionals attribute depression to biological causes and note that the relation between age and depression is "confounded" by factors such as disability, income status, and social isolation, implying that the influence of these variables interferes with and masks the "true" relationships. In contrast, psychologists and sociologists tend to view depression as *caused* by disability, income status, and social isolation and might consider medical or biological conditions as "confounding" the true relationship between depression and an aversive environment.

Regardless of theoretical interpretation, physical health does seem to be more closely associated with depression as one ages. Koenig and Blazer (1992) reviewed much of the research on this topic and concluded:

> Physical health status has a major impact on the adjustment of older adults. Regardless of how it is measured (self-rated, functional status, number of chronic conditions, number of physician visits, or number of prescribed medications), health has been consistently related to depression in virtually all studies on community-dwelling elders. Although true for both sexes, the relationship may be particularly strong in women. (p. 240)

The strong association between health and depression in the aged is apparently due to the psychological and social consequences of illness rather than to the biological correlates of the illness since the authors estimated that less than 2% of depressions in the elderly are due to biological changes associated with the physical illness or to medication side-effects.

A similar focus characterized a large cross-national study conducted by the World Health Organization (Simon *et al.*, 1996) in which physical complaints and psychological distress were measured at fifteen intervention sites. At all sites, the number of current physical complaints (medically explained or not) was significantly correlated with psychological distress. There were no clear patterns of influence associated with geography or economic development. Indications that poor physical health is *causing* psychological distress, rather than occurring coincidentally, are noted in a study by Kennedy *et al.* (1991). These authors assessed elderly women and men over 65 years old twice at two-year intervals. Not only was worsening health associated with a persistence of depressive symptoms, but a remission of depressive symptoms was associated with improved health.

The question remains as to why physical health seems to cause, or at least be associated with, depression and why this relationship increases with aging. Although a variety of explanations present themselves, the most parsimonious is, perhaps, that physical illness reduces one's control in everyday life. There is a large literature (discussed more fully above) documenting the strong and persistent association between control and depression. In the young, most physical illnesses are not chronic and are not associated with long-term or permanent disability. However, as one ages, the probability of suffering from an illness or chronic condition that results in disability, reduced functional capacity, or chronic pain increases, and these outcomes result in a reduced ability to exert control over everyday and future events. The consequent feelings of helplessness are typically manifest in depression. Since women exhibit a greater incidence of chronic disease than do men, this may partially explain the greater incidence of depression in women.

The importance of menopause

The belief that menopause is a major cause of psychological problems has been popular for at least the last century. According to Formanek (1990), the 1888 Surgeon General's Catalogue directs readers interested in menopause to "See also: insanity in women." In 1909, the German psychiatrist Kraepelin coined the term *involutional melancholia* to refer to the unavoidable full-blown depressive episode of menopause. This belief continues today: "Anxiety, depression, irritability, and fatigue increase after menopause" (Marshburn and Carr, 1992, p. 145).

The empirical research suggests a different conclusion. Data from large surveys of women of menopausal age indicate that depression does not vary predictably with menopausal status (Ballinger, 1975, 1976; Holte, 1992; Kaufert and Gilbert, 1986; Leiblum and Swartzman, 1986; Lennon, 1987; McKinlay *et al.*, 1987). A recent and thorough review by Nicol-Smith (1996) summarized 94 articles from the past 30 years and concluded that menopause does *not* cause depression. Further evidence is found in studies failing to demonstrate strong relationships between hormonal levels and psychological states. An early study by Abe *et al.* (1977) found no significant relationships between the severity of psychological symptoms and serum levels of estrogen, progesterone, FSH (follicle-stimulating hormone), and LH (luteinizing hormone) in menopausal women. In reviewing this research area, Pearce *et al.* (1995) concluded that there were no notable relationships between psychological problems and serum levels of hormones – either endogenous or exogenous. The one exception is that castration appears to be associated with depression (Porter *et al.*, 1996). McKinlay and McKinlay (1989) found, in their large community sample, that women who had been castrated reported twice the rate of depression than the rest of the sample. Castration, *per se*, and the associated hormonal changes may, however, not be causing depression as these women reported poorer health both before and after the surgery.

The stereotype of the menopausal woman as depressed, irritable, wrinkled, and asexual is just that, a stereotype. In spite of the research discussed above, medical and mental health professionals continue to portray menopause as a time of heightened vulnerability to physical and psychological symptoms (Hay *et al.*, 1994). These stereotypes are passed on to the public through the media and are exacerbated by the unrealistic credibility Western cultures ascribe to medical professionals. In 1993, a colleague and I (Gannon and Ekstrom, 1993) examined attitudes toward menopause in a large sample of community women and men aged 18 to 85 years. Attitudes were assessed under three conditions: menopause portrayed as a "medical condition," as a "life transition," or as a "symbol of aging." The "medical condition" elicited significantly more negative attitudes toward menopause than the other contexts. In general, women's attitudes were more positive than men's and attitudes became increasingly positive with age and/or the experience of menopause. Because menopause is not a major concern for most men and younger women, their attitudes are most likely determined by the cultural stereotype. As women age, they begin to anticipate the event and seek information by talking to friends and relatives who have experienced menopause; gradually, their attitudes take on a more personal and idiosyncratic nature, and women who have actually experienced menopause would be most likely to base their attitudes on their own experience. In our study, women who had experienced menopause had more positive attitudes than any other group; those women who had experienced menopause and who had expressed their attitudes toward menopause in a life transition and aging context – as opposed to the medical context – were the only participants to express attitudes that were, on balance, positive. Thus, professionals who insist on equating menopause and depression, despite evidence to the contrary, are perpetuating a stereotype that is neither true nor beneficial to aged women.

Consistent with the lack of association between menopause, hormone levels and psychological symptoms is research failing to demonstrate the effectiveness of hormonal therapy in treating such symptoms. As early as 1950, Fessler noted that hormonal therapy did not relieve irritability and depression. Psychological symptoms, particularly depression are notoriously responsive to placebo effects, that is, any form of treatment, including sugar pills, tends to reduce the frequency and severity of symptoms. This may be because persons who believe they are being treated expect to feel better, resulting in a central nervous system response of increased secretion of endorphins which may, in turn, cause relative euphoria. Furthermore, untreated depression is typically time-limited and the spontaneous remission of symptoms frequent. In any case, research evaluating the effectiveness of any form of treatment for depression necessitates the use of placebos in a control group. A study evaluating the effectiveness of hormone therapy on depression and satisfying these methodological requirements was reported by Utian (1972). He found that hot flashes and vaginal dryness were relieved by estrogen, but not by placebos, whereas symptoms of depression, irritability, insomnia, and palpitations responded significantly both to estrogen and placebo therapies; the response to estrogen was not different from the response to placebos. These results have been replicated (George *et al.*, 1973; Gerdes *et al.*, 1982; Poller *et al.*, 1980).

In spite of such clear and consistent evidence, studies are still being published (at least one per year) that do not use a placebo control, and conclude that hormone therapy does significantly elevate mood (e.g., Best *et al.*, 1992). The results of this inadequate and misleading research are passed on to medical consumers. Ettinger (1988) wrote: "estrogen therapy can alleviate menopause-related sleep disorders, psychological problems and sexual dysfunction" (p. 31S). Brenner (1988) stated: "Estrogen replacement therapy enables postmenopausal women to sleep better, wake rested, perform better, and feel less irritable and depressed" (p. 7S), and cited early research by Thomson and Oswald (1977) who did, indeed, find estrogen to relieve depression, but not as effectively as did a placebo! The widespread belief among medical professionals that hormones determine the psychological well-being of women is incredibly persistent. In spite of considerable evidence to the contrary, the US National Institutes of Health funded research in 1996 to study the effects of estrogen on depression (Bishop, 1996). In 1997, Studd stated: "These wretchedly depressed women in their 40's usually respond well to oestrogen treatment" (p. 1229).

The belief that hormones cure depression is so insidious that it serves as an *assumption* – a phenomenon that is obvious to all and questioned by no one. Ferin *et al.* (1993) admitted that not all aging depressed women are effectively treated with estrogen; rather than conclude that estrogen is not a panacea, the authors blame the patient. They suggest that hormones may not cure psychological problems in all menopausal women because some women have always been mad: "psychological symptoms are not always alleviated [by hormones]. Many of the symptoms that appear around the climacteric have deep roots in the distant past" (p. 102). In such cases they recommend tranquilizers be added to the hormones.

Most recently, Zweifel and O'Brien (1997) conducted a meta-analytic review of twenty-six studies that had examined the treatment effectiveness of hormone therapy on depressed mood. The authors concluded that hormone therapy is effective in reducing depressed mood among menopausal women. However, an examination of their evidence indicates the opposite conclusion. Of the 26 studies included, only *two* met the criteria that the women were naturally menopausal, the hormone therapy consisted of both estrogen and progesterone (the regimen universally recommended in order to avoid an increased risk of uterine cancer), and a placebo-control group was used. Neither of these two studies reported a significant benefit from hormone therapy. In spite of such inadequate and contradictory evidence, Schmidt and Rubinow (1991) argue for the existence and formal recognition of a "menopause-related affective syndrome." These authors acknowledge the considerable research that has failed to identify increased depression associated with menopause and those studies that have documented significant relationships between contextual factors (poverty, discrimination, violence) and mood/behavior changes at all ages, including menopause. Yet, they conclude, "However this evidence is far from conclusive in refuting the existence of a menopause-related affective syndrome" (p. 846). Why does a syndrome that has never been empirically, clinically, or epidemiologically validated need to be refuted?

The persistent efforts to demonstrate that menopause causes depression in the face of evidence to the contrary is, at least partially, motivated by the misogynistic values of our culture – values that limit women's roles to biological, particularly reproductive, ones. In the nineteenth century, women's physical and psychological well-being were believed to be determined by the health of their uterus; in the twentieth century, the focus has moved from the uterus to hormones. Since, in patriarchal societies, women are valued largely for their reproductive capacity, their fertile years are designated as "normal," and the end of fertility as abnormal. Thus, women are assumed to be at their happiest and most fulfilled when pregnant, giving birth, or taking care of small children and to experience grief and depression when no longer able to reproduce.

The politics behind these beliefs are illustrated by contrasting the scholarly literature on depression during pregnancy and depression during menopause. Since the low rate of depression during menopause contradicts the stereotype, Schmidt and Rubinow (1991) argue that the standard criteria for depression be *less* stringent when applied to menopausal women: "the use of excessively stringent criteria for severity may result in failure to identify clinically significant mood disturbances during menopause" (p. 847). In contrast, Holcombe *et al.* (1996) found that 43% of their sample of pregnant women were depressed according to traditional criteria. Since a high rate of depression during pregnancy contradicts the stereotype of the happy, pregnant young woman, the authors suggest using a *more* stringent criterion resulting in fewer pregnant women being labeled as depressed. Thus, the definition of depression is conveniently modified so that the outcomes are consistent with and support misogynist cultural values. The persistence of this belief is unfortunate since it detracts attention from the social, interpersonal, economic, and occupational causes of women's distress at all ages in a patriarchal society.

Summary

The treatment of depression in mid- and old-age women is complicated by the large array of life circumstances that may contribute to or cause the depression, such as poor physical health, chronic financial strain, bereavement, sexism, racism, ageism, and disability. There is little individual psychotherapy can do in the way of eliminating these causes. On the other hand, psychotherapy may be useful in helping women accept, adjust to, and/or effectively work to diminish certain stressors, such as the onset of a disabling disease, and in facilitating quality of life. A psychotherapist may also aid the elderly woman by identifying modifiable sources of depression and by focusing the therapy on achieving these modifications. The decreasing incidence of depression with aging in women may be even more pronounced when the current 40-year-olds reach their elder years. Compared to Western women of the 1950s, women today are less likely to have some of the risk factors that are thought to predict depression, such as low education levels (Gallo *et al.*, 1993), chronic poverty (Keith, 1993), and strong adherence to the culturally-defined female sex role (Bromberger and Matthews, 1996).

The elderly are often thought to be not good candidates for successful psychotherapy. This belief may well be motivated by therapists' preferences for young, physically healthy, and psychologically minded clients, since research documenting a poor response by the elderly to psychotherapy is lacking. None the less, antidepressant medication is frequently prescribed. Financial considerations enter into choice of treatment and, for those on fixed incomes and inadequate health insurance, medication may be more cost-effective. The choice of medication presents complications not present in younger populations. The standard dose for young adults tends to produce higher plasma concentrations in the elderly because the drugs are cleared from the system more slowly due to aging processes in the kidney and liver and co-existing physical illnesses. Potentially serious complications are related to adverse drug interactions as most of the elderly are taking a number of medications.

The traditional antidepressants are tricyclic antidepressants, which block reuptake of norepinephrine and serotonin, and monoamine oxidase inhibitors, which increase the effectiveness of norepinephrine, serotonin, and dopamine. Norepinephrine, serotonin, and dopamine are neurotransmitters in the central nervous system; increasing the quantity, quality, or impact of any of these tends to be associated with increased arousal and activity. Both of these drug types are not particularly suited to the elderly because of potentially severe side-effects and a high probability of interactions with other drugs and foods. Both have the potential to cause orthostatic hypotension (feelings of dizziness when standing up), making the individual susceptible to falls and fractures. Selective serotonin reuptake inhibitors are a newer form of antidepressant drug. These drugs are relatively free of *serious* side-effects, produce fewer drug interactions, do not cause sedation or falling, have been found to be effective in the elderly, and do not require therapeutic monitoring (adapted from Preskorn, 1993).

COGNITIVE DEVELOPMENT

Cognitive development refers to several phenomena – typically intelligence, memory, attention, and concentration. In general, these components of cognition tend to be associated with one another, that is, an individual who has difficulty attending and concentrating is likely to also exhibit intellectual deficits. Until fairly recently, the general consensus has been that all forms of cognitive functioning decline during the middle and elder years and that research efforts in this area should be directed toward determining the details of this inevitable decline. This was the position of one of the most prominent of the theoreticians, David Wechsler, author of the most widely used intelligence tests since the 1940s: "nearly all studies dealing with the age factor in adult performance have shown that most human abilities...decline progressively, after reaching a peak somewhere between ages 18 and 25" (Wechsler, 1958, p. 135). As is the case with many scholarly knowledge bases, the research and theories of cognitive development have been largely developed and tested on young men; the application of this knowledge toward the understanding of mid- and old-age women is questionable. In the last decade, there has been an increased interest in scholarship on aging. Consequently, researchers have begun to explore development, as opposed to deterioration, in mid- and old-age persons.

The importance of age

Today, many scholars of cognition and aging are challenging the assumption that a decline in cognitive functioning is inevitable. While average intellectual performance on standardized tests does decline with age, researchers note tremendous variability among the aged. In one study, a third of the octogenarians performed as well as younger adults on eleven separate cognitive tests (Powell, 1994). It seems that the cognitive decline with aging is, indeed, not universal. Advances in this area include the use of increasingly sophisticated and appropriate research strategies. Earlier research on aging was typically addressed in cohort studies; for example, one might test groups of persons – some in their twenties, others in their thirties, and so forth – and then compare the various groups on measures of performance. More recently, longitudinal studies have been undertaken. Such studies consist of identifying a group of individuals at a young age and then testing these individuals repeatedly and at regular intervals across the life span. While the latter yields more definitive information, they are relatively uncommon as they require considerable commitment of time and resources.

Decreasing cognitive functioning with age is typically found in cohort studies but not in longitudinal studies. According to Schmid (1991):

> cohort studies on intelligence parallel neurobiological studies of dementias in that they suggest a loss that is not found in longitudinal studies....[Longitudinal studies]...found that individuals remain on a stable course even during the critical periods of 67 to 74 years of age, but...the cohort born later in the century (birth cohort) retained higher positions throughout a lifespan. The investigators observed that the differences found in cohort studies reflected variations stemming from non-age-related rapid technological–cultural changes, not from intrinsic (ontogenetic) decline. (p. 360)

Thus, comparing today's 70-year-olds to today's 30-year-olds will probably suggest a cognitive deficit in the older persons – yet, this "deficit" may not be age-related but rather due to differences in educational level and other relevant cultural factors.

Not only are age-related declines in cognitive function apparently limited to some individuals, they are also limited to certain skills. Memory is a case in point. The construct of memory can be divided into short-term memory and long-term memory: the former, remembering a phone number while dialing, is time-limited and capacity-limited; the latter refers to memory of the relatively distant past and is permanent and unlimited. There are fairly consistent data indicating that these aspects of memory are differentially influenced by age. In general, short-term memory seems to decrease with age while long-term memory appears to remain constant or to increase with age (Horn and

Donaldson, 1980). Relatively consistent evidence has indicated aging declines in attention; but this general statement requires qualification. Effortful attention is the label given to the processing and performance of new tasks while automatic attention refers to tasks that are overlearned and frequently performed. The former apparently declines with age while the latter does not (Hoyer and Pludes, 1980).

Those skills that deteriorate with age may do so because they become less salient to the tasks and goals of aging people and, thus, are not practiced: the forms of intelligence most salient to the pursuits of a person 20 years of age are not necessarily those most useful to a person aged 70 (Blanchard-Fields, 1989). Two forms of intelligence have been distinguished: fluid intelligence is one's ability to reason abstractly while crystallized intelligence represents an individual's accumulated knowledge and verbal skills. Fluid intelligence decreases with age and crystallized intelligence increases with age (Horn, 1975). Certain types of careers and achievements may rely more on one type of intelligence than the other. Lehman (1964) noted that mathematicians, musicians, chemists and poets are most productive at a relatively young age while historians, astronomists, philosophers, and psychologists exhibit more creativity later in life, implying that the former may rely on fluid intelligence while the latter rely on crystallized intelligence.

Since the decline in cognitive skills with aging seems not to be universal, scholars have studied the contextual aspects of aging in an attempt to understand the sources of variability. US studies of healthy people aging in their own communities, as opposed to those residing in institutions, do not show the "inevitable" decline in memory and intelligence (Daniel, 1994). Similarly, Cockburn and Smith (1991) found greater participation in social and domestic activities to be associated with better verbal, visual, and spatial memory. Thus, as one might expect, elderly people who are able and willing to remain active are less likely to show deficits, since these individuals continue to gain practice and experience. Because cultural demands and expectations may yield a "self-fulfilling prophecy," this information should be widely disseminated in order to dispel the myth of universal age-related cognitive deterioration.

In persons of all ages, physical and psychological well-being are obviously associated with cognitive performance. Because physical health is, in part, determined by diet and exercise, Nolan and Blass (1992) proposed that these factors are also related to cognitive functioning: those persons whose physical health and lifestyle quality allow the retention of a high level of physical activity are also those unlikely to show cognitive deficits with age. On the other hand, elderly persons who suffer from physical disease, who require the use of medication with cognitive side-effects and those who suffer from psychological disorders requiring sedatives or psychotropics are more likely to exhibit cognitive impairment (Simoneau and Leibowitz, 1996). Many diseases common to the elderly, such as arthritis and back injuries, are accompanied by chronic pain which has been shown to disrupt concentration, memory, and performance (Crombez *et al.*,

41

1996). Conversely, those persons whose psychological health facilitates motivation, challenge, and engagement are more inclined to retain, and even enhance, cognitive functioning as they age.

Lyness *et al.* (1996) identified elderly persons suffering from major depression and reported that the main cognitive decrements attributed to depression were in the performance of complex tasks, particularly perceptual motor skills. Similarly, Rabbitt *et al.* (1995) studied a large group of community residents, aged 50 to 90 years, who varied on a measure of depressive symptoms. Although none of the participants was clinically depressed, those reporting higher levels of dysphoria exhibited significantly poorer scores on both crystallized and fluid intelligence. Finally, Deptula *et al.* (1993) studied the influence of depression, anxiety and social withdrawal on memory. Each was found to be significantly related to memory among those over 60 years of age. Of interest were the analyses estimating that anxiety accounted for 8% of the variance, depression 12%, and withdrawal from social and physical activities 30% of the variance in memory. A common dimension characterizing those physical and psychological difficulties found to be associated with decline in cognitive function is activity level. A reasonable conclusion from the available research is that if the elderly are not prevented from remaining physically active – due to either disease, medication, pain, lack of motivation, despair, or social alienation – they have a relatively high probability of retaining cognitive skills.

The importance of menopause

Cognitive function has not escaped the trend of the decade – the automatic reattribution of aging processes to menopause (see Chapter 4). As with cardiovascular disorders, diminishing libido, and weight gain, deteriorating cognitive function in aging men is attributed to age or boredom, while in women, these problems are said to be caused by menopause. And, again, this reattribution takes place in the absence of empirical support and in the context of an ideology that is consistent with women being determined and guided by hormones. Research on cognitive changes associated with menopausal status is inadequate. However, the absence of a hormonal influence on cognitive performance is suggested by research on the menstrual cycle. Several major reviews have concluded that cognitive performance does *not* vary predictably, consistently, or significantly across the menstrual cycle (Cockerill *et al.*, 1994; Gannon, 1985; Sommer, 1973).

In spite of the clear absence of any supporting research, deterioration in cognitive function is believed to accompany the menopausal transition; the public, as well as scholars, are victims of these stereotypes (Gannon and Stevens, in press). Matthews *et al.* (1997a), attempting to justify and explain the huge financial and personnel commitment for the Women's Health Initiative, claim that hormone therapy may alleviate "Declines in memory [which] have been reported during menopause" (p. 111). In support, they cite two sources: the first is a 1972 article in German (Kopera, 1972), which, from the English abstract, seems to have little to do with menopause; the second was published in 1953 (Malleson, 1953) and consists of a series of opinions and several case studies with rather archaic views, such as that masochism in women is natural and useful and that all employers are aware that middle-aged women are difficult employees because of menopause. The absurdity of referring to these articles as "evidence" for a hormonally caused deterioration of cognitive function simply emphasizes the lack of valid evidence!

In spite of the absence of supporting data documenting a cognitive deterioration associated with menopause, hormone therapy has been advocated. Kampen and Sherwin (1994), in an observational study comparing users and nonusers of hormone therapy, assessed performance on six tasks – tapping visual, spatial, memory, language, and attention functions. Hormone users were significantly better than nonusers on two of the six, whereas, on the remaining four, nonusers scored better, although not significantly so. In spite of the clearly ambiguous results and in spite of the observational nature of the study which precludes causal inferences, the authors (inappropriately) concluded, "the results of our study argue for a direct effect of estrogen on memory functioning" (p. 982). In another study, Phillips and Sherwin (1992) used random assignment to hormone and placebo groups. They found hormone users to perform better on immediate recall of paragraphs, but there were no hormone effects on immediate or delayed recall of visual material, delay of recalled paragraphs, or digit span. Not only are these results highly equivocal but the participants were limited to castrated women and the dose of estrogen was extremely high, resulting in supra-physiologic levels of serum estrogen – four to five times that of premenopausal levels. In contrast, a large observational study was reported by Barrett-Connor and Kritz-Silverstein (1993) in which cognitive function was measured with eight standard instruments. Their conclusions apply equally well to other studies on this topic: "No compelling or internally consistent evidence for an effect of estrogen on cognitive function was found in these older women. These data do not support the hypothesis that estrogen use after the menopause preserves cognitive function in old age" (p. 2637).

This brief overview of research on cognitive development in mid- and old-age women must be interpreted with caution. Most of the research on cognitive function has focused on young male participants; consequently, the instruments, tasks, and interpretations have been normed and developed on a population considerably different from the one of interest here. Similarly, the skills and abilities assessed are those which are of greatest use to the activities and lifestyles of the young. The young are more likely than are the old to be required to learn new tasks and to be in a situation in which time is crucial. Perhaps, certain skills decline with age because they are no longer useful and practical in one's everyday life. Denney (1986) evaluated the practical aspects of problem solving in aging adults by examining their methods of solving practical problems, such as their landlord being unwilling to fix a stove or not receiving their pension check. She found that the ability to deal with practical problems actually *increased* in middle age. Schmid (1991) points out that to interpret age *differences* in cognitive skills as reflecting deterioration is to place additional burdens on the elderly. The expectation that they perform poorly on all tasks, suffer from various cognitive deficits, and are in a general and continuous state of decline may impact their performance as well as our interpretation:

> Indeed, the best way to conceptualize the manner in which the deficiency model is generated is as a cascade of circular thought processes, each step influenced by bias. This self-propagating cascade has an inner coherence that makes bias so systematic as to legitimize it.
>
> (Schmid, 1991, pp. 358–9)

Without our agist perspective, we might recognize that individuals of both genders and all ages develop and maintain skills and abilities in response to need and usefulness rather than age, *per se*.

Cognitive development (rather than deterioration)

The "aging" model and the "menopausal deficiency" model are the most popular perspectives on cognitive function in aging women. By their titles, both are clearly models of decline and deterioration. There are, on the other hand, many cultures and subcultures, both historical and current, in which the elderly are viewed with respect because of their greater accumulated experience and wisdom. "Wisdom *is expert knowledge about the practical aspects of life*....This practical knowledge involves exceptional insight into human development and life matters, good judgment, and an understanding of how to cope with difficult life problems" (Santrock, 1992, p. 595, emphasis in original). Western cultures today seem to place little value on the wisdom of the elderly. Daniel (1994) notes that the accelerated cultural changes brought about by rapid technological advancement encourage the young to dismiss elderly wisdom as no longer relevant to life: "We have confounded the accumulation of data with its appreciation, or even an understanding of it. Wisdom, on the other hand, always puts information back in the context of human life" (p. 68).

Neither an aging model which is based on deterioration due to cell loss or a menopause model which is based on deterioration due to hormonal changes can provide a perspective with which to study wisdom as a characteristic of the aged. A crucial component of such a model is the assumption that the cognitive skills most relevant to an individual's life change across the life span. Piaget's model of cognitive development, one of the more prominent and famous, recognizes the importance of different skills at different ages (Inhelder and Piaget, 1958). Although his theory of development ends with early adulthood, Piaget's basic model of conceptualizing cognitive function as dynamic and developmental has created the structure in which theories of cognitive development in adulthood have emerged.

Kramer has developed and researched a model of cognitive development that spans adolescence through maturity to old age; three stages, each defined by a particular thinking style, are recognized (Kramer and Melchior, 1990; Kramer *et al.*, 1992). The most basic thinking style, absolute thinking, is mechanistic and reductionistic in outcome; absolute thinking is based in dichotomies (right, wrong; weak, strong). The second level of adult cognitive development is relativistic thinking which is based on a world view which defines reality as contextual, unpredictable, and continually changing (Stevens, 1994). Some authors have suggested that relativistic thinking functions as a temporary bridge between absolute and dialectical thinking rather than a stage, *per se*, since this thinking style precludes commitment, development and growth – a state most individuals find stressful. Whether stage or bridge, relativistic thinking hopefully progresses to the most sophisticated form – dialectical thinking. Dialectical thinking allows for the confrontation and integration of contradictory ideas.

> The "old" belief is transformed by integrating the new, contradictory information....A synthesis has occurred which allows for the growth of one's knowledge by integration of new information....Dialectical thinking is a continuous, creative process whereby new beliefs are born out of the synthesis of contradictory knowledge.
>
> (Stevens, 1994, p. 3)

Kramer's model is a developmental one – persons are thought to progress from absolute thinking to dialectical as they age, with thinking styles being appropriate to developmental tasks. For instance, the tasks of persons in late adolescence are absorbing information in educational and vocational contexts; absolute thinking may facilitate the learning of "facts" and "procedures." In contrast, the tasks of middle-aged persons are complex and require integration: decisions and actions are ideally the product of a synthesis of facts, beliefs, values, financial constraints, health, and prior experience. Kramer *et al.* (1992) examined thinking styles in persons aged 17 to 83 years. Relativistic styles peaked during late adolescence and early adulthood, declining thereafter, whereas, dialectical styles increased linearly into old age. Kramer's concept of dialectical thinking style is remarkably similar to Blanchard-Fields' (1989) description of positive aging. According to the latter, mature thinking reflects growth in many aspects: (a) the integration and regulation of cognitive and affective systems; (b) an increase in autonomy and a decreased reliance on external authority and social conventions; (c) an increase in cognitive complexity and integration; and (d) a decrease in hostility and escapism when confronted with challenging situations.

Kramer and Melchior (1990) proposed that, due to their greater role conflicts, women, compared to men, develop more readily into the dialectical stage. In testing young adults, they did, indeed, find women to be more relativistic and dialectical in their thinking style than were men. In discussing their results, the

45

authors speculate that the conflicts expressed by women surrounding work and family may facilitate the earlier development to dialectical thinking: "Some women expected an integrated solution, others expected a tradeoff, while others expected to redefine traditional sex roles in order to forge egalitarian marriages. Fewer men expected such conflicts, and consequently few had plans for resolving them" (p. 570). These findings are consistent with Gilligan's (1982) work on moral development. She noted that women's moral beliefs emerge from seeing oneself in relation and connection to other people while men's morality is reflected in rights and rules; the former is theoretically consistent with dialectical thinking and the latter with absolute thinking. The theory, research, and interpretation here clearly locate gender differences in cognitive function in a cultural context rather than a biological one.

The appreciation of wisdom as emerging from a lifetime of experience and the emergence of newer models of positive aging and developmental thinking styles change the landscape within which aging is viewed and valued. The dominant model of aging in Western cultures is a medical or physical one in which mid- and old-age are necessarily times of reduced energy, increased probability of disease, and chronic, disabling illnesses. Regardless of one's endorsement of this model for physical health, the model does not necessitate accepting a model of biological deterioration for cognitive function. The evidence is accumulating that increased age is associated with greater complexity, integration and sophistication in thinking.

CONCLUSIONS

The research literature concerned with psychological well-being has been developed and interpreted in a social context in which young adult men have represented the "standard" human. Since the definition of psychological well-being and the pathways leading to its achievement vary with gender and age, this research is clearly inadequate and unacceptable as a basis for understanding psychological well-being in mid- and old-age women. Until the women-centered research of the last decade, information on psychological well-being in mid- and old-age women was based on stereotypes – stereotypes consistent with a patriarchal ideology. In this tradition, women were believed to be biologically motivated to sexually attract men and to bear and raise children; it was assumed that when these primary and essential roles became no longer possible, the women must necessarily become morose and depressed. The research studies documenting an absence of psychological and cognitive decline in middle-aged women have been difficult for traditional scholars to accept; their response has been to develop new methods of pathologizing elderly women by modifying the criteria for the diagnosis of depression and by medicalizing menopause.

In spite of sexist and agist cultural imperatives, women fare well when progressing through mid- and old-age: (a) women adapt well to life transitions and role changes; (b) psychological well-being in women does not appear to be dependent upon a high level of control over others; (c) the traditional gender roles accorded to women have facilitated highly developed social skills – skills of considerable value in maintaining psychological well-being in the elderly years; and (d) women derive satisfaction from roles that continue into old age, such as friend, partner, caregiver, and parent. None the less, these skills and values can only be fully expressed and can only be fully beneficial when women have the financial resources and physical health to maintain a minimum level of independence. The same tradition that facilitates these qualities and abilities in women also places women at risk with regard to material resources. Because of women's roles and values, their position in society often precludes maintaining the professional constancy required for high salaries and adequate pensions (see Chapter 8).

Psychological and physical well-being typically are discussed and researched as independent of one another. While this allows a certain structure and organization in conceptualizing these constructs, psychological and physical well-being are not dichotomous or independent in theory or practice. Psychological distress and stress are typically studied in the realm of psychology and, in the past, have been thought to impact primarily psychological well-being. More recently, psychological distress has been found to cause diminished immune competency which, in turn, increases vulnerability to physical disease. Similarly, while control has been studied primarily in the realm of psychology and in the context of psychological problems, the psychological distress resulting from a lack of control may ultimately diminish physical well-being. More directly, control is crucial in determining one's physical health throughout life: in order to subscribe to a healthy lifestyle, an individual must have sufficient control over their everyday life to buy and eat nutritious food, to avoid polluted environments, to exercise in safety, and to access medical care. The mutually interacting association between physical and psychological well-being seems to accelerate with age. The major predictors of psychological distress or depression in mid- and old-age persons are health and functional capacity. As the probability of chronic disease and disabling conditions increases, so does one's appreciation of good health. One recognizes that good health is necessary in order to be motivated to perform and take pleasure in any activity. Thus, in persons of this age and life stage, physical and psychological well-being are inextricably linked.

3

PHYSICAL WELL-BEING

> If a society puts half its children in dresses and skirts but warns them not to move in ways that reveal their underpants, while putting the other half in jeans and overalls and encouraging them to climb trees and play ball and other active outdoor games; if later, during adolescence, the half that has worn trousers is exhorted to "eat like a growing boy," while the half in skirts is warned to watch its weight and not get fat; if the half in jeans trots around in sneakers or boots, while the half in skirts totters about on spike heels, then these two groups of people will be biologically as well as socially different. Their muscles will be different, as will their reflexes, posture, arms, legs and feet, hand–eye coordination, spatial perception, and so on.
>
> (Hubbard, 1990, p. 115)

Stating that physical health is crucially important to people is, perhaps, self-evident. None the less, the relative importance of physical health varies among individuals and, predictably, increases with age: injuries and illnesses in the young may result in a two-week vacation from work, whereas, in the elderly, injury may result in permanent disability and illness or chronic pain. Scholars have recognized the necessity of going beyond the physical in the search for physical well-being. Burnside (1993) has identified other areas of "health" in additional to physical: intellectual – the ability to take advantage of opportunities for learning; social – forming and maintaining good personal relationships; and, purpose – having feelings of self-esteem and control over one's life. Gatz *et al.* (1995) add functional health – the physical ability and psychological set to remain independent – and economic health – the resources to provide oneself with nutritional food, housing, and safety. These "healths" interact in a mutually enhancing manner so that the strength of the relationships among various dimensions of health grows and the progressive and ultimate impact on physical health and mortality accumulates with experience and age. Consequently, old age tends to be characterized by high individual variability but predictable consistency across domains of health – the extremes being the individual who reports poor health is likely to have few friends and family, have insufficient financial resources, exercise little, have low self-esteem, eat poor quality food, and have insufficient access to medical care; the individual who has excellent health is likely to have close friends and family, have adequate resources, exercise regularly, feel self-confident, eat nutritional food, and have access to quality medical care.

The last several decades have brought medical and technological advancements that have significantly increased life expectancy, particularly for women. Unfortunately for many, this has resulted in a longer period of morbidity, creating an extended old age of disability and degeneration. According to Fries (1989), continued medical and technological advancements are unlikely to further extend life expectancy. Rather, the target is more likely to be a delay in morbidity and an enhancement in quality of life until an age older than is currently probable. He notes that four of the most prominent primary prevention studies, including those assessing the consequences of smoking cessation, dietary fat reduction, and cholesterol reduction, found no differences in mortality between the intervention and control groups but did find morbidity of chronic diseases to be far less in the intervention group than in the control group. He refers to this as the "compression of morbidity" and proposes that the primary method of compression is lifestyle change: "With chronic diseases accounting for the great majority of morbidity, and with the 'incubation period' for most of these chronic illnesses spanning many decades prior to first symptoms, the potential for preventive strategies is manifest" (Fries, 1989, pp. 208–9). An 80-year-old individual who practiced a healthy lifestyle is likely to be strong, flexible, energetic, and alert, whereas a similarly aged individual at the other end of the continuum of lifetime behaviors may be alive, but disabled and in pain. The value of compressing morbidity is unquestionable: most would rather have diabetes for 2 years than for 30 years; most would prefer one month, rather than 10 years, as an invalid. Prevention of chronic disease, rather than chronic treatment of chronic disease, is the key to preserving quality of life.

The prevention of physical illness, disability, and psychological distress takes several forms in the scientific literature. Tertiary prevention applies to those individuals whose health has been already compromised; it refers to rehabilitation and prevention of further disease progression in order to maximize remaining functions, given the restrictions imposed by the disease. An example might be a cardiac rehabilitation program for persons who had suffered from a heart attack. Secondary prevention refers to the early detection of disease or to the recognition and modification of highly salient risk factors. An example might be the use of screening mammograms or the dietary treatment of high cholesterol. Finally, primary prevention refers to disease prevention through health promotion. An example might be an educational effort to reduce smoking and alcohol abuse, improve diet, and increase exercise (Primomo, 1995). The importance of lifestyle is relevant to all three forms of prevention although the effectiveness is maximized if employed as primary prevention.

Recognizing poor health in old age as the cumulative effects of lifelong poor health habits underscores the futility of the medical contention that distinguishing normal aging and illness is possible and desirable. Distinguishing between acute illness and aging poses few problems since the symptoms of acute illness tend to be sudden, obvious, and time-limited. Chronic diseases, on the other hand, typically have an insidious onset, are often difficult to diagnose, and are, by definition, not curable. Many, if not most, chronic diseases develop in the context of chronic causes, many of which are lifestyle factors and life conditions. Thus, the accumulated effects over a lifetime of poor diet, sedentary activity level, substance abuse, and environmental pollution are expressed as chronic, progressive conditions such as hypertension, obesity, asthma, and osteoporosis. The vast majority of the elderly have some form of chronic disease that renders them difficult to treat and, therefore, they are not favorites of physicians. "Doctors question why they should even bother treating certain problems of the aged; after all, the patients are old. Is it worth treating them? Their problems are irreversible, unexciting, and unprofitable" (Butler, 1989, p. 140).

The insurance industry developed in tandem with the medical profession and, consequently, their policies and guidelines agree with and reinforce that of the medical profession. The general goal of US Medicare is to provide treatment for acute illness and for care in hospital settings (Cunningham and Brookbank, 1988). Rather than meet the needs of the increasing aged population, medicine, particularly in the United States, has created needs to fit their traditions. Because the medical paradigm is designed for acute problems, chronic diseases are commonly treated late in the disease course when irreversible consequences have occurred. Clearly, the most obvious treatment for chronic disease is prevention. The implementation and evaluation of primary prevention interventions, however, do not fit the tradition of heroic medicine, do not win political votes, and are not rewarded with financial profits. Rather than a system that emphasizes improved lifestyle in order to prevent or limit chronic disease, medicine treats the consequences of a lifetime of poor health habits as they would acute illness – with expensive and invasive high-technology procedures. According to Fries (1989), "behavioral and preventive initiatives required are relatively low in technological content and may prove to be less expensive than traditional medical approaches" (p. 226).

With increasingly aged populations, the distinction between normal aging and disease becomes increasingly blurred. Recognizing the theoretical confusion, scholars have offered a variety of solutions. Aging has been variously defined: (a) increased biological vulnerability and reduced reserve capacity (Staudinger et al., 1989; Albert and Cattell, 1994); (b) reduced adaptive capacities and speed and excellence of performance and increased susceptibility to disease and pathological processes (Shock et al., 1984); (c) loss of complexity in the dynamics of organ system function, leading to an impaired ability to adapt to stress (Peterson, 1994); and (d) biological deterioration that is universal in old age. Others have attempted to clarify the distinction by creating vague classification systems. Elias et al. (1990) proposed distinguishing among three categories: universal, progressive, and irreversible with age (e.g., atherosclerosis); common with age but not universal and not inevitable (e.g., cancer); and not necessarily related to age but more harmful in the elderly (e.g., pneumonia). A similar system was proposed by Brody and Schneider (1986) who suggested two classes: age-dependent diseases in which the pathogenesis seems to be located in normal aging (coronary artery disease); and age-related diseases that may be temporally related to age but not related to the aging process (multiple sclerosis).

Another approach to distinguishing aging from disease is to define successful or optimal aging – all else is then disease. Shock *et al.* (1984) proposed to study aging in well-educated, affluent subjects who had good access to medical care. Age deterioration emerging from this group could then be classified as pure aging and free of sociodemographic and lifestyle factors. They wished: "to examine all subjects in great detail and to exclude from the analysis of age trends data from any subjects who show evidence of pathology or disease" (p. 1). Taken to its logical conclusion, all persons would eventually be eliminated. Although delineating optimal aging and disease may be a theoretically interesting dilemma, it is not particularly practical. Defining normal aging as that which changes over time in individuals who have no genetic abnormalities, have experienced no traumatic physical or psychological stress throughout their life, have had a continuously nutritious diet, have never abused alcohol, nicotine, or caffeine, have never inhaled second-hand smoke, have lived their entire lives away from polluted environments, and have not been exposed to pesticides, contaminated foods or foods preserved with unhealthy substances may provide a definition of successful aging but one that would apply to no one.

Each of these attempts at defining normal aging is intentionally vague, reflecting the practical difficulty of distinguishing between aging and disease in clinical settings. Theoretically, if not always in practice, scholars tend to agree on the universal and inevitable nature of the deterioration that accompanies old age. The maximum life span potential (MLP) is defined as: "that age beyond which no member could survive even in a protected environment" (Weiss, 1981, p. 28). Human MLP has not changed in the last 100 000 years; it is estimated to be between 90 and 100 years (Amoss and Harrell, 1981). The increase in life expectancy over the last century is due to the reduction in deaths from infection and maternity at relatively early ages; today, the vast majority of mortality in Western societies is caused by intrinsic, degenerative diseases of later life (Weiss, 1981). There is no cure for these chronic conditions but the implementation of prevention strategies can delay disability and pain and prolong quality of life.

In the US, women are twice as likely as are men to seek prevention services. Unfortunately, the cultural imperative of patriarchy tends to denigrate what women do. As a consequence, rather than being commended for taking care of themselves, women are negatively and stereotypically portrayed as whiners, complainers, and hypochondriacs. While stoicism, supposedly a characteristic of men, may enhance feelings of masculinity, it may be a trait detrimental to one's health. If women are more likely to notice a headache and to report a headache, they may also be more likely to seek prevention services such as mammograms and flu shots. Perhaps, the whining and complaining and the many visits to the doctor keep women healthier than men. Women's more frequent contact with the medical profession might be more appropriately viewed as pursuing and receiving proper help rather than attention-seeking.

Compared to men, women suffer from a greater incidence of minor physical illness (Popay *et al.*, 1993), visit health care professionals more often, suffer from more chronic diseases, perceive their health to be poorer, and have greater rates of disability. Yet, women live longer (Huyck, 1990; Lorber, 1997). This has long been a puzzle to epidemiologists – logic seems to dictate that the greater risk for morbidity should translate into greater risk for mortality. A partial answer may lie in the distinction between objective and subjective assessment of health. In a research context, objective health is typically assessed by medically verified pathology, functional status, cardiovascular fitness, consumption of pharmaceuticals, and/or visits to doctors while subjective health is typically assessed by evaluating an individual's *perception* of their health. This is variously referred to as self-reported health status, subjective health status, or perceived health status. Although one might expect objective health and subjective health to be highly correlated, this is not necessarily the case. In addition, subjective and objective health differentially predict mortality and psychological status and are differentially predicted by factors such as race, sex, psychological status, economics, stress and personality. In elderly women, subjective health is a better predictor of mortality (Gatz *et al.*, 1995; McCallum *et al.*, 1994; Wolinsky and Johnson, 1992) and depression (Beekman *et al.*, 1995) than is objective health. The unexpected salience of subjective health has led researchers (who tend to prefer an "objective" world) to appreciate and study constructs that have, thus far, eluded researchers' attempts at measurement and analysis – constructs such as "zest for life," "attitude toward aging," and the "will to live."

DIET AND EXERCISE

Since Roman times, exercise and moderation in food and drink have been recommended as a way to preserve vitality and energy (Cunningham and Brookbank, 1988). In spite of this ancient wisdom and in spite of public health efforts to discourage sedentary lifestyles and poor diets, poor nutrition and inactivity characterize the life course of most individuals in Western societies. Among middle-aged women in the US, 32.5% are obese or overweight (B.M. Posner, *et al.* 1995), and 58.5% report a sedentary lifestyle (Marcus *et al.*, 1995a). Why do people choose not to have healthy lifestyles? Clearly, many of the poor do not have the choice. They may not have access to healthy food or the facilities and the time to prepare it; they do not have the time, freedom, or safety to engage in regular exercise. But this does not explain why middle- and upper-class persons make similar choices nor does it explain why hospitals and schools pay little attention to the nutritional value of the food they provide.

The public's apparent preference to be medically treated for illness rather than prevent illness through lifestyle changes is evident. Prevention efforts are often dismissed as a fad, a "health craze," or vegetarian fanaticism. I recently viewed a television program on the early detection of diabetes. The medical community was promoting the screening of basically healthy people in order to detect the early stages of diabetes with the hope of preventing progression to the more severe forms that are associated with disability and early mortality. The physician being interviewed described a simple, inexpensive blood test for all persons who had any of a number of minor symptoms thought to characterize pre-diabetics. The journalist asked what treatment would be recommended for the individual who was found to be pre-diabetic. The physician responded by saying, "modifications in diet and increased levels of physical activity." The journalist expressed astonishment at this response and trivialized the recommendation, saying, "You mean that all you would do is recommend diet changes and exercise?" Obviously, the journalist wanted a magic pill – a desire all too common in the general population.

Diet

The Western diet has changed somewhat over the last 25 years. Liebman (1997) has documented some of these changes in the United States: (1) a small increase in consumption of fruits and vegetables; (2) decreased beef and increased chicken consumption; (3) sugar and other refined sweeteners up from 120 to 150 pounds/person/year; (4) a small decrease in coffee and milk and a dramatic increase in soda; (5) egg consumption down from 310 to 235/person/year; (6) cheese purchases up from 12 to 28 pounds/person/year; (7) whole milk consumption down from 25 to 7 gallons/person/year with a modest rise in 2% milk and even less increase in skim milk. Public health efforts can be recognized in these trends: eggs, beef and whole milk have been stigmatized as sources of cholesterol and to be avoided; caffeine has been cast as an addictive substance and a contributor to tension and stress; and carbohydrates have been promoted as a quick source of energy. Public health efforts have focused on foods to avoid but have been less forthcoming in the recommendation of healthy foods. Thus, many persons substitute cheese for meat even though cheese can be a major source of cholesterol. Similarly, eliminating whole milk without substituting other sources of calcium can be detrimental to bone health. Many foods, such as vegetable proteins, have not been promoted in spite of the demonstrated health benefits. None the less, the trends that have occurred over the last 25 years seem to indicate that public health campaigns can be, at least moderately, successful. (The impact of diet on the incidence and progression of cardiovascular disease and osteoporosis is discussed in detail in Chapters 6 and 7, respectively.)

Dietary trends relevant to cardiovascular risk have been somewhat discouraging. Reporting on the Framingham Study, a large-sample longitudinal study, B. M. Posner *et al.* (1995) highlighted several results from analyzing dietary profiles and risk factors over a 30-year period (1957–60, 1966–9, and 1984–8): (a) while 35 to 60% of the participants reported decreasing their consumption of animal fat, the total fat intake remained relatively stable; (b) despite reductions in cigarette smoking, blood pressure and low-density cholesterol levels, and despite both men and women reporting higher levels of physical activity, the prevalence rates of overweight and hypertension increased; (c) only 56% of men and 63% of women reported making healthy changes in their eating habits; and (d) commercial vegetarian products were among the most infrequently consumed food.

The popularity of vegetarian diets has, in the past, been compromised by the lack of available information and the absence of readily available food products. While these problems continue somewhat for vegans (those who do not include dairy products in their diet), lactovegetarians (those who do consume dairy products) have welcomed the increased information and research concerning the health benefits and risks of a vegetarian diet. Appropriate food products are increasingly available, even in traditional supermarkets. Marsh *et al.* (1988) compared bone mineral density in omnivores (those who eat meat) and lactovegetarians. In young adults, there were no differences in bone density; on the other hand, between the ages of 50 and 87, differences emerged with omnivores having 35% less bone density than younger persons while lactovegetarians had only 18% less bone mass. Those with the lowest bone density when entering the eighties were vegans and omnivores who consumed meat regularly. Comparing the diets of a sub-sample in detail, the authors found similar nutritional value in the diets of omnivores and lactovegetarians. However, the diets of omnivores had a greater sulfur content, causing a shift toward more acidic urine, which, in turn, may have caused calcium to be lost through excretion. Similar conclusions were reached by Stini (1995) who noted that, because of the enhanced loss of calcium in omnivores, lactovegetarians require less dietary calcium to maintain bone density.

Reviewing the research on the adequacy of a vegetarian diet in providing adequate calcium requirements, Weaver and Plawecki (1994) concluded that, if dairy products are included, vegetarian diets maintain good bone health. The use of soy products greatly eases the difficulties persons encounter in adopting a vegetarian diet, and, today, these are readily available throughout the world. The most popular soy product, tofu, is an excellent source of protein and calcium.

Soy products are of special interest to mid- and old-age women because they are a source of phytoestrogens – compounds with estrogen-like action. Murkies *et al.* (1995) studied the effects of adding soy flour to the diet of middle-aged women who were experiencing hot flashes. At six weeks, there was a significant reduction in hot flashes and by 12 weeks, hot flashes were reduced by 40%. In a more recent study (Albertazzi *et al.*, 1998), soy protein was compared to placebo in a randomized, controlled study. Those women consuming soy reported a 33%

reduction in hot flashes by the fourth week. Others (e.g., Somer, 1997) have hypothesized that the high consumption of soy products in China and Japan is responsible for the low incidence of hot flashes reported by women in these countries.

Exercise

> If we could put exercise into a pill, we would have one of the best medicines available (Butler, *et al.*, 1995, p. 39).

In the last two decades, we have witnessed a wide-spreading and deepening interest among the public and among scientists in the effect of exercise on physical and psychological well-being. An increasing number of persons in Western societies engage in regular aerobic exercise, such as running, swimming, and dance. Reinforcing this popular interest has been an ever-expanding data base representing a variety of disciplines including psychology, behavioral medicine, physiology, and endocrinology within which the biochemical, hormonal, behavioral, and psychological consequences and correlates of exercise have been examined. The benefits of exercise have been accepted by health care workers across disciplines as an important component in good health. Exercise is often a core component of wellness programs and is increasingly accepted by the medical profession as prevention and treatment of some health problems. At the same time, exercise is often dismissed as a "fad" and the outcome trivialized by attributing the motive to vanity rather than to health: "By the late 1970's as the baby boomers who had fostered the youth culture aged, the struggle to maintain a youthful appearance had fostered a nationwide fitness craze" (Dinnerstein and Weitz, 1994, p. 7). Such comments trivialize the effort by attributing the motive to vanity rather than to health and label a desire to be healthy as an obsession.

The primary cause of disability in the elderly is the progressive nature of chronic diseases such as arthritis, osteoporosis, diabetes, and cardiovascular disease, as well as simple frailty – a consequence of the loss of reserve capacity that epitomizes aging. The beneficial effects of exercise on chronic diseases, and therefore, on subsequent disability is well-known: maintaining strength and aerobic capacity through exercise remains the most effective method of delaying functional incapacity. None the less, few studies have directly examined the impact of exercise on disability. Lane *et al.* (1987) compared long-distance runners to community controls (aged 50 to 72) on rates of musculoskeletal disability. Runners had less physical disability and greater functional capacity than controls. Fries *et al.* (1994) examined the development of disabilities in groups of runners and sedentary individuals – age approximately 60 years – over an 8-year period. The rate of acquiring disability was several times lower in runners than in controls. Finally, J.D. Posner *et al.* (1995) studied the relationship between muscle strength and peak oxygen consumption and the ability to perform activities necessary to daily living in women with an average age of 69. Significant correlations were found between the strength of the calf muscle and oxygen consumption and successful performance of tasks. Although the temptation is to attribute the enhanced functional status to exercise, the methodology of these studies is observational, precluding such precise interpretations. Persons who are strong and are able to exercise may well be those who are not vulnerable to disability.

In addition to preventing and lessening osteoporosis and cardiovascular disease (see Chapters 6 and 7), exercise has been found to be associated with other health benefits as well: a reduction in the risk of cancer (Colditz, 1996), specifically, breast cancer (Thune *et al.*, 1997); the maintenance of metabolically active tissue, the prevention of intraabdominal adipose tissue, the decrease of fat mass, and the prevention of the decline in lean mass (Campbell *et al.*, 1994; Ryan *et al.*, 1996); lowered probability of developing severe chronic diseases (Laukkanen *et al.*, 1998); reduction in breathlessness and enhancement of psychosocial function in chronic obstructive pulmonary disease (O'Donnell *et al.*, 1993); reduction in subjective back complaints (Preisinger *et al.*, 1996); enhancement of self-rated health (Gregg *et al.*, 1996; Stewart *et al.*, 1993); reduction in the rate of developing age-related disability (Fries *et al.*, 1994; Lane *et al.*, 1986); decreased probability of premature mortality (Kushi *et al.*, 1997); reduction in hyperinsulinemia and improvement in insulin action (Evans, 1995; Kirwan *et al.*, 1993); alleviation of depression (Klein *et al.*, 1984; Slaven and Lee, 1997); reduction of perceived stress, anger and anxiety (King *et al.*, 1993; Markoff *et al.*, 1982); reduction in obesity and hypoglycemia (Rauramaa, 1984); and, of particular interest to women, a slowing of the natural decline in estrogen levels during middle age (Garrison, *et al.*, 1994). Some of these benefits are listed in Table 3.1.

Although exercise confers benefits at all ages, the habits, roles, and customs of most societies demand more physical activities from children and young adults while making fewer physical demands on individuals as they age. Thus, the aged are more likely to be sedentary than those younger, yet, these are precisely those who could benefit the most from *increasing* their level of physical activity. O'Brien and Vertinsky (1991) reported that the proportion of those who never exercised nearly doubled from 19% for those under the age of 55 to 36% for those aged 55 and older. Only 5 to 7.5% of those over 65 engaged in adequate levels of exercise. The authors interpret these data in light of what they consider the consequences of inactivity to be: after the age of 85, 20% of the women needed assistance to walk across the room, 69% needed help with housework, and 25% needed assistance to climb stairs. These discouraging statistics may be descriptive of cohorts of women who matured in the 1950s, when the ideal woman was sedentary and lazy. Many women maturing today have a healthier, more active ideal. When today's 40-year-olds who are presumably more physically fit than their predecessors reach their eighties, they can, perhaps, anticipate greater functional capacity and less disability.

Given a constant level of activity, maximal aerobic capacity decreases at the

Table 3.1 Beneficial effects of exercise on chronic conditions of aging

Condition	Recommended exercise	Effect(s)
Coronary heart disease	Aerobic, endurance type	Reduction of BP; Increase in HDL and reduction in body fat; Increased cardiac output; Increased maximal oxygen consumption; Increased insulin sensitivity
Hypertension	Aerobic, endurance type; leisure-time activity	Decreased systolic BP; Decreased total peripheral resistance
Osteoarthritis	Resistance stretching; endurance	Maintain range of motion and muscle mass; Increased muscle strength
Osteoporosis	Resistance; weight-bearing	Strengthened postural muscles; Stimulated bone growth; Decreased rate of bone loss
Diabetes mellitus	Aerobic, endurance type	Fat loss; Increased insulin sensitivity; Decreased glucose intolerance risk
Cognitive dysfunction	Aerobic	Improved cerebral function; Increased cerebral perfusion; Increased beta-endorphin secretion

Source: Reproduced with permission from E. W. Kligman and E. Pepin (1992) Prescribing physical activity for older patients. *Geriatrics*, 47: 33–47. Copyright by Advanstar Communications Inc. Advanstar Communications Inc. retains all rights to this article.

rate of approximately 1% per year. Physiological changes causing and correlating with this gradual deterioration are decreased maximal cardiac output, lower maximal heart rate and contractility, decreased muscle mass, and decreased oxidative capacity of skeletal muscle (Evans, 1995). Consequently, maintaining a constant level of activity as one ages becomes increasingly difficult and aversive since the same task represents a larger and larger percentage of the maximum reserve capacity. Although these aging changes are universal, exercise provides the individual with a higher "set point" so that dependency is delayed:

> The impact of a regular exercise program upon such functional deterioration can be illustrated by age-related changes in the maximum oxygen intake, which expresses the ability of the body to transport oxygen from the atmosphere to the working muscle....If oxygen delivery is inadequate to meet metabolic demand, work must be performed anaerobically, which quickly causes fatigue....The rate of functional loss remains essentially constant, regardless of whether an individual is an active exerciser or sedentary. A sedentary person thus reaches the threshold where institutional support is needed between the ages of 80 and 85. However, regular endurance training increases the peak oxygen transport by 5 to 10 ml/mim/kg BM at any given age....In the active individual, therefore, it takes 10 to 20 years longer for oxygen transport values to drop to the threshold where independence can no longer be sustained.
>
> (Shephard, 1993, p. 63)

Given such extensive and impressive benefits, we must ask why everyone does not exercise. A partial explanation for the low levels of physical activity among women is that, historically and currently, women have received contradictory information on the benefits and risks of exercise. In the second half of the nineteenth century:

> A successful man could have no better social ornament than an idle wife, her delicacy, her culture, her childlike ignorance of the male world gave a man the "class" which money alone could not buy. A virtuous wife spent a hushed and peaceful life indoors, sewing, sketching, planning menus, and supervising the servants and children.
>
> (Ehrenreich and English, 1979, p. 106)

And the forced inactivity did not begin with marriage: in 1916, Dr Winfield Scott Hall recommended:

> all heavy exercise should be omitted during the menstrual week...a girl should not only retire earlier at this time, but ought to stay out of school from one to three days as the case may be, resting the mind and taking extra hours of rest and sleep.
>
> (Ehrenreich and English, 1979, p. 111)

These views and lifestyle prescriptions for middle- and upper-class women were not only motivated by sexual politics but also by medical profits:

> better-off women were sickly because of their refined and civilized lifestyle. Fortunately, however, this same life-style made them amenable to lengthy medical treatment. Poor and working-class women were inherently stronger, and this was also fortunate, since their life-style disqualified them from lengthy medical treatment anyway. The theory of innate female sickness, skewed so as to account for class differences in ability to pay for medical care, meshed conveniently with the doctors' commercial self-interest.
>
> (Ehrenreich and English, 1979, p. 115)

The classic perfection of the frail, weak woman has continued, albeit with various modifications and manifestations, to the present day. Post-World War II romanticism and consumerism idealized the woman who "did not have to work" and who had modern time- and energy-saving gadgets. In the late 1950s, the girls in my junior high school class were not expected to participate in physical education classes when menstruating. Gender-role socialization continues today to the detriment of women's health. The assumption that women are weak and should remain so slowed the progress of incorporating women into professions requiring strength and endurance such as the military and the police and fire forces.

Since regular, strenuous exercise has not been expected of women, indeed even considered dangerous, there has been little research on the benefits of exercise in women. The little information available has been focused on the consequences of highly stressful and competitive athletics on reproductive function. Researchers have reported that women athletes often experience amenorrhea; they express concern that, if amenorrhea is accompanied by lowered levels of estrogen, then harmful consequences may ensue (Cann *et al.*, 1984; Drinkwater *et al.*, 1984). These studies found that extremely high levels of physical activity, particularly if performed in a competitive atmosphere, are likely to diminish some aspects of health. Others (Hale *et al.*, 1983; Russell *et al.*, 1984; Tortiola and Mathur, 1986) reported a return to normal reproductive functioning when intensive training was reduced to moderate levels and the psychological stress of competition was removed. Unfortunately, the results of these early studies of extreme and unique groups have been used to caution all women against all exercise (Block *et al.*, 1987). Shangold *et al.* (1981) have pointed out the necessity of separating the effects of exercise, *per se*, from the effects of the physical stress of intensive training and the emotional stress of competing.

The practice of defining physical health in women solely as reproductive health is consistent with women's roles in patriarchal societies and should be questioned. Ellison and Lager (1986) studied menstrual function in recreational runners (12.5 miles per week) and sedentary women. Although the runners and controls had similar cycle lengths and progesterone profiles during the luteal phase and there were no differences in the timing of the luteal phase, runners exhibited lower peak progesterone levels and lower average progesterone levels during the luteal phase of the cycle. The authors conclude: "our results suggest that exercise may modulate female reproductive function in a continuous fashion, with mild exercise leading to mild impairment of function" (p. 1003). Yet, the differences found between these two groups are not indicative of any disorder or disease, causing one to question the designation of "impaired." With regard to other health parameters – especially cardiovascular and bone health – a sedentary life-style is clearly associated with low levels of physical and psychological well-being, particularly during middle and old age. In a more enlightened context, sedentary individuals are more deserving of the "impairment" label than the recreational exercisers. Fentem (1994) comments, "inactivity must not be accepted as normal" (p. 1294); clearly, utilizing sedentary individuals as an "optimal standard of health" is absurd given the current level of knowledge on the benefits of exercise.

Although research on the timing, type, and amount of exercise required to maximize benefits and minimize risks is of considerable importance in recommending exercise programs, there seems no question as to the benefits of moderate exercise for overall health and well-being. Research efforts are needed on methods of increasing compliance with exercise programs and of developing environmental, work, and personal milieus that encourage the initiation and maintenance of exercise. Available statistics indicate that approximately 50% of mid- and old-age women comply with prescribed exercise programs (Preisinger *et al.*, 1995; Williams and Lord, 1995). This may sound discouraging but, perhaps, less so if considered in comparison with compliance rates for other recommendations from health professionals: the compliance with exercise appears better than compliance with hormone therapy (see discussion on compliance in Chapter 4). Studies that have examined compliance with exercise regimens, although few in number, have noted particular barriers to exercise associated with noncompliance: unemployment (Eaton *et al.*, 1993); high levels of anxiety (Stones and Kozma, 1996); lack of time, responsibility for young children, safety problems, and embarrassment (Marcus *et al.*, 1995a).

King *et al.* (1988) evaluated the effectiveness of quite simple strategies for increasing compliance. Individuals were provided with 30 minutes of initial instruction for a moderate-intensity, home-based exercise program. Subsequently, half of the people received continuing instruction and support through 10 staff-initiated telephone contacts of 5 minutes each every 2 weeks; the other half received no calls. The phone-contact group significantly increased their peak oxygen uptake after 6 months while the noncontact group did not. Half of those in the phone-contact group were then randomly selected to be instructed on adherence and daily self-monitoring while the remaining participants did weekly self-monitoring. Those with daily self-monitoring reported significantly greater exercise compliance than did those with weekly self-monitoring during the next 6 months. The functional capacity in both groups remained higher than before training. In a similarly motivated study, Perri *et al.* (1997) examined compliance under supervised and unsupervised exercise regimens for forty-nine obese women. All participants were expected to complete a walking program of 30 minutes per day, 5 days per week. The supervised individuals participated in three group sessions per week for 26 weeks, and two per week thereafter. Unsupervised participants were expected to complete all exercise sessions on their own. At six months, both groups were similar in exercise participation, fitness, eating patterns, and weight loss while at 12 and 15 months, unsupervised individuals achieved more gains than did supervised individuals. In a third study of initially sedentary individuals, Swinburn *et al.* (1998) compared the effectiveness of physicians providing verbal instructions (average time of 5 minutes) and verbal instructions plus a written ("green") prescription on level of physical activity 6 weeks later. While the written prescription was superior on a number of variables, the average increase was in excess of one hour per week for both groups. Although preliminary, these studies indicate that, even with minimal professional effort and time, exercise compliance can be enhanced. Given the potential health benefits, research designed to develop methods of increasing compliance deserves high priority.

Taking into consideration the available research as well as the goals of primary prevention, a variety of methods to increase exercise participation have been proposed: (1) health professionals need to increase their appreciation of the benefits of exercise and to consider exercise as an effective method of treatment and prevention for many disabling and life-threatening problems; (2) health professionals need to recognize that compliance with exercise regimens is possible and to behave in a manner likely to enhance compliance, such as continued contact, problem-solving, and reinforcement; (3) the structures and policies of work environments should facilitate regular exercise by providing on-site shower and changing facilities, safe exercise equipment and outdoor tracks, flexible time, and child-care; and (4) local governments should provide safe parks, recreational sites, and adequate public transportation. In order to accommodate those individuals who are more likely to participate if the exercise is social, medical clinics, wellness centers, and work place sites could schedule group sessions and organize social events around exercise activities.

OBESITY

Obesity has multiple adverse consequences that span all areas of an individual's life. Obesity lowers self-esteem and quality of life, is a source of oppression and discrimination, and is a risk factor for many disabling and life-threatening diseases. In spite of the negative consequences and in spite of public health efforts to facilitate healthy lifestyles, trends in the US suggest an increased prevalence of overweight over the last 30 years (B.M. Posner et al., 1995). At least 25% of the US population is overweight or obese. Although this overall figure has changed little, rates of obesity and overweight among persons aged 45 to 54 years have increased. The prevalence of overweight in men increased from 28.1% in 1960–2 to 31.0% in 1976–80, while for women in this age group the prevalence has increased from 30.9 to 32.5% (B.M. Posner et al., 1995). Possible causes for the increased prevalence of obesity in middle age were examined by Poehlman et al. (1995). They assessed body fatness, physical activity in leisure time, aerobic fitness, and resting metabolic rate in women and men aged between 17 and 90. Fat mass increased with age; the rate of increase was greater in women than in men. The increases in fat mass were closely associated with decreased physical activity and lower aerobic capacity but were not related to resting metabolic rate, menopausal status, or nutritional intake. These results imply that the increase in fat mass, weight, and/or obesity often occurring in middle age is most likely the consequence of preventable lifestyle changes (i.e., decreased participation in physical activity, particularly aerobic activity) rather than endocrinological, metabolic, or physiological processes associated with aging.

Obesity has been studied primarily in young adults. Since the social, cultural and psychological milieu change dramatically from young adulthood to old age, the data from this research are not readily applicable to older adults. Hetherington and Burnett (1994) compared young and elderly normal-weight women on measures of dieting and attitudes. The two groups were similar in discrepancy between current weight and desired weight; both groups averaged a desired weight loss of approximately 10 pounds. However, the elderly were significantly more satisfied with their bodies than the young. These data, as well as considerable anecdotal data, indicate that elderly women are less concerned with physical attractiveness than are younger women. Elderly women's interest in maintaining normal weight probably derives from the motivation to enhance health and mobility and minimize disability rather than from the motivation to achieve a physically and sexually attractive appearance. This is not to say that mid- and old-age women do not desire to be attractive, only that they revise their priorities, and major priorities for most elderly are physical health and functional capacity. Differences between African American and European American women in behavior and attitudes related to weight were the focus of a study by Stevens *et al.* (1994). Black women were less likely to feel guilty after overeating, less than half as likely to diet and 2.5 times as likely to be satisfied with their weight and to consider themselves to be attractive than were White women. Although the attitudes of the Black women toward weight are psychologically "healthier" in the sense that they may promote self-esteem and reduce the risk of eating disorders, in other respects these attitudes may not promote improved physical health since the prevalence of obesity in Black women is twice that of White women.

Adipose tissue is a primary site for the conversion of androgens to estrogens in postmenopausal women. Consequently, overweight and obese women tend to have higher levels of estrogen than do normal-weight and thin women (Erlik *et al.* 1982). Several of the health correlates of obesity may be related to the higher levels of estrogen among the obese: obesity is a risk factor for breast cancer, particularly after menopause (Coney, 1994), and weight loss reduces the risk of breast cancer (Schapira *et al.*, 1991). On the positive side, heavier women seem to have some protection from osteoporosis. Harris and Dawson-Hughes (1996) examined a large group of postmenopausal women and reported a positive association between body weight and bone mineral density. Tremollieres *et al.* (1993), comparing vertebral bone loss between obese and normal-weight postmenopausal women, concluded: "within the first years after menopause, moderate excess body weight significantly reduces vertebral post-menopausal bone loss" (p. 683). In addition to the increased levels of estrogen associated with obesity, the extra weight of the obese places mechanical stress on the skeleton, which serves as a physiological stimulus for increased bone remodeling.

> Obesity is the oldest identified risk factor for cardiovascular disease in men and women. Seventy percent of cardiovascular disease in obese women and 40% in all women is attributed to obesity. Obesity itself does not seem to be the culprit; instead, it is the...hypertension, hyperlipidemia, hyperinculinemia, insulin resistance, and diabetes mellitus.
>
> (Hammond, 1996, p. 10S)

Diabetes is undoubtedly the primary pathway between obesity and cardiovascular disease. Of people with adult-onset diabetes, 80 to 90 percent are overweight or obese, and the increased risk of cardiovascular disease from diabetes is so strong in women as to negate the gender differences in morbidity and mortality of heart disease (American Diatetic Association, 1995). Predictably, obesity is associated with increased mortality (O'Brien, 1996). Manson *et al.* (1995) examined the association between body-mass index (BMI: weight in kilograms divided by the square of the height in meters) and mortality in a prospective study of over 100,000 women. The women were aged 30 to 55 years in 1976 and followed for 16 years. These authors concluded that:

> Body weight and mortality from all causes were directly related among these middle-aged women. Lean women did not have excess mortality. The lowest mortality rate was observed among women who weighed at least 15 percent less than the US average for women of similar age and among those whose weight had been stable since early adulthood. (p. 677)

Recently, cardiovascular researchers have emphasized a particular type of obesity as contributing to the risk of disease. This has been variously referred to as "central obesity" or "waist-to-hip ratio." Essentially, central obesity describes a fat pattern with most of the excess weight carried in the center of the body (Wild, 1995). Gardner and Poehlman (1995) studied predictors of age-related increases in blood pressure in women and men; for women, the distribution of fat (i.e., central obesity) was the primary correlate of blood pressure increases. Bengtsson *et al.* (1993) examined the cholesterol–obesity–mortality pathway in mid- and old-age women. The authors concluded that the distribution of adipose tissue was more important than obesity *per se* as a risk factor for mortality. The distribution of added weight and the salience of this factor on physical and psychological well-being may be influenced by exercise habits and genetics, neither of which have been studied sufficiently in this context.

SUBSTANCE USE AND ABUSE

Caffeine

As a potential risk, caffeine has been studied in the context of osteoporosis and fractures. According to Kiel *et al.* (1990), caffeine increases urinary calcium output and may reasonably be expected to increase one's risk of osteoporosis. They recorded caffeine intake and fracture incidence in mid- and old-age women for 12 years. Consumption of more than 2 cups of coffee or 4 cups of tea per day was associated with an increased risk of hip fractures. The link between caffeine and calcium is supported in two further studies. Harris and Dawson-Hughes (1994) reported an interaction between dietary calcium and caffeine on bone density: women consuming more than 800 mg of calcium per day did not show an association between caffeine and bone density, whereas those women with a low dietary calcium intake tended to have lower bone density if heavy coffee drinkers. Lifetime diet was examined in a study by Barrett-Connor et al. (1994). Bone density did not vary with lifetime coffee intake in women who reported drinking at least one glass of milk per day during most of their adult lives. However, among those who did not drink milk on a daily basis, the caffeine equivalent of two or more cups a day of coffee was associated with decreased bone density. In each of the three studies relating caffeine to osteoporosis or bone density, the risk seemed to begin when coffee consumption exceeded two cups of coffee per day.

On the other hand, it is possible, perhaps even likely, that the association between caffeine and any health outcome is correlational rather than causal. For example, women who are thin may be heavy coffee drinkers and their low weight may not place sufficient stress on the skeleton to maintain integrity. Physicians and other health workers may advise all their clients to eliminate caffeine "just to be safe." Caffeine, however, may confer benefits. In a large US survey, Kawachi et al. (1996) found a strong inverse association between caffeine intake and suicide – high caffeine intake was related to low risk of suicide. Furthermore, caffeine may be beneficial to the aged in helping them maintain alertness and concentration. Finally, caffeine may be a source of pleasure to persons who find they must increasingly forego pleasures – alcohol, rich foods, nicotine – in order to maintain health as they age.

Cigarette smoking

The most serious consequences of cigarette smoking are increased risks of cardiovascular disease and lung cancer. Considerable information has been published on this topic and will not be repeated here. However, smoking has been found to have additional influences that are particularly relevant to aging women. Garrison et al. (1994) reported that the normal decline in estrogen levels between the ages of 30 and 54 years was accelerated in women who smoked. These data may explain the frequent finding that women smokers tend to have an earlier menopause. In one of the largest prospective studies of middle-aged women, McKinlay et al. (1992) found that smokers experienced natural menopause on average of 1.8 years earlier than did nonsmokers and that the perimenopausal transition was of shorter duration in smokers compared to nonsmokers. In a rather unique sample composed of female twins discordant for smoking, Hopper and Seeman (1994) concluded that: "Women who smoke one pack of cigarettes each day throughout adulthood will, by the time of menopause, have an average deficit of 5 to 10 percent in bone density" (p. 387). Finally, although not a health risk *per se*, increased risk for facial wrinkling was found to be associated with smoking in Caucasian women over 40 (Emster *et al.*, 1995).

Alcohol

The cost–benefit ratio of alcohol consumption on physical and psychological well-being varies with the population being studied and the quantity of alcohol being evaluated. In general, among the elderly, small to moderate amounts of alcohol are thought to increase sociability, cognitive performance, appetite, and bowel regularity, while heavy drinking impairs nutritional status, cognitive performance, and sleep (Dufour *et al.*, 1992).

Reduced bone density and osteoporosis have been cited as one of the consequences of alcohol use. The initial studies were those finding a high risk of osteoporosis among men with alcoholic cirrhosis (Chappard *et al.*, 1991). These results are not readily applicable to aging women who are not alcoholics. Felson *et al.* (1995) recorded alcohol consumption and bone density every two years for 20 years in mid- and old-age persons. For women, alcohol consumption of at least 7 oz per week was associated with significantly higher bone densities than those who had less than one ounce per week. Similar results were found by Holbrook and Barrett-Connor (1993) who concluded that social drinking is associated with higher bone mineral density in both women and men. In contrast, Tuppurainen *et al.* (1995) compared middle-aged women with and without fractures and found that those with fractures had a higher alcohol intake than those without fractures. If the data in these studies are reliable and valid, they indicate that, despite the positive association between alcohol consumption and bone density, drinking alcohol may increase the risk of fractures. One hypothesis to account for these contradictory results is that alcohol consumption contributes to fractures by increasing the probability of falling (Moniz, 1994; see Chapter 7).

Heavy alcohol consumption is associated with premature death from cardiovascular disease in both women and men when "heavy drinking" is defined as more than 14 drinks per week (Hanna *et al.*, 1992). Gronbaek *et al.* (1995) examined the effects of different types of alcohol on all-cause mortality in women and men. They reported that while low-to-moderate intake of wine was associated with lower mortality, consumption of spirits tended to increase mortality, and beer had no effect. Fuchs *et al.* (1995), focusing on mid- and old-age women, assessed alcohol consumption in 1980 and analyzed these data with a 12-year follow-up of mortality. They concluded, "Light-to-moderate drinking...was associated with a decreased risk of death from cardiovascular disease; heavier drinking was associated with an increased risk of death from other causes, particularly breast cancer and cirrhosis" (p. 1245).

In mid- and old-age women, the mechanism through which alcohol influences osteoporosis and breast cancer may be via an effect on estrogen levels. A major source of estrogen in postmenopausal women is the conversion of androgens to estrogens in adipose tissue, and this process is enhanced with the consumption of alcohol. Gavaler and Van Thiel (1992) examined the relation-ship between alcohol consumption and estrogen levels in postmenopausal women. The estradiol levels of abstainers averaged 100.8 pmol/liter, signifi-cantly lower than the 162.6 pmol/liter of those reporting alcohol use. The average weekly intake of alcohol in those who drank was 4.8 drinks. Thus, alcohol may influence mortality through its effects on estrogen which, in turn, is known to have a positive impact on bone density but to increase the risk of breast cancer.

Health professionals need to use caution in recommending that mid- and old-age women regularly drink alcohol. Alcohol potentiates the effects of many drugs and opposes the effects of others. Since the majority of elderly are taking some kind of medication, the interaction of alcohol with medications is a potential health hazard. Practicing these precautions, however, the consumption of low-to-moderate amounts of alcohol may reduce the risk of osteoporosis and cardiovascular disease. High levels of alcohol intake are, on the other hand, associated with decreased quality of life and increased morbidity and mortality. The definition of low, moderate, and high intake needs to be individ-ually determined since weight, fat-to-lean body mass ratio, health status, and age may moderate the quantity of alcohol necessary to achieve a particular blood alcohol level.

CONCLUSIONS

We often assume that the reason persons do not seem to welcome aging is that the end point is death. Perhaps, what is more frightening and dreaded is disability and dependence. As we age and care for our aging parents, we are forced to acknowledge the possibility of disability in our future. For many, disability means institutionalization and, in many Western societies, institutions for disabled and/or dependent elderly people conjure up visions of neglect, dete-rioration, and dementia. Biologists believe that the human life span, estimated to be approximately 100 years, has not changed in the last 150,000 years and is unlikely to do so in the near future (Amos and Harrell, 1981). Once longevity approaches the life span – as has happened for women in Western societies – further medical and technological advances act primarily to improve the quality of life in the aging population by diminishing disability and functional inca-pacity:

> The "compression of morbidity" hypothesis envisions reduction of the national illness burden by postponing the age of onset of chronic infir-mity relative to average life duration so that the period of morbidity is compressed between an increasing age of onset and a relatively fixed life expectancy.
>
> (Fries, 1989, p. 208)

The manner in which persons choose to live their lives clearly impacts their physical well-being. There is a growing appreciation by both professional health workers and the public of the benefits of a healthy diet and regular physical exercise and the risks associated with obesity, smoking, and excessive alcohol and caffeine. Public health efforts have focused on educating the public on health risks and encouraging the adoption of healthy lifestyles. Voluntary lifestyle changes at the individual level are, according to McKinlay (1993), receiving attention and resources disproportionate to their effectiveness because this focus is congruent with traditional medical approaches. McKinlay points out that expecting individuals to change their behaviors in a sociopolitical environment that encourages, rewards, and profits from people engaging in at-risk behavior is impractical and illogical. He advocates *"social system contributions,* including governmental policies, organizational priorities and professional behaviors, …[which] offer considerably more promise for intervention and beneficial change" (p. 110, emphasis in the original). Perhaps, the epitome of the individual, voluntary approach is the "Just say no" campaign by the US government initiated to prevent adolescents from abusing drugs. In this campaign, there was no appreciation for the sociological, political, and economic context within which drug use occurred and was encouraged.

In his proposal to switch the emphasis of prevention from the individual to the system, McKinlay notes: "Adding only 8 cents to US cigarette taxes apparently caused 2 million adults to stop smoking and prevented 600 000 teenagers from starting" (p. 113). Other suggestions by this author include the removal of price supports for sugar and strengthening clean-air and antipollution policies. Of high salience for the population of concern here are the rules and regulations governing reimbursement for health care by governments and private insurance companies. Few individuals have the financial resources to privately fund their medical care. When a physician prescribes a reimbursable pain killer for a back problem, the patient will probably take the medicine rather than pay for her/his own physical therapy even though the latter may prevent future injury and disability. Given a choice between a free anti-hypertensive medication or paying for a high-priced health club, the drug is tempting. Although prevention is praised by every medical profession and government agency, preventive health practices are not logistically or financially encouraged. Perhaps, Western societies have gone as far as practical in promoting individual voluntary efforts towards improving health: "Our challenge is to move beyond personal attributes and find ways to bring planned and gradual changes in the sociopolitical system into efforts at primary and secondary prevention" (McKinlay, 1993, p. 113).

4

MENOPAUSE

After approximately 30 years of menstrual cycles in order to provide transitory fertility, ovarian serenity is restored, estrogen once again becomes stable and levels return to normal, menstruation ceases. The woman experiences release from reproductive pressures and is able to participate fully in her career, social, and family activities as she need no longer be concerned about the problems associated with menstruation, birth control and pregnancy and is no longer at a heightened risk for endometriosis, uterine fibroids, and breast cancer.

(Gannon, 1996, p. 243)

In the last decade, a woman's menopausal status has become a crucial component of her identity. In many disciplines, a woman's career, roles, accomplishments, and lifestyle are being reconstructed within a hormonal paradigm. Research which, in the past, might have been titled "career changes in young adult women" might today be titled "career changes in premenopausal women." Age-related physical changes, such as diminished energy and cardio-vascular changes, have been re-defined as part of the "menopausal syndrome." The transformation of menopause from a predictable, expected, and normal life event to a progressive disease with manifestations in every sphere of life is consistent with sexual politics – defining women according to their reproductive status and as biologically disadvantaged –and medical politics – pathologizing a universal event.

One of the many unfortunate consequences of medicalizing a normal life event is the consequent usage of dualistic theory and absolute thinking that characterize medical theory and practice. Within the medical paradigm, there is a clear tendency to view the life cycle as consisting of abrupt, distinct phases rather than gradual and continuous development. The "normal" menstrual cycle portrayed in the research literature is one based on the study of women primarily between the ages of 18 and 30; the description of menopause found in the medical and popular literature is typically the hormonal profile of a 55- to 60-year-old woman. Because they are separated by 25 years of continuous developmental changes, these two hormonal profiles are, indeed, distinctly different. However, the continuity that represents lifetime reproductive development in women is lost when such medical categories are imposed. Since castration is associated with an abrupt decline in hormonal levels, the common practice of equating castration and natural menopause has contributed to the misconception that the latter is also discrete and abrupt.

The dualism of medical theory is readily accepted because it seems consistent with the everyday experiences of girls and women. Hormonal and associated biochemical and physiological changes are, for the most part, silent. A 13-year-old girl is not aware that during the last several years, estrogen levels have been increasing and internal organs developing. Menarche clearly announces its presence, and the cultural and social response to menarche bestows added drama to the "event." Similarly, at age 35, women tend not to notice minor decreases in menstrual blood loss, an occasional missed period, or the gradual hormonal changes. They *do* notice when menses ceases, reinforcing the perception of a dichotomy – one is fertile when premenopausal and infertile when postmenopausal – when, in fact, fertility begins to slowly diminish in the early thirties.

Women have complained for decades that the medical community has trivialized their complaints of premenstrual and menopausal problems. Medical professionals have responded with PMS (premenstrual syndrome or premenstrual tension) clinics and menopause specialists. So what is the problem? Why are we still complaining? The "problem" is that, within the patriarchal medical ideology, a woman is not seen as a normal, healthy individual with one or several complaints, symptoms, or illnesses; she is regarded as essentially and basically flawed because of her biological sex. Osteoporosis, cardiovascular disease, mood swings, and Alzheimer's disease are, in men, disorders or diseases determined by genetics, lifestyle, and environment. In women, however, these are not regarded as diseases but as manifestations of an underlying disease process – the disease being femaleness. In aging men, osteoporosis is the purview of bone specialists, cardiovascular disorders of cardiologists, mood swings of psychologists, Alzheimer's disease of neurologists, and all such disorders are treated with specific medications and/or advice on lifestyle modifications. In aging women, these disorders, as well as others, are deemed the consequence of menopausal hormonal changes, and all are readily treated by a gynecologist who is likely to recommend hormone therapy as a panacea. Women don't have problems, women are the problem.

ENDOCRINOLOGY

The endocrinology of women's reproduction develops in a predictable fashion from before birth through to old age. Our knowledge of this development varies with the stage of life. While there is minimal information and research on development prior to and through puberty, considerable research has been published outlining the endocrinology of the normal menstrual cycle, pregnancy, and, more recently, menopause.

In prenatal development, fetal differentiation of the sex organs is complete by three months and, by the sixth month, the structures of the uterus, Fallopian tubes, and vagina are complete. At birth, the ovaries contain about 2.5 million primitive eggs or follicles. Only about 500 of these will develop and be released as mature oocytes. The rest are lost through absorption; by puberty 200 000 to 300 000 remain. Although puberty is thought of as a distinct event, gradual changes throughout childhood and adolescence occur in preparation. The systems of reproduction are quiescent through much of childhood but, several years prior to puberty, begin to become active. The impetus for this change is unknown. Gradually, these structures increase their sensitivity to various activating agents and increase their secretion of hormones. The beginning of menstrual cycles in girls, or menarche, does not necessarily signal the onset of fertility since ovulation does not typically occur in the early cycles, and these cycles tend to be irregular. After about 40 cycles over a period of 3 or 4 years, a predictable pattern is achieved and the young adult menstrual cycle is established.

The normal menstrual cycle

The events that characterize normal menstrual function rely primarily on the activities of the hypothalamus and the anterior pituitary in the brain and the ovaries. Beginning arbitrarily with menstruation and the preovulatory phase, the hypothalamus produces gonadotropin-releasing hormone (GNRH), which, in turn stimulates the anterior pituitary to release the gonadotropins – follicle stimulating hormone (FSH) and luteinizing hormone (LH). FSH triggers the initial growth of follicles in the ovary. As these follicles develop, they begin to produce estrogen; eventually, one follicle assumes dominance and continues to develop while the others regress and are absorbed. The dominant follicle increases its production of estrogen. Estrogen causes proliferation of the endometrium (the lining of the uterus) and proliferation of breast cells, exerts a feedback effect on the anterior pituitary, and is responsible for the mid-cycle surge of LH. This surge is followed by ovulation, which is the release of the mature ovum from the follicle. LH also transforms the ruptured follicle into the corpus luteum.

In the postovulatory or luteal phase, the corpus luteum, a short-lived secretory organ, produces estrogen and progesterone. Progesterone transforms the endometrium into a secretory organ in preparation for implantation of the embryo should conception occur. Progesterone also exerts a negative feedback effect on the release of gonadotropins from the pituitary, precluding further follicular growth during this phase. Although somewhat controversial, current consensus on the action of progesterone on breast tissue seems to be that it continues to enhance mitosis (cell division) and proliferation of cells (Weinstein *et*

70

al., 1990). If conception does not occur, the corpus luteum degenerates, accompanied by decreasing levels of estrogen and progesterone. Since the secretory endometrium requires these hormones for maintenance, it also regresses and menstruation occurs. With low levels of estrogen and progesterone, inhibition of the hypothalamus and the anterior pituitary is lifted and a new cycle begins. Testosterone rises during the follicular phase, peaks around ovulation, and then decreases. However, the role of testosterone in the menstrual cycle is not clear.

Perimenopause

The menstrual cycle continues throughout young adulthood with gradual and subtle changes occurring mostly unnoticed. With age, and influenced by numerous health, lifestyle, and environmental factors, continued development brings noticeable changes. In their thirties or early forties, women begin to experience changes in their menstrual cycle in terms of duration, frequency, and amount of bleeding. The cause of these changes has generally been attributed to a considerable reduction in the number of remaining follicles and a lessened responsiveness to gonadotropin stimulation in those remaining (Studd *et al.*, 1977). However, extrapolating from follicle counts in menstruating women, one would predict that women at menopausal age would have several thousand follicles remaining. More recently, Richardson *et al.* (1987) examined the follicular presence in ovaries of women at various ages. The rate of follicle loss appears to accelerate dramatically in the last decade before menopause, but the cause of this acceleration is yet to be clarified. Indeed, given the intricacies of the hypothalamic–pituitary–ovarian system, isolating one cause of the developmental changes that characterize the hormonal environment in middle-aged women is, perhaps, impossible. As women traverse their thirties and forties, an increasing number of menstrual cycles are anovulatory, and hormonal levels gradually change. This transitional period, the perimenopause, conversely parallels that of puberty and progresses over a period of five to ten years. More and more cycles become anovulatory until menstruation stops completely; the medical profession defines menopause as the absence of a menstrual period for 12 months.

The hormonal environment during the perimenopause has only recently been a focus of research interest. Previously, the concept of discrete phases prevailed, leading to the view that an abrupt disruption of regular menstrual cycles occurred at menopause. That is, previously high levels of estrogen and progesterone and low FSH and LH were believed to undergo an abrupt alteration, and the sudden onset of menopause was characterized by the absence of estrogen and progesterone, as well as dramatically increased levels of FSH and LH. This misconception is partially due to (1) previous disinterest in conducting research on menopause, which has resulted in ignorance of the processes involved; and (2) to the medical profession's tendency to equate natural menopause with surgical castration. Castration in premenopausal women produces an abrupt discontinuity with quickly diminishing levels of estrogen and an increasing production of gonadotropins. The traditional research strategy of combining naturally menopausal and castrated women in studies of menopause biases the averaged data toward finding more accelerated and sudden hormonal changes than those that truly characterize natural menopause. This is, perhaps, the background for the frequent assumption that a woman's hormonal profile changes abruptly during mid-life, creating chaos and illness, while a man's sex hormones diminish in a continuous manner, allowing gradual adaptation. In fact, both women and men experience similar mid- and old-age changes in reproductive function. The manifestations of the hormonal changes differ in that reproduction in men tends to end due to changes in sexual activity, whereas reproduction in women ends due to infertility.

Recently, researchers have studied the reproductive differences between young (20–30) and old (40–50) menstruating women. This research has begun to provide documentation of the gradual development leading eventually to the cessation of menstruation. Fitzgerald *et al.* (1994) compared older and younger women and found ovulation to occur several days later, less follicular development, and greater endometrial thickness during the luteal phase in older women. FSH and LH were higher in the older women during the follicular or preovulatory phase, but estrogen and progesterone levels were similar between the two groups. These gonadotropin and sex hormone findings were replicated in a study by Batista *et al.* (1995); these authors noted that estrogen peaked earlier in the follicular phase and dropped more abruptly after ovulation in the older group compared to the younger women. Blake *et al.* (1997) reported that both young and old menstruating women had a similar pattern of hormonal fluctuations across the cycle but, interestingly, the older women had *more* estrogen than the younger women. The authors suggest that the older ovaries may be less sensitive to stimulation and thus require greater hormonal stimulation to ovulate. This recent documentation of perimenopausal changes has created more questions than answers. For example, the rise in FSH during perimenopause has been traditionally attributed to the diminishing levels of estrogen but, in fact, the initial increment in FSH is not associated with diminished estrogen (Chang *et al.*, 1994) Clearly, the structures and hormonal environment influencing the reproductive and sexual development of women during their mid-years are not static but are instead continually and slowly changing.

Menopause

Natural menopause and castration have traditionally been viewed as having identical outcomes; in other words, having totally inactive ovaries in the former is equated with having no ovaries in the latter. None the less, the ovary during and after natural menopause is not inactive. The ovary consists of two types of secretory cells. The outer cortex contains granulosa cells, which are the primary source of ovarian estrogen (Longcope *et al.*, 1980); these cells are reduced in number and productive capacity after menopause. However, the ovarian stroma cells are capable of synthesizing the androgens – androstenedione, dehydroepiandrosterone, and testosterone – and continue a similar rate of hormone production after menopause (Hunter, 1976). Direct data regarding the hormone production of the postmenopausal ovary come from a study by Judd *et al.* (1974). They compared the concentrations of testosterone, androstenedione, estradiol, and estrone in peripheral and ovarian vein blood from ten postmenopausal women. A higher concentration of all these hormones was found in the ovarian vein than in the peripheral vein; the magnitudes of the differences were 15-fold for testosterone, fourfold for androstenedione, and twofold for both estradiol and estrone. The authors concluded that the postmenopausal ovary secretes primarily androgens while retaining a diminished but detectable amount of estrogen secretion. Table 4.1 provides the reader with a relative comparison of various hormone levels during the various life phases. Estradiol, the most potent estrogen, is present at similar levels in young women and those who are perimenopausal; natural menopause is associated with approximately a 50% reduction in estradiol, while castration is associated with a 75% reduction. Levels of estrone are similar across these life phases. Estrone, a less biologically active compound than estradiol, is the major estrogen in postmenopausal women.

Table 4.1 Hormonal levels seen during the reproductive life[a]

Stage	E_2 (pmol/L) (pg/ml)	E_1 — —	P_4 (nmol/L) (ng/ml)	FSH (IU/L) —	LH (IU/L) —	T (nmol/L) (ng/dl)	AND — —
Prepubertal	<5 <10	<5 <10	<0.5	<5 —	<5 —		
Reproductive age							
Early follicular	10–80	15–50	<0.5	2–10	2–10	15–40	100
Late follicular (ovulation)	200–600	75–200	0.5–2.0	20–60[b]	30–70[b]	15–70	150
Luteal	100–300	50–150	10–30	<10	<10	15–70	150
Perimenopausal							
Follicular	20–75	15–50	—	<20	<20	—	—
Mid-cycle (ovulation)	150–600	50–200	—	20–70	30–80	—	—
Luteal	75–200	40–100	—	<20	<20	—	—
Menopause (ON NO HRT)							
Postoophorectomy	5–20	5–40	<0.5	>30	>20	15–70	20–150
Natural/early	10–40	5–10	<0.5	>30	>20	15–70	20–150

Source: Taken from R. J. Chang *et al.*, 1994. Reprinted by permission of Springer-Verlag Publishing.
Notes:
[a] Levels are given to show relative ratios. Actual levels will vary greatly between laboratories.
[b] Represents mid-cycle surge.
E_2 = estradiol; E_1 = estrone; P_4 = progesterone; FSH = follicle stimulating hormone; LH = luteinizing hormone; T = testosterone; AND = androgens.

The sources of estrogen in postmenopausal women are ovarian cells (described above) and the conversion of androgens to estrogen in peripheral tissue, particularly adipose tissue. Research investigating the percentage of total estrogen produced via peripheral conversion has not yielded consistent results. In one study (Grodin *et al.*, 1973), the quantity of estrone derived from conversion of androgens was essentially the same as the absolute levels of estrone, suggesting that all estrone was derived in this manner. In contrast, Judd *et al.* (1982) assessed the metabolic clearance rate, conversion ratios, and production rates of androgens, estrone, and estradiol. They found the peripheral conversion of androgens accounted for 24.6% of circulating estrone but accounted for only minimal quantities of estradiol, whereas the peripheral conversion of estrone accounted for 21.5% of estradiol. The participants in this study had experienced natural menopause, but it is unclear whether the estrogens unaccounted for by peripheral conversion were ovarian or were due to an age-related increase in conversion efficiency. Hemsell *et al.* (1974) found a significant relationship between the efficiency of conversion and age; as one ages the body becomes more efficient at converting androgens to estrogens. Most likely, all of the estrogen in castrated women is from peripheral conversion.

Research, then, indicates that the postmenopausal woman has detectable levels of plasma estrogen and that the naturally menopausal woman has higher levels of plasma estrogen than castrated women. Since the adrenal cortex (of the adrenal glands) is capable of synthesizing and secreting androgens, these glands may also be capable of synthesizing estrogen or may contribute significantly to the pool of precursors available for peripheral conversion. There is some indication that the adrenal cortex of castrated women secretes more androgen than that of naturally menopausal women, partially making up for some of the androgens lost when the ovaries are removed (Chang *et al.*, 1994). Adipose tissue is the primary site of the peripheral conversion of testosterone and androstenedione to estradiol and estrone in postmenopausal women (Archer, 1982), and this is consistent with research findings that demonstrate that circulating levels of estrone and estradiol are significantly correlated with body weight and excess fat (Badawy *et al.*, 1979; Judd *et al.*, 1976).

Sex hormone binding globulin (SHBG) may influence this association between estrogen and body weight. SHBG is a circulating plasma protein produced by the liver that binds with sex hormones (estrogen and testosterone) and renders them biologically inactive (Erlik *et al.*, 1982). The biological role of SHBG is unknown, but fluctuating levels of SHBG are relevant to the hormonal profile since only unbound, or free, sex hormones are metabolically active. Research on SHBG and aging is limited to studies examining the fluctuations in SHBG with menopause, a rather imprecise correlate of aging. Walsh and Schiff (1990) note that obese women tend to have lower levels of SHBG than normal-weight women. Since lowered levels of SHBG would leave more estrogen free, this may account for the higher levels of biologically active estrogen in obese women. Pasquali *et al.* (1997) found SHBG to be stable across groups of women defined by menopausal status, while other researchers have found SHBG to drop significantly after menopause but only in lean women (Bruschi *et al.*, 1997). Perhaps, since obese women already have low levels of SHBG prior to menopause, the range for potential change is restricted.

The drop in SHBG after menopause in lean women may be due to physiological feedback mechanisms. Lean women tend to have lower levels of estrogen throughout life than do obese women. The diminishing estrogen of menopause may activate homeostatic mechanisms, resulting in lowered levels of SHBG and, consequently, more biologically active, or free, estrogen. The presence of this protein and its biological actions present a dilemma for those interpreting research on sex hormone levels associated with menopause. Most researchers do not distinguish between bound sex hormones (inactive) and free sex hormones (active) despite the obvious importance. Chang *et al.* (1994) note a further complication. According to these authors, estradiol is the primary estrogen of premenopausal women while estrone is the primary estrogen of postmenopausal women; SHBG binds estradiol but not estrone which implies that SHBG may be more relevant to estrogen activity in premenopausal, compared to post-menopausal, women. The paucity of factual knowledge of these interrelationships and their relevance to women's health is one more indication that current knowledge of the aging process, particularly in women, is inadequate.

An integral component of the reproductive cycle in women is the secretion of gonadotropins – luteinizing hormone (LH) and follicle stimulating hormone (FSH) – by the anterior pituitary. Menopause is characterized by increased levels of gonadotropins but consensus is lacking as to the cause. Given the feedback mechanisms necessary for normal menstrual cycling during the premenopausal years, it is possible that: (1) the decreasing estrogen causes reduced negative feedback to the hypothalamus, resulting in greater production of gonadotropin releasing hormone (GnRH) and, ultimately, increases FSH and LH; (2) the levels of GnRH remain the same but the sensitivity of the pituitary to GnRH increases, resulting in greater production of LH and FSH; (3) both hypothalamic and pituitary activity is similar to that of premenopausal years but the metabolic clearance rates of LH and FSH are reduced; or (4) the gonadotropins increase with age rather than in association with menopause.

There is no information on endocrinological changes that may take place past the first few years after menopause. Since postmenopausal women do not experience obvious reproductive "events," the assumption has been that no further hormonal or gonadotropin changes occur. The lack of interest in the endocrinology of postmenopausal women is consistent with the patriarchal construction of womanhood – once reproduction is over, women's unique physiology is of little interest.

Menopause versus aging

Since menopause typically occurs in women between the ages of 45 and 55, the physiological changes that occur in middle-aged women may be attributed to menopause or to the aging process. If endocrinological changes are primarily due to aging, then one would expect to find a significant relationship between the levels of various hormones and age; alternatively, if such endocrinological changes are due to menopause, one would expect to find relatively constant levels prior to menopause, an abrupt shift coincident with menopause, and a steady but altered state subsequent to menopause. Within a restricted age range, the likelihood of menopause increases with age, so that the relative importance of age and menopause is not readily discernible.

The patterns noted for estrogen are consistent with a menopausal hypothesis; that is, estrogen levels decrease at the time of menopause and are not significantly correlated with age (Meldrum *et al.*, 1981). On the other hand, the research on androgens and gonadotropins is less clear. Meldrum *et al.* (1981) assessed hormonal levels in women aged 34 to 83, all of whom had experienced menopause. They found a strong negative relationship between age and levels of the androgens dehydroepiandrosterone (DHEA) and dehydroepiandrosterone sulfate (DHEAS). In contrast, androstenedione and testosterone were significantly lower than levels found in premenopausal women, and these androgens were uncorrelated with age. These authors concluded that adrenal androgen secretion decreases as a function of age. Unfortunately, this study suffers from the methodological problem still common in research on menopause today – it involved noncomparable research samples consisting of women who were castrated, naturally menopausal, or prematurely menopausal. As discussed above, androgens are secreted by the adrenal cortex and the ovary in postmenopausal years. Clearly, if the ovaries are removed, androgen secretion diminishes. In postmenopausal women who have experienced natural menopause, the cessation of menstruation does not appear to be associated with reductions in androgen production (Chang *et al.*, 1994).

As with other aging patterns, the increase in gonadotropins is not abrupt but gradual and begins many years before menopause. In an early study (Reyes *et al.*, 1977), FSH was found to be primarily related to age while LH was unrelated to age but higher during the postmenopausal years. More recently, Ebbiary *et al.* (1994) assessed serum levels of gonadotropins in women aged 20 to 44 years. There was a significant and progressive increase in FSH levels beginning at age 30, continuing throughout the thirties, and becoming steeper in the early forties. LH levels increased from the mid-thirties to the mid-forties. Since all of these women were premenopausal, the data point to age, rather than menopause, as the source of change. Gonadotropin levels in women aged 45 to 57 were assessed by Burger *et al.* (1995). FSH was found to increase in a linear fashion across this age span and was significantly associated with menstrual markers of menopause; women who had not menstruated for 12 months had higher FSH than those who had not menstruated for 3 months who, in turn, had higher FSH than those who had experienced some irregularity in their cycles. In contrast, Stellato *et al.* (1995) found no differences in perimenopausal women who were still menstruating and postmenopausal women. Thus, the research indicates both age and menopausal status contribute to the changing levels of gonadotropins. Indeed, in naturally menopausal women the effects of age and menopause are probably not separable either practically or statistically. As noted previously, important information on continued development and change after menopause has, for the most part, not been gathered.

In summary, the endocrinology of natural menopause is consistent with a gradual process characterized by a progressive increase in anovulatory cycles and eventual cessation of menses. The hormonal changes accompanying this process probably originate with a decrease in estrogen production by the ovaries. The increased levels of gonadotropins found in postmenopausal women may be a consequence of aging, the cessation of menstruation, or both. Although much reduced, estrogen continues to be detectable in the serum after menopause. The sources of this estrogen are most likely the ovaries and the adrenal cortex. Although the less active ovaries of menopausal women probably influence the gradually changing hormonal profiles of elderly women, other factors – such as physiological changes due to aging, percentage of body fat, and general health – appear to have considerable influence.

DEVELOPMENTAL ASPECTS OF MENOPAUSE

Traditionally, menopause has been associated with a variety of unpleasant symptoms and changes – hot flashes, profuse sweating, headaches, increased weight, dryness and thinning of the vaginal walls, increased incidence of vaginal infections, loss of breast firmness, dizziness, sensations of cold in the hands and feet, irritability, depression, insomnia, pruritus of the sexual organs, and constipation, to name but a few (Weideger, 1977). In the last decade, cardiovascular disorders, osteoporosis, cognitive decline, memory problems, and incontinence have been added. This picture of menopause originates in the medicalization of this life transition. Medicalization of menopause has created a context within which any and all aversive correlates of aging, chronic illness, and destructive lifestyle habits are attributed to menopause. The language may be different but the sentiment is similar to that of 150 years ago:

> "There is a predisposition [during menopause] to many diseases, and these are often of a melancholy character," one physician noted in the 1830's. The host of diseases that might develop as a result of the cessation of menstruation included, as one doctor lamented, "almost all the ills the flesh is heir to."
>
> (Smith-Rosenberg, 1985, p. 191)

Models of menopause

The primary theoretical model for conceptualizing menopausal symptoms has been a biomedical one. In this context, both physical and psychological changes associated with mid-life in women are viewed as the direct result of estrogen withdrawal or the result of biochemical changes concomitant with estrogen withdrawal, such as the elevated gonadotropin levels found in menopausal women. Since medical science is focused on the identification and treatment of problems, only changes reflecting loss or deterioration are studied, whereas positive aspects of menopause have been outside the purview of medicine. Unfortunately, the medical view of menopause has become the public view of menopause. In a recent study, Gannon and Stevens (in press) examined the portrayal of menopause in the popular print media in the United States between 1981 and 1994. The data revealed that menopause, according to the media, is a disease with universal, aversive consequences. In the 50 articles analyzed, there were 350 instances of 39 different negative experiences said to be associated with menopause; there were 27 instances of 11 different positive experiences said to be associated with menopause. Aging, castration, stress, lifestyle factors, race and ethnicity, exercise and diet were, with few exceptions, ignored or trivialized. Although the medical profession often criticizes the mass media for conveying false images by simplifying and sensationalizing medical findings, the media version of menopause and the medical version of menopause are surprisingly similar and neither is consistent with the picture that emerges from careful examination and interpretation of the scholarly literature.

Research conducted in a medical context has taken several forms. For example, there have been numerous large surveys of middle-age women who have been categorized as premenopausal, perimenopausal, and postmenopausal according to self-reported information on the presence and regularity of menses. These groups are then compared to one another on a large number of symptoms with the goal of determining which of these symptoms are related to menopausal status. An early report by McKinlay and Jeffreys (1974) was based on a survey of 638 women between the ages of 45 and 54. Hot flashes and night sweats were consistently associated with menopause and occurred in the majority of women; headaches, dizzy spells, palpitations, sleeplessness, depression, and weight increase showed no relationship to menopause. More recently, McKinlay et al. (1992) followed 2,570 women for five years during perimenopausal years. A wide variety of symptoms and complaints were assessed with only hot flashes, night sweats, and insomnia occurring together and in relationship to menopausal status. Two surveys directed by Holte (Holte and Mikkelsen, 1991; Holte, 1992) assessed a wide variety of physical and psychological symptoms. They reported that: "vasomotor complaints associated with excessive sweating, hot flushes and vaginal dryness, constituted the only variable significantly related to menopausal development" (Holte and Mikkelsen, 1991, p. 193). Interestingly, Holte (1992) is one of the few authors to comment on positive changes associated with menopause. Almost half of the women reported fewer headaches and less breast tenderness while a sizable minority reported fewer vasomotor complaints and less dryness of the vagina after menopause as compared to before menopause.

Whether treatment studies can provide information relevant to etiology is questionable since one cannot infer the cause of a disease from findings on the effectiveness of a treatment (e.g., headaches are not due to a lack of aspirin). None the less, effective treatment need not necessarily alter causes in order to be useful and, with this caveat, the benefits of hormone therapy are addressed here. Research designs considered adequate with regard to methodology are those that compare the effects of hormone therapy to the effects of placebos; ideally, neither the research participants nor the evaluators are aware of which compound a woman has been given. There have been numerous studies meeting these criteria; consistently, the results have been that only hot flashes and vaginal dryness are relieved by estrogen, but not by placebos, while symptoms of depression, irritability, insomnia, and palpitations respond significantly to both estrogen and placebo therapies (Gerdes et al., 1982; Utian, 1972).

Other theoretical models of menopause have received less attention by researchers since the profit motive, and therefore the funding resources, have been absent. The "coincidental stress model" hypothesizes that particular stresses, common in mid-life, such as children leaving home or the illness or death of a parent, predispose women to aversive physical and psychological changes. The most comprehensive study designed in the context of this model was published by Greene and Cooke (1980). They interviewed 408 mid-life women to determine stressful life events, psychological and physical symptoms, and menopausal status. The contribution of stress was significant for both psychological and somatic symptoms and accounted for 38% and 43% of the variance in psychological and somatic symptoms, respectively. The contribution of menopausal status in accounting for the variance in symptomatology was small and nonsignificant. In a later analysis (Cooke and Greene, 1981), the authors noted that women experience the greatest number of stressors and the most severe ones between the ages of 35 and 54. Theorists have concluded that hot flashes, and perhaps atrophic vaginitis and osteoporosis, are caused by the changing hormonal environment of menopause, whereas other somatic and psychological symptoms are the result of aging, personal history, and stress factors (Fogel and Woods, 1995; Rakoff, 1975).

According to the "cultural relativism model," women's roles in Western society are limited not only in number, and not only to roles of relatively low status, but also primarily to biological roles. Women are valued for their youthful attractiveness and for their capacity for bearing and raising children. Given such culturally defined roles, it is not surprising that women view menopause negatively and that they experience adverse psychological and physical consequences when they are no longer capable of fulfilling the major roles available to them. Scholarly work conducted in the context of this model renders even hot flashes and vaginal dryness questionable as menopausal symptoms. The most relevant research approach in the context of this model is cross-cultural; unfortunately, there are few such studies. Studies of mid-life women in Western societies have yielded results similar to those conducted in the United Kingdom and the United States. Porter *et al.* (1996) studying Scottish women and Holte (1992) studying Norwegian women concluded that only the classic menopausal symptoms (hot flashes, vaginal problems) were related to menopausal status while other reported difficulties were due to stress or aging.

NonWestern cultures present a different picture. Flint and Samil (1990), studying postmenopausal Indonesian women, reported the most common mid-life complaints to be fatigue, weight gain, atrophic vaginitis, and hot flashes, although the percentage of women reporting hot flashes was about half that in the US. Seven Far Eastern cultures were compared in a study by Boulet *et al.* (1994). On the whole, there was a low rate of complaints and considerable variability. For example, women in only two countries complained of anxiety, and women in five countries complained of painful sexual intercourse. The influence of researchers' values and expectations on research outcomes was clearly demonstrated when these authors interpreted the results as if women in Western societies provided a kind of "standard" for the rest of the world: they suggested that the relative lack of menopausal complaints in other cultures is due to the women being unwilling to acknowledge the climacteric. Typically, when health differences are found between two cultures, in the absence of evidence to the contrary, the culture found to be healthier is examined for the source of the health benefit. However, Western scientists are so convinced that menopause is a universally aversive experience that, rather than examine cultural parameters consistent with a positive menopausal experience, they pathologize those who are not reporting symptoms.

Bart's (1969) research suggests a different interpretation. She examined ethnographic material from six societies – three in which women's status went up at mid-life, one in which it remained the same, and two in which it went down. In societies where aging increased one's status and perceived wisdom, where the desexualization associated with menopause made women less threatening to men, or where women's freedom increased with menopause, there was little evidence of psychological and emotional difficulties associated with menopause and the end of fertility was often met with relief. On the other hand, in Samoa, where most of the heavy work on plantations is done by women aged between 45 and 55, menopause was marked by temporary instability, being finicky with their food, and whims.

If the type and severity of changes at mid-life are culturally determined, then this effect is most probably mediated by attitudes toward menopause. According to Bowles (1990) the beliefs and expectations inherent in the prevailing sociocultural paradigm are responsible for the formation of specific attitudes toward menopause, which in turn influence the actual experience of menopause. That is, depending upon the cultural beliefs, values, and attitudes, menopause may be experienced by individual women as trivial or traumatic, negative or positive.

This model consists of two causal pathways: the cultural values influence attitudes, and attitudes influence experience. Support for the latter causal path has been noted in several studies (Abraham *et al.*, 1995; Avis and McKinlay, 1991; Hunter, 1990; Meltzer, 1974): attitudes, beliefs, and expectations – all, according to Bowles (1990), derived from the sociocultural paradigm – were predictive of reported distress at the time of menopause. Negative attitudes were associated with negative experiences, whereas positive attitudes were associated with positive experiences.

The initial causal path – sociocultural paradigm influences attitudes – was the focus of a study by Gannon and Ekstrom (1993). In order to evaluate paradigmatic influences on attitudes toward menopause, a large sample of women and men between the ages of 17 and 88 were assigned to one of three groups distinguished by the context within which they expressed their attitudes toward menopause. For one group, menopause was described as a medical illness, in another as a symbol of aging, and in the third as a life transition. The results indicated that the medical context elicited significantly more negative and fewer positive attitudes than did the other two contexts, particularly among the older participants. This research suggests that the cultural evaluation of menopause dictates individuals' attitudes toward menopause. Furthermore, the perspective that menopause is a deficiency disease and should be treated medically is likely to facilitate negative attitudes characterized by pessimism and fear when anticipating mid-life and menopause. An interesting aside from this study was that, compared to younger women and men of all ages, older women (those past menopause) had the least negative attitudes – indeed, only this group expressed attitudes that were, on balance, positive – suggesting that, perhaps, the actual experience of menopause is more positive than is the stereotype.

Menopausal symptoms: hot flashes

Research investigations across models and disciplines have been surprisingly consistent in Western societies in supporting a distinction between mid-life changes due to menopause and mid-life changes due to aging and stress. Thus, theorists have concluded that hot flashes, and perhaps atrophic vaginitis and osteoporosis, are caused by the changing hormonal environment of menopause whereas other somatic and psychological symptoms are due to other factors. Since atrophic vaginitis and osteoporosis are discussed in other chapters of this book (Chapter 5 and Chapter 7, respectively), the current discussion is limited to hot flashes. Logically, if the only cause of hot flashes were menopause, then all menopausal women would experience hot flashes and this is not the case. Beyene (1986) evaluated the menopausal experience among Greek and Mayan women; the Mayans reported no hot flashes while the Greeks reported hot flashes but did not consider them a problem. In the study by Boulet *et al.* (1994), women in five of the seven Far Eastern countries reported hot flashes. Taken as a whole, the scholarship on hot flashes is consistent with an increased vulnerability to vasomotor instability associated with the hormonal changes associated with menopause; however, whether or not this increased vulnerability is manifested as hot flashes depends, perhaps, upon diet, physical activity, chronic illness, genetics, and the particular cultural valuation of aging women.

Hot flashes are characterized by sensations of heat usually in the face, neck, and chest and sometimes followed by perspiration, shivering, or both. They are frequently noticed prior to the complete cessation of menses and continue through the early years after menopause. They seem to be most frequent and most intense shortly after cessation of menses in natural menopause or shortly after castration surgery. There is surprisingly little reliable information on the percentage of women who experience hot flashes during menopause or on the length of time the symptoms persist. It has been assumed that this symptom occurs in the majority of women (60 to 75%) in Western societies and that, without treatment, hot flashes abate over time and eventually cease completely. In the only published descriptive study of the menopausal hot flash, Voda (1982) had twenty menopausal women keep records of their hot flashes for two weeks. She presented the following summary information based on 912 hot flash records: the mean duration was 3.31 minutes; the majority started in the neck, head, scalp, and ears while the rest started in the neck and/or breast area; the time of day or night varied, with no particular time for the majority; and there did not seem to be a common trigger such as eating or stress.

Until recently, the only information on hot flashes came from self-report data. However, in the past several years, attempts have been made to develop objective indices of hot flashes. One of the first studies was reported by Meldrum et al. (1979) who recorded finger temperature in postmenopausal women who were experiencing frequent hot flashes; temperature elevations were found to coincide with subjectively reported hot flashes. Tataryn et al. (1981) took continuous recordings of finger temperature, skin conductance, and core temperature. The physiological sequence associated with a hot flash began with increased skin conductance, then a rise in finger temperature, followed by a decrease in core temperature. Ginsburg et al. (1981) assessed cardiovascular accompaniments of hot flashes. Increases in hand blood flow preceded the hot flash and an increase in heart rate occurred subsequent to the subjective sensations. Finally, de Bakker and Everaerd (1996) reported that the most specific and most sensitive physiological marker of hot flashes was sternal skin conductance. Although these data are interesting, they are not particularly useful. The coincidence of the subjective report of hot flashes and these physiological changes approaches 100%, which simply confirms that the least expensive and time-consuming method of assessing hot flashes is with self-report rather than technology. Initially, researchers expressed hope that studying these physiological accompaniments may reveal etiology. This has not occurred, nor is it likely to since the physiological markers are those associated with the autonomic nervous system, which is notoriously nonspecific, variable, and slow to activate and recover.

The popular belief that declining levels of estrogen are the cause of hot flashes has been perpetuated because of the coincidental occurrence of hot flashes and menopause in many women and because estrogen therapy alleviates hot flashes in most of the women that suffer from them. None the less, Aksel *et al.* (1976) noted that the occurrence of hot flashes after castration was not related to plasma estrogen levels. Similarly, Hutton *et al.* (1978) found women experiencing hot flashes did not have lower levels of estrogen than those symptom-free. Indeed, several researchers (Maddock, 1978; Casper *et al.*, 1979) have argued against estrogen as the cause of hot flashes since other conditions that are characterized by lower levels of estrogen, such as primary gonadal failure or the rapidly falling levels of estrogen during the premenstrual phase or prior to labor, are not typically associated with hot flashes. More recently, the high rate of hot flashes in men who have been castrated (Karling *et al.*, 1994; Loprinzi *et al.*, 1994) is further argument against the lack of estrogen being the only cause of hot flashes.

Regardless of etiology, estrogen therapy is effective in relieving vasomotor complaints in menopausal women. Furthermore, obese menopausal women are less likely to experience hot flashes. Obese women have higher levels of plasma estrogen than normal-weight women due to the conversion of androgens to estrogen in adipose tissue. Such findings implicate estrogen as a relevant factor in the causal pathway to hot flashes. Quite recently, phytoestrogens have received attention. These are compounds with estrogen-like actions and are found in large quantity in certain foods particularly soy products. Murkies *et al.* (1995) compared the effectiveness of soy- and wheat-flour additions to the diets of post-menopausal women. Those women adding soy flour had significant reductions in frequency of hot flashes after 6 weeks and, by 12 weeks, recorded a 40% reduction. These data may partially explain the absence of hot flashes among Japanese women, since their diet contains a considerable number of soy products. Thus, estrogen is obviously related to hot flashes as a cause, correlate, or predisposing factor but the specific pathways remain a mystery.

Research on the physiological correlates of subjective hot flashes suggests that hot flashes may be associated with changes in levels of stress, since activity of the autonomic nervous system tracks stress. Although stress has been said to exacerbate almost every problem and illness people experience, there has been amazingly little research on the association between stress and hot flashes. Stress as a causal factor in hot flashes is implied in a study by Freedman and Woodward (1992) who successfully treated hot flashes by stress-reduction techniques. Gannon *et al.* (1987) required menopausal women reporting frequent hot flashes to monitor their hot flashes and stressful life events for 6 weeks. The association between frequency of daily stressors and frequency of hot flashes was highly significant for some women and not for others, suggesting individual differences in the causes and enhancers of hot flashes.

Other research on hot flashes has not been systematic but offers tantalizing bits of information deserving further investigation. Frey (1982) reported that employed women had fewer menopausal symptoms than did unemployed women. More recently, Schwingl *et al.* (1994), evaluating a community sample of African–American and European–American women, compared lifestyle factors and reproductive histories of those with and without hot flashes. High rates of hot flashes were associated with having less than a high school education and with smoking, while race and parity were unrelated to hot flashes. These authors also noted that women reporting natural menopause before the age of 52 were more likely to experience hot flashes than those with a later menopause. This finding may be relevant to the concept of "timing." There are hints throughout the literature implying that life events (menarche, pregnancy, menopause) which are "on time" may be less stressful than those that are early or late. The Mayan and Greek women studied by Beyene (1986) commented that menopause occurring "on time" was not associated with problems but early menopause (in this case, under 40 years old) was associated with ill health.

Summary

There are several conceptual models that aid our understanding of the menopausal transition and the changes in health that accompany it. It is probable that no one model is sufficient, and all are necessary to explain the complex experience of menopause. Koeske (1982) argues for the necessity of embracing complexity and diversity in understanding menopause:

> It is important to acknowledge that sociocultural factors also influence the actual levels of important biological variables, thereby indirectly influencing bodily experience and behavior: gene pools, diet, exercise, obesity, sleep, physical and emotional stress, parity, lactation, disease history, available medical care – all are influenced by social and cultural factors in complex and probably unknown ways. The estrogen decline that comes with increasing age may not be associated with identical body changes and body experiences when the accompanying physiological context varies. Thus, such characteristics of the menopause as age at last menstrual period, length of perimenopause, pattern of endocrine-hormone changes, and types of patterns of associated body changes may covary with such factors as obesity, current and lifetime stress, speed of role loss or role change, current diet, exercise, or sleep patterns, and pre-existing disease states or propensities. And influences such as these will in part reflect the operation of sociocultural factors that have been translated into a lifetime of multiple influences.
>
> (Koeske, 1982, p. 12)

MENOPAUSE AS A CULTURAL PHENOMENON

The medicalization of menopause

At the time in life when women become free of dysmenorrhea, premenstrual syndrome, endometriosis, birth control worries, and, for some, childrearing, they are labeled by the medical profession as chronically ill and are advised to take powerful and potentially dangerous drugs for the rest of their lives. Menopause, a biologically normal and universal phenomenon, has been transformed into a medical problem: the 1990 Merck Manual of Geriatrics (Abrams and Berkow) lists menopause under "metabolic and endocrine disorders" and the 23rd edition of the *Physicians' Handbook* (Krupp *et al.*, 1985) describes menopause as a "clinical disorder of the ovary" characterized by estrogen deficiency. Although the medical profession has had opinions about menopause and advice for menopausal women for at least the last century, only with the availability of a "treatment" has menopause been labeled a disease. Forty years ago, hot flashes were considered a temporary and unpleasant manifestation of an inevitable life transition; today hot flashes are considered a symptom of an underlying disease process. Current medical opinion recommends that all women, when suspecting the beginning of menopause, be evaluated by their physician and be treated with estrogen for the rest of their lives (Mishell, 1989; Studd, 1989). This recommendation is reflected in the use rate in the United States. An estimated 13.6 million prescriptions were given for oral menopausal estrogens in 1982 compared to 31.7 million in 1992, a 2.3-fold increase. Prescriptions for oral progestins increased from 2.3 million in 1982 to 11.3 million in 1992 (Wysowski *et al.*, 1995).

Historically, women have been valued for their youthful beauty and fertility and their essential roles have been wife/sex partner and mother. Considerable attempts to change women's roles have occurred in the last several decades resulting in unprecedented educational and career opportunities for women. However, five thousand years of patriarchy are not so easily eradicated. Perusal of any popular magazine collection informs us that the emphasis on traditional femininity and women's roles continues: "the postmenopausal body is overdetermined by imagery signifying shame and disempowerment" (Zita, 1993, p. 74). As is typical for victims of political oppression, there has been a general acceptance of this perspective by those who suffer most from it – mid- and old-age women. Thus, when menopausal women are given a view of their future as one of isolation, alienation, redundancy, and perhaps poverty, can we really expect them to refuse a "miracle drug," which, according to advertisements, restores youth, beauty, and health? Social scientists have frequently described the medicalization of menopause as an instance of medical imperialism: the motivation is profit and power; and women and the elderly are easy targets since they lack status and influence in our society (Reissman, 1983; Strong, 1979).

Menopause as wellness

The view that the fertile, menstruating woman is the "norm" or the "ideal" state of womanhood serves both sexual politics by defining normal women as those capable of reproduction and medical profits by labeling every woman over 50 as ill and in need of medical attention. In contrast, one could argue, as I do below, that women's and men's reproductive years are neither biologically nor socially ideal – that fertility, although necessary for the perpetuation of the species, is neither "normal" nor healthy but is, instead, a temporary state characterized by high risk of disease and death. In men, testosterone, the primary androgen, is generally believed to facilitate the expression of various behaviors associated with mating in the males of many species. Testosterone is associated with copulatory behavior, aggressiveness, sexual promiscuity, and fighting (McEwen, 1981) – all of which increase the probability of injury, disease, and/or death. The ages when testosterone is highest are between 16 and 50 – the ages when men are most vulnerable to cardiovascular disease, death by accident and violence, and prostate cancer. The rate of death from cardiovascular disease increases with age in men but this rate of increase slows with the decline of testosterone in mid-life (this is illustrated in Chapter 6 in Figure 6.1). The mid-life decrease in testosterone is also associated with a decreased rate of death associated with risk-taking behaviors.

Similarly, one could well argue that, compared to the postmenopausal woman, the menstruating woman is at heightened risk for disease, injury, and death. Until the mid-twentieth century, the major causes of death for women under 50 were complications of pregnancy and childbirth. It was only after these causes of death were rendered less dangerous that women began to experience the surprising longevity of today. While women are menstruating, they produce high levels of estrogen; estrogen promotes cancers, particularly breast cancer and those of the reproductive tract, and stimulates autoimmune diseases (Mayer, 1994). When estrogen diminishes during mid-life in women, they are then at lesser risk for these diseases as well as endometriosis, and the dangers associated with birth control, pregnancy, and childbirth.

In a recent article, Strassman (1997) proposed a theory in which the cessation of menstruation in mid-life is a healthy, adaptive strategy. In order to develop this theory, she first discusses a characteristic that tends to distinguish human from nonhuman animal species – that of cyclic fertility. According to Strassman, cyclicity is adaptive in that it allows for conservation of resources so that metabolic fuels are utilized to maintain the endometrium in a preparatory state for implantation only when ovulation occurs. When, for whatever reason, the menstrual cycle ceases, resources are not wasted in maintaining the endometrium. Evidence in support of this hypothesis comes from studies indicating that the postovulatory endometrium is indeed more resource-consuming than the endometrium prior to ovulation. The luteal phase of the menstrual cycle has been found to be associated with greater food intake (Gong et al., 1989), a higher basal metabolic rate

(Solomon *et al.*, 1982), and a higher sleeping metabolic rate (Meijer *et al.*, 1992) than other phases. Strassman's hypothesis implies that the cessation of ovulation with menopause is associated with a saving of the resources required for endometrial preparation and menstruation. "If a woman forgoes the cost of the luteal phase for 12 months during amenorrhea, she saves...her food supply for half a month" (Strassman, 1997, p. 158). With age, diminished immune competence is common and the probability of degenerative and chronic disease increases. The metabolic fuels saved by the absence of fertility may be utilized to counteract these trends and to maintain health during the aging process. Given other age-related changes as diverse as reduced efficiency in nutrient absorption and increased levels of poverty, conservation of metabolic fuels with age can only be beneficial. In this context, menopause is a resource-conserving strategy with considerable biological adaptiveness.

In addition to the biological advantages of diminished hormone secretion, culture-specific rituals and behaviors have been identified which render the fertile years far less than the romanticized ideal. In ancient times, menstruating women were sent to menstrual huts and not allowed to perform certain activities; today, menstruation continues to be a source of embarrassment, and consumer products designed to hide the sight or smell of menstruation fill the pharmacy shelves. In the !Kung San culture:

> All during their reproductive years both men and women had to avoid certain foods and any contact with certain kinds of supernatural power. Most of these restrictions were lifted from people past the age of begetting or bearing children....those beyond the reproductive period were released from the ritual disabilities and impurities it generated.
>
> (Amoss and Harrell, 1981, p. 16)

In the latter part of the nineteenth century, scientific theories emerged that excluded fertile women from educational institutions and professions in order to protect the delicacy of their reproductive processes. Today, in spite of almost three decades of a strong feminist movement, "women are considered unfit for certain kinds of work and physical activity because of their procreative physiology. What supposedly makes females 'real' women – their menstrual cycles – makes them unreliable workers, thinkers, and leaders" (Lorber, 1997, p. 55). Culture, as well as biology, places limitations and restrictions on individuals who are responsible for reproductive activities. Thus, ideology rather than health promotion motivates the labeling of the hormonal state associated with fertility in women and men as "normal."

The endocrinology of hormone therapy

Estrogen therapy became popular in the 1940s when its production became cost-effective. Estrogen was promoted as being beneficial for diminishing wrinkles and depression and for enhancing sexual arousal and all aspects of "femininity" (Wilson, 1966). By the mid-1970s, researchers had documented a 4 to 8 times increased risk of uterine cancer in women taking estrogen (Smith *et al.*, 1975; Gambrell *et al.*, 1980). Although initially dismissed as "alarmist" by physicians, research noting that dose and duration of estrogen therapy bore a linear relationship to risk (Rosenwaks *et al.*, 1979; Stavraky *et al.*, 1981) was eventually accepted as definitive evidence. The mechanism through which estrogen therapy increases uterine cancer risk seems to be via a direct effect on the endometrium. Aycock and Jollie (1979) compared the cellular response of the postmenopausal endometrium to estrogenic stimulation with the cellular activity in endometrial cancer and found close similarities. Natrajan *et al.* (1981) have suggested that unopposed estrogen stimulation increases the concentration of estrogen receptors and results in a state of hyperreceptivity to estrogen, the consequence being hyperplasia – a condition amenable to malignancy.

The subsequent concerns over uterine cancer led women to refuse hormones, and physicians were reluctant to prescribe them. In response, the pharmaceutical companies modified the drug to more closely follow the hormonal profile of premenopausal women. The effect of estrogen on the endometrium is growth, and continual estrogen causes continual growth with haphazard shedding when the lining outgrows its blood supply. According to Budoff (1980), in the natural menstrual cycle, hyperplasia is avoided because progesterone causes the cells lining the uterus to differentiate from the uterus and become secretory. Thus, when progesterone and estrogen levels decline, prior to menstruation, the lining cleanly and precisely sloughs off. The pharmaceutical equivalent is, most commonly, to administer estrogen on a cyclic basis and to add progesterone the last 10 days of the cycle. This form of treatment does not cause hyperplasia and does not increase the risk of uterine cancer (Sturdee *et al.*, 1978; Whitehead *et al.*, 1978). Estrogen therapy without progesterone, however, continues to be prescribed for castrated and hysterectomized women because they do not have a uterus and, therefore, cannot develop uterine cancer.

There are a variety of different estrogens used in hormone therapy. In most European countries, natural estrogens – estradiol, estrone, and estriol – dominate while in the United States, most hormone therapies include conjugated equine estrogens (so-called because they are derived from the urine of pregnant mares). Synthetic estrogens, such as ethinyl estradiol, are used primarily in oral contraceptives. Similarly, there are several compounds possible for the progesterone component of hormone therapy; the most common ones are synthetic. The progesterone component is thought to be responsible for many of the negative side-effects of hormone therapy; consequently, there are currently efforts on the part of the pharmaceutical companies to modify the chemical composition and develop new forms. In the last two decades, the doses of estrogen and progesterone in both oral contraceptives and menopausal hormone therapy, have been dramatically reduced in an effort to reduce side-effects while maintaining effectiveness. In spite of this, the doses remain pharmacological rather than physiological – that is, the doses are considerably higher than those found natu- rally in a woman's body. According to Voda:

> thirty-five micrograms of ethinyl estradiol found in the birth control pill is greater than the naturally synthesized concentration of picogram quantities of estradiol found in the blood. The daily dose of estrogen (Estrone) prescribed for postmenopausal women is in the milligram quantities, which is, theoretically, *more than a million times the concentration of natural estrogens*. Progesterone replacement at menopause in the form of medroxyprogesterone acetate (MPA) is prescribed in ten-milligram quantities. *This dose is one million times greater than the concentration of proges- terone measured in the blood.*
>
> (Voda, 1993, p. 169, emphasis in the original)

Information has recently been published indicating that the ingestion of alcohol by women taking hormone therapy may lead to significant and sustained eleva- tions of serum levels of estrogen over and above that achieved with hormone therapy alone (Ginsburg *et al.*, 1996). The justification for hormone therapy is frequently that the hormones replace those which are natural in premenopausal women: "women need to know that estrogen is 'natural' and that living for 30 years or more without it may be less so" (Ettinger, 1988, p. 34S). Yet, the blood levels of estrogen and progesterone created by hormone therapy far exceed that which is natural for a woman at any age.

The most common form of hormone therapy in the past has been oral medi- cation in a sequential fashion – estrogen for 4 weeks with progesterone added the last 10 days followed by a week of no medication. Currently, hormone therapy is also available in implant and patch forms as well as a new oral form which provides estrogen and progesterone on a combined, continuous basis. Only the oral sequential form of hormone therapy has been approved by the US Federal Drug Administration. The newer schedules and routes have not been adequately tested for effectiveness and safety. For example, Gordon *et al.* (1995) published a study with a title proclaiming both efficacy and safety of transdermal hormone therapy; the research participants were studied for only 11 weeks of hormone therapy, effectiveness was measured only by hot flash frequency, and only minor side-effects, such as bleeding and breast pain, were assessed. For most women who are considering hormone therapy, hot flashes are not the major indication, and the major safety concerns are uterine cancer, breast cancer, and thrombosis – all of which require 10 years of follow-up to demonstrate safety. Gambrell (1995) suggested that the current regimen for combined, continuous hormone therapy carries a greater risk of uterine cancer than has been reported and that one reason for underreporting this risk is the inadequate duration of the trials. The practice of prescribing medications without adequate research demon- strating safety and effectiveness is misleading and dangerous.

Benefits of hormone therapy

Many of the hypothesized benefits and risks of hormone therapy, such as reduced risk of cardiovascular disease, reduced risk of osteoporotic fractures, increased risk of breast cancer, and increased risk of thrombosis, require at least 10 years to assess. With very few exceptions, estrogen therapy alone has been studied in these contexts; adequate information on the impact of adding progesterone to the regimen is not available. However, on the basis of known pharmacological action of progesterones, various researchers have predicted that adding progesterone to hormone therapy will adversely affect lipids (Schwartz *et al.*, 1995; Grodstein and Stampfer, 1995; Derman, 1995), cause deterioration in glucose tolerance (Lindheim *et al.*, 1993) and increase the risk of heart disease (Voda, 1993).

The indications for the use of hormone therapy vary with the prescriber and with national medical practices, but most current medical literature proposes hormone therapy as a treatment for hot flashes and vaginal dryness and as a preventative intervention for osteoporosis and cardiovascular disease. The US Federal Drug Administration has approved hormone therapy for hot flashes, vaginal dryness, and osteoporosis only. Although hormone therapy is advocated and prescribed for cardiovascular problems, the FDA has not approved this indication. The effectiveness, or lack of effectiveness, of hormone therapy for each of these is discussed fully in chapters on these topics. To briefly summarize, hormone therapy effectively treats hot flashes and vaginal dryness, although the benefits of the latter are questionable since sexual activity and sexual satisfaction are not apparently impacted (see Chapter 5). The overall benefit of hormone therapy on bone health is questionable. Although hormone therapy slows menopausal loss of bone density, it has not been found to impact age-related bone loss, has not been demonstrated to prevent fractures, and does not diminish the probability of falling – a major cause of fractures in the elderly (see Chapter 7). Finally, with regard to cardiovascular disease, hormone therapy tends to reduce total cholesterol (TC) and low-density lipoproteins (LDL), but does not increase high-density lipoproteins (HDL) nor reduce triglycerides – the changes of the lipid profile of greatest concern to women (see Chapter 6).

Beneficial effects on the skin have been proposed: Maheux *et al.* (1994) concluded that estrogen therapy prevents skin aging, but examination of their results indicated that estrogen therapy was associated with increased skin thickness only on the thigh – not on the neck or abdomen. In contrast, in a large-sample, observational study, Bauer *et al.* (1994) noted that estrogen users had significantly *thinner* skin compared to those who had in the past used or were currently using estrogens. Similar contradictions are found in the research on weight gain. Two studies found no weight change with hormone therapy (Krtiz-Silverstein and Barrett-Connor, 1996; Reubinoff *et al.*, 1995), whereas two other studies found hormone therapy to be associated with weight gain and acceleration of loss of lean body mass (Aloia *et al.*, 1995; Hartmann *et al.*, 1996). In any event, the lack of consensus on the effects of hormones on skin and weight is, perhaps, of minor concern when considering a drug reputed to be life-extending as well as life-threatening.

Many of the benefits claimed for hormone therapy derive from observational studies and seem to emerge from improperly interpreting one of many differences between large groups of women taking hormones and not taking hormones. For example, Calle *et al.* (1995) and Newcomb and Storer (1995) found hormone users to have less incidence of colon cancer than nonusers in observational studies. Later, Potter *et al.* (1996) mistakenly conclude that these studies demonstrate a reduced risk of colon cancer from hormone therapy; they reach this conclusion even in the absence of any plausible physiological or biochemical mechanism:

> There is an increasing disparity in the rates of colon cancer between men and women beginning in the last 20 years. Women in the United States are now clearly doing something different from men. A plausible candidate is HRT use. (p. 781)

This absurd logic would also suggest that women's lesser rate of prostate cancer can be attributed to hormone therapy. The authors do not take into consideration that users and nonusers differ on many factors, any of which may be the source of the association. Hormone users are more likely to exercise and exercise is associated with a reduced risk of colon cancer to a similar or greater extent than is hormone therapy (Colditz, 1996).

The effects of hormone therapy on cognitive variables and Alzheimer's disease is a further example of exaggerated claims for hormone therapy that are based on inadequate research. In one observational study, Robinson *et al.* (1994) found hormone therapy to be associated with better recall of proper names but not of words while, in a similar research format, users of hormones were better on two of six memory tests but worse, though not significantly so, than nonusers on the remaining four tests (Kampen and Sherwin, 1994). In a more recent study, one that illustrates the limitations of observational research, Jacobs *et al.* (1998) found women who had used hormone therapy to score higher on cognitive tests than those who had never used the drug. However, the latter group of women had, on average, less education than the users, and there was a greater percentage of ethnic minorities in the nonuser group. The evaluation instruments were traditional ones that do not provide a valid assessment of cognitive abilities in minority persons; the influence of education is obvious.

The randomized, controlled study is the only research method that can establish the efficacy of a drug. In one such study (Phillips and Sherwin, 1992), hormone-treated groups were better on only one of six cognitive tests even though the hormone-treated women had four to five times the serum estrogen levels of normal premenopausal women. More recently, Polo-Kantola *et al.* (1998) randomly assigned women to 3-month treatments of estrogen or placebo;

after a one-month wash-out period, the women were crossed over to the other regimen for an additional three months. Cognitive speed and accuracy as well as attention and memory were assessed throughout the study. The authors found no evidence to support the hypothesis that estrogen aids cognitive activity. Indeed, effects on two of the subtests were statistically significant in the opposite direction, suggesting that estrogen supplements may be detrimental to cognitive activity.

The association of hormone therapy and Alzheimer's disease was studied in an observational study by Tang *et al.* (1996); women who developed Alzheimer's disease were less likely to have used hormone therapy than those who were free of this disease. However, those with Alzheimer's were also older and less educated so there is no logical reason to select hormone therapy as the essential group difference. After conducting a meta-analysis of ten studies investigating the effects of hormone therapy on cognitive function, Yaffe *et al.* (1998) concluded that there is insufficient evidence to justify a recommendation of hormone therapy for the prevention or treatment of Alzheimer's disease. Labeling menopause as a hormone deficiency disease does, indeed, provide a readily available attribution for any and all age-related problems women might encounter; the potential profits provide the motivation to do so.

The risks of hormone therapy

A variety of side-effects have been reported to be associated with hormone therapy, including abnormal uterine bleeding (Ettinger *et al.*, 1993), a doubled risk of urinary tract infections (Orlander *et al.*, 1992), a doubled risk of lupus (Sanchez-Guerrero *et al.*, 1995), migraine headaches (Silbertein, 1995), and a worsening of asthma (Lieberman *et al.*, 1995; Troisi *et al.*, 1995). Akkad *et al.* (1995) and Sener *et al.* (1996) note that myomas and fibroids that are associated with excessive uterine bleeding diminish with natural menopause but hormone therapy prevents these benefits from occurring.

Cancer

Of major concern with hormone therapy is the increased risk of cancer. The research in the 1980s on the effects of adding progesterone effectively silenced concerns regarding uterine cancer associated with estrogen therapy. However, this safety has only been demonstrated with oral, sequential forms; the assumption cannot be made that all forms of hormone therapy with progesterone are safe with regard to uterine cancer. The type of progesterone, the dose, the duration, the schedule, the route – all may impact the frequency and severity of negative side-effects (Grady *et al.*, 1995). Since receptors for estrogen and progesterone are found throughout the reproductive tract, all reproductive organs are potential cancer sites with longer-term hormone therapy. Despite this, cancer of the ovary has not been a major research focus. Helzlsouer *et al.* (1995) reported that low FSH is associated with an increased risk of ovarian cancer. Since hormone therapy reduces FSH levels, ovarian cancer is a reasonable concern. Rodriquez *et al.* (1995) noted that long-term hormone therapy (greater than 11 years) was associated with a 70% increase in risk of fatal ovarian cancer. Given the high rate of mortality associated with ovarian cancer, the impact of hormone therapy deserves considerable research attention.

Breast cancer is, perhaps, the most controversial consequence of hormone therapy. Randomized, controlled studies designed to evaluate increases in the risk of breast cancer from hormone therapy are unlikely to occur, since assigning women to a treatment group would be viewed as unethical by those who believe hormone therapy to be associated with life-threatening side-effects and assigning women to the placebo group would be viewed as unethical by those who believe hormone therapy to be a miracle drug. Given this dilemma, relevant information may be obtained from experimental studies in animals and observational studies in humans. In the former category, Cline *et al.* (1996) studied hormone treatment in adult female macaques who had been castrated, assigning a third to each of three groups – no-treatment, estrogen, and estrogen-plus-progesterone. The combined hormone induced greater proliferation of breast tissue than did the estrogen alone, which suggests that the risk of breast cancer from combined hormone therapy may be greater than that found for estrogen therapy alone. The authors comment that, rather than protecting the breast from the carcinogenic impact of estrogen as it does in the uterus, progesterone *enhances* carcinogenic potential in the breast.

Observational studies in humans cannot establish a causal relationship between hormone therapy and breast cancer but do provide one source of information. The breast cancer–hormone therapy controversy began in earnest with the publication by Bergkvist *et al.* (1989) of Swedish data. Although this was an observational study, it is somewhat better than most since medical and pharmaceutical records are available in a national registry, freeing researchers from relying on retrospective self-reports for information on dose, duration, and type of drug. These researchers reported a 70% increased risk of breast cancer with estrogen therapy for nine years or more. Of considerable relevance was their finding that women taking combined (estrogen plus progesterone) hormone therapy for longer than 6 years had a 4.4 times greater risk of breast cancer than those not taking hormones. This report caused considerable criticism from the advocates of hormone therapy. One (Gambrell, 1990) accused *The New England Journal of Medicine* of sensationalism for publishing it and lamented the potential hardship on those women who, as a consequence of their fears of breast cancer, may refuse hormone therapy. Although this initial study has been criticized as being flawed (sample too small, wrong type of estrogen), the results seem to be reliable. Persson *et al.* (1996) provided a further four-year follow-up of the initial data and reported that the risks associated with the combined therapy were larger than previously reported.

The results of Bergkvist and colleagues have since been replicated many times (e.g., Colditz *et al.*, 1993; Gorsky *et al.*, 1994; Harris *et al.*, 1992). Most recently, the Collaborative Group on Hormonal Factors in Breast Cancer (1997) in the UK combined the data from 90% of the worldwide epidemiological studies on the association between breast cancer and hormone therapy. The combined sample consisted of over 160,000 women from 51 studies in 21 countries; a third of the women suffered from breast cancer. Analyses of these data revealed a clear increase in the relative risk of breast cancer among current or recent users of hormone therapy for more than 5 years and indicated that risk increased with duration of use. Since only 12% of the hormone users had been exposed to progestagens, these data are directly relevant only to those women who are prescribed estrogen regimens.

Those who continue to defend hormone therapy as effective and safe have dealt with this information with a sort of pseudoscientific double-talk. According to Ferin *et al.* (1993), "after at least 9 years of treatment with estradiol, the risk of breast cancer doubled. The most disturbing finding...was a fourfold increase in the risk of breast cancer in women treated for more than 4 years with estradiol and progestins" (p. 164). Yet, on the same page, these authors state: "The latest consensus is that estrogen treatment does not pose an increased risk of breast cancer" (p. 164). Similarly, Marshburn and Carr (1992) review the research linking breast cancer and hormone therapy and conclude that there is a "theoretical risk of breast cancer" that should not stop women from lifelong hormone therapy; the authors do not explain what a "theoretical risk" is, exactly.

Several authors have criticized this research because of the observational nature of the studies: "Epidemiologic studies such as this [Bergkvist *et al.*, 1989] can never show a true cause and effect, only a possible association" (Gambrell, 1990, p. 202). Corson (1995) and Cobleigh *et al.* (1994) express similar sentiments. This is a legitimate concern but these critics of the breast cancer research readily accept the findings of the observational studies (often the same studies) regarding the benefits of hormone therapy for the cardiovascular system. Indeed, observational studies may actually underestimate the risk of breast cancer. Typically, these studies compare users of hormone therapy to nonusers without regard to the type of menopause. Those who have been castrated have less risk of breast cancer (Parazzini *et al.*, 1997), and women who have been castrated are more likely to use hormones than those who have experienced a natural menopause (Ettinger *et al.*, 1996). Thus, when comparing the incidence of breast cancer in those who take hormones and those who do not, the former are initially at lower risk of breast cancer, biasing the results in favor of not finding an association between breast cancer and hormone use. A similar biasing effect results from including women with simple hysterectomy (Pike *et al.*, 1998).

There is considerable empirical documentation supporting a link between estrogen – endogenous or exogenous – and breast cancer: (1) an increase in breast cancer was associated with diethylstilbestrol (DES), a synthetic estrogen prescribed in the 1960s (Greenberg *et al.*, 1984); (2) an increase in breast cancer is associated with estrogen in oral contraceptives (Price *et al.*, 1997); (3) between the mid-1970s to the mid-1980s – a decade of steadily increased use of hormone medications – the incidence of estrogen receptor-negative breast cancers rose from 22% to 27%, while the incidence of estrogen receptor-positive cancers rose 131% (Glass and Hoover, 1990); (4) estrogen stimulates the proliferation of breast tissue (Voda, 1993); (5) breast cancer is more common in women with a longer-duration reproductive span (early menarche, late menopause); (6) premature menopause and castration are associated with reduced risk of breast cancer (Parazzini et al., 1997); (7) serum levels of estrogen are correlated with breast cancer risk; (8) cessation of hormone therapy may induce regression of breast cancer (Eden and Wren, 1996); and (9) Tamoxifen, an anti-estrogen agent, is used successfully to prevent a reoccurrence of breast cancer (Balducci et al., 1994).

Aware that breast cancer is of primary importance in women's willingness to take hormones, advocates of hormone therapy for aging women have claimed that these drugs are not associated with an increased risk of breast cancer or that the increase is so small as to be negligible, and they challenge critics to prove otherwise (Couzi et al., 1995). In response, Jacobs and Loeffler (1992) comment that the evidence for a causal link between estrogens and breast cancer is so persuasive that "the aim of a scientific evaluation of the link is to try to fault the hypothesis rather than to attempt to prove that oestrogens cause cancer of the breast" (p. 1404). That is, the evidence is so strong that we should *assume* that estrogens cause an increased risk of breast cancer unless there is convincing evidence that it does not.

A third, middle-of-the-road position acknowledges the risk of breast cancer, yet advocates hormone therapy with frequent, regular medical surveillance so that any cancer is detected early. Bonnier et al. (1995) suggest that the increased medical attention to hormone users improves the survival rate of those who may develop breast cancer. Unfortunately, hormone therapy seems to reduce the effectiveness of mammography. Two case studies of increased mammographic density after hormone therapy were described by Doyle and McLean (1994), and a larger study (McNicholas et al., 1994) found that 27% of the hormone users had increased density on mammograms versus none of the control women. According to Laya (1997), the increased density reduces the sensitivity (some cancers would not be detected) and specificity (some positive outcomes would not be cancerous) of mammography in women who are hormone users. The decreased usefulness of mammography in hormone users is a particular problem, since the most common age to begin hormone therapy (over 50) is also the age for which mammography is apparently the most successful as a diagnostic aid (Kerlikowske et al., 1995).

Further complicating an already complex picture is the use of the anti-estrogen drug, Tamoxifen, to treat breast cancer. The logic of denying that the administration of estrogen is associated with an increased risk of breast cancer while treating breast cancer with a drug that reduces serum estrogen is rather untenable. One gets the impression that oncologists specializing in women's reproductive organs and gynecologists specializing in cancer do not talk to one another. O'Leary Cobb (1992) summarizes the odd result:

> otherwise healthy women who are frightened of the idea of breast cancer are being asked to take a drug which will induce menopausal ailments (but which may protect them against a cancer they may never get). At the same time, otherwise healthy women who experience menopausal ailments are being persuaded to take a drug which will alleviate these complaints (but which may increase their risk of breast cancer). (p. 3)

The US Federal Drug Administration became the center of a controversy over the issue of requiring pharmaceutical companies to include patient inserts in all prescriptions of hormone therapy in order to inform the users of the increased risk of cancer and other possible side-effects. The arguments were not about "scientific facts," research, data, methodological issues, or sampling problems. The real issues were about medical politics and power, which is readily apparent when one considers the "players." Those organizations in favor of the inserts were the National Woman's Health Network Association, the Consumer's Union, the Consumer's Federation of America, the Women's Equity Action League, the Coalition for Medical Rights for Women, and the National Action Forum for Older Women, whereas those against the inserts were the pharmaceutical manufacturers, the American College of Obstetrics and Gynecology, the National Association of Chain Drug Stores, and the American Society of Internal Medicine (McCrea, 1983).

Thrombosis

Thrombolytic disorders involve a clot or thrombosis that attaches to the wall of a blood vessel causing occlusion and, in the case of a coronary artery, infarct and death. In thromboembolism, a clot is carried by the blood stream as an embolus, potentially causing occlusion anywhere in the vasculature. Emboli lodging in the coronary arteries or in the vasculature of the lungs or brain may result in death. Venous thrombosis is a major health problem with an incidence rate of one per 1000 annually – a rate equivalent to that of stroke (Silverstein *et al.*, 1998). Early forms of oral contraceptives were found to significantly increase one's risk of blood clots, stroke, and heart attack (Seaman and Seaman, 1977). It is generally believed that the newer forms of oral contraceptives with reduced dosages do not increase the risk of thrombosis. However, seven studies published in 1990 indicate that, although the adverse effects on the cardiovascular system are lessened with lower doses of oral contraceptives, they are still substantial and include harmful changes in cholesterol levels (Clarkson *et al.*, 1990; Leuven *et al.*, 1990; Simon *et al.*, 1990) and increased risk of thrombosis (Daly and Bonner, 1990; Hirvonen and Idanpaan-Heikkila, 1990; Kelleher, 1990). Most recently, in a review of the research literature on this topic, Douketis *et al.* (1997) indicate that, with the newest form of oral contraceptives (i.e., "third generation"), the risk of thrombosis is actually higher than that with older forms of oral contraceptives.

Given these findings, claims that hormone therapy benefits the cardiovascular system are somewhat paradoxical since oral contraceptives and hormone therapy have similar chemical compositions. Until recently, the published medical literature has rarely addressed this issue. When it has been mentioned, the dilemma is dismissed as "irrelevant" or explained away by pointing out that women at an age when they take oral contraceptives have different body chemistry than those at an age appropriate for hormone therapy, that the dosages of the hormones in oral contraceptives differ from those in hormone therapy, and that the type of estrogen in the two is different. Although these points appropriately indicate that it would be illogical to *assume* that hormone therapy is associated with the same risks as oral contraceptives, it is equally illogical to ignore the potential for risk. Until quite recently, medical professionals have claimed hormone therapy to be free from an increased risk of clotting disorders. Yet, women taking hormone therapy are advised to take aspirin every day to prevent clotting problems (Notelovitz, 1989). And the British National Formulary recommends hormone therapy be discontinued four to six weeks prior to major surgery because of concerns over postoperative venous thromboembolism.

Directors of large longitudinal studies spanning the last two decades had, until recently, neglected to examine the risk of thrombolytic disorders associated with hormone therapy. Finally, in 1996, attention was directed toward this potential risk. Daly *et al.* (1996) examined the risk of venous thromboembolism in women aged 45 to 64 years and found current users of hormone therapy to have 3.5 times the risk of nonusers; they also noted a nonsignificant trend for a dose–response relationship. In a study of younger women between the ages of 30 and 55 years, Grodstein *et al.* (1996) studied the influence of both oral contraceptives and hormone therapy on primary pulmonary embolism; both hormone regimens were associated with a doubling of risk. Similarly, Jick *et al.* (1996), studying women aged 50 to 74, noted a 3.5 times risk among current users compared to nonusers of hormone therapy. These authors also reported a clear dose–response relationship. Gutthann *et al.* (1997) found current users to have double the risk of thromboembolism than nonusers. Interestingly, the greatest risk appeared to be in the first year of therapy with a 4.5 times risk in the first 6 months, indicating that, perhaps, even short-term hormone therapy may have substantial risks. Finally, Varas-Lorenzo *et al.* (1998) noted similar increased risk for thrombosis when hormone therapy was delivered transdermally. In response to the fact that these data had been available for years but only recently published, Vandenbrouche and Helmerhorst (1996) comment: "It is intriguing that such information buried in databases has only just surfaced" (p. 976).

Advocates of hormone therapy tend to minimize the importance of this risk. Whitehead and Godfree (1997) argue that the risk estimates of thrombosis from hormone therapy is based on flawed research and should be "weighed against the established benefits of hormone replacement therapy, including relief of menopausal symptoms, prevention of osteoporosis and arterial vascular disease" (p. 587). Yet, the "flawed" estimates of thrombosis risk and the "established" benefits for arterial vascular disease are derived from the same studies. In contrast, Rosenberg *et al.* (1997) expressed concern that the risk of thrombosis due to hormone therapy has been underestimated. They argue that women susceptible to venous thromboembolism may have developed clotting problems in conjunction with oral contraceptives and, therefore, would refuse further exposure to hormones. Thus, these studies may underestimate the risk because women at higher risk for thrombosis than the general population have been excluded.

Risk–benefit comparisons

The multiple benefits attributed to hormone therapy and the multiple adverse consequences of hormone therapy have caused considerable confusion among professional and lay populations. Attempting to clarify these issues, researchers have studied the all-cause mortality of users and nonusers of hormone therapy and have conducted risk–benefit analyses. Three mortality studies have been published and each reported lowered all-cause mortality among users of hormones compared to nonusers. The primary difficulty in interpreting these results is that the groups differ, not only on their use of hormones, but on other, highly relevant, factors. Ettinger *et al.* (1996) noted that the hormone users had less hypertension, were less likely to have had an abnormal electrocardiogram, were less likely to drink alcohol excessively, and were more likely to have been castrated compared to those naturally menopausal. Schairer *et al.* (1997) commented that had they been able to control for exercise level, education, castration, urban–rural residence, and fat mass, the effects of hormone therapy would have been attenuated. Any or all of these factors, as well as others not yet identified, may be responsible for the differences in mortality. Noteworthy is the continued research practice of combining castrated and naturally menopausal women in these studies. Castrated women can reasonably be described as estrogen deficient and, therefore, have a clear benefit from hormone therapy. On the other hand, the need for or the overall benefit of hormones for naturally menopausal women remains highly questionable.

In the last several years, there have been numerous cost–benefit discussions of hormone therapy published (Andrews, 1995; Gambrell *et al.*, 1993; Greendale and Judd, 1993; Hopkins, 1996; Lobo, 1995b; Smith and Studd, 1993; Thorneycroft, 1995). Unfortunately, these might be more accurately described as advertisements for hormone therapy. There are several elements common to each of these cost–benefit analyses: (1) in the absence of supporting research, the risk of cardiovascular disease is said to be increased with menopause; (2) the

SYLVIA   by Nicole Hollander

Source: Reproduced with permission from Nicole Hollander.

descriptive nature of the observational studies on hormone therapy and cardio-vascular disease is ignored or minimized; (3) emphasis is given to the consistency of the results of the observational studies, as if reliability yields validity; (4) breast cancer risk is dismissed; (5) the fact that most of the research has been based on estrogen therapy and the effects of adding progesterone to the regimen are unknown is given, at most, a brief aside; and (6) the differences in the endogenous hormonal profile between castrated and naturally menopausal women is ignored as are the differences in the subsequent needs of these two groups. None recommended that use be limited until further research on these issues can be completed; none pointed out that the US Federal Drug Administration has approved hormone therapy for hot flashes, vaginal problems, and osteoporosis, only; none compared the effectiveness of hormone therapy to standard medical treatments or lifestyle interventions; and none made a serious attempt to deal with the complex issues surrounding relevant individual differences, such as age and preexisting risk. Gambrell *et al.* (1993) note that there is a consensus that the benefits of hormone therapy outweigh the risks but they provide no references to support this highly exaggerated claim.

I believe that an essential difficulty with the medical view of menopause and hormone therapy is one of oversimplification – postmenopausal women are incredibly diverse in terms of age, hormonal status, chronic illnesses, lifestyle habits, roles, economic conditions, psychological well-being, and so forth. To claim that an increased risk of heart disease, osteoporosis, depression, sexual problems, cognitive difficulties, and hot flashes characterizes all mid- and old-age women, and that hormones are, universally, an effective treatment for all problems for all women is simply irrational and reminds one of the "tonic" remedies popular in the early twentieth century. Colditz (1996) authored a cost–benefit discussion of hormone therapy in which he acknowledged some of these issues. He suggests, for example, that women are likely to benefit from heart disease treatment of proven success in men, such as aspirin. He notes the difficulty in determining cost–benefit since most fractures occur after age of 80 but taking hormones for 30 years is likely to increase the risk of breast cancer dramatically. He concludes that long-term hormone therapy is clearly indicated only for those women with a high risk of cardiovascular disease. Love and Lindsey (1997) point out that, although true, the claim that the major cause of death for women is heart disease is misleading. Below the age of 75, there are three times as many deaths from breast cancer as from heart disease and, if smokers are excluded (most of the early cardiac deaths), the factor increases to six. These authors further provide some cost–benefit comparisons with health promoting activities such as improving diet and increasing exercise.

The most recent "advertisements" for hormone therapy offer mathematical calculations for the risk–benefit analyses. An example is one by Lobo (1995b). The author points out that, according to observational studies, estrogen use *appears* to benefit the cardiovascular system, but definitive evidence is lacking. He then goes on to use the results of observational studies in calculating the risk–benefit ratios. The qualifying comments at the beginning of the paper are lost by the time he concludes: "Overall mortality is known to decrease with duration of estrogen use. Thus, it is important that a woman be encouraged to maintain treatment with the understanding that 15 or more years of estrogen use will bring her the most benefit" (p. 988). The conclusions of a similar analysis by Stanford (1996) reveal a somewhat more careful word choice: "the *hypothesized* effect of current, longer-term…HRT use on mortality from coronary heart disease and breast cancer, *assuming* various relative-risk estimates" (p. 42, emphasis added). Such wording subtly acknowledges the uncertainties surrounding the risks and benefits of hormones but these are easily dismissed by those seeking miracles.

Crouch and Wilson (1982) have published criteria with which to assess the validity of risk–benefit analyses: (1) general agreement over the basic facts among experts; (2) a good experimental basis for the facts; (3) a good theoretical basis for the facts; (4) direct experience with the same or similar system; (5) the facts apply directly to the specific design or situation being assessed; (6) the risks and benefits of alternatives are considered. Applying these criteria to the question of risks and benefits of hormone therapy, we find none of these criteria has been met: (1) there is considerable disagreement among the experts; (2) there is no experimental basis, there are only results from observational studies; (3) there are numerous and conflicting theories surrounding the characterization of menopause as a disease and as requiring medical treatment; (4) previous experiences with oral contraceptives, DES, and estrogens suggest considerable caution; (5) most of the data are from estrogen therapy with castrated women, but are applied to hormone therapy with naturally menopausal women; and (6) alternatives are typically not considered in risk–benefit discussions of hormone therapy. One must conclude that, not only have the published risk–benefit analyses and discussions fallen far below the standard, but the current lack of knowledge on menopause and hormone therapy precludes the possibility of meeting established scientific criteria at this time.

The politics of hormone therapy

Compliance

Compliance with hormone therapy has been a disappointment to the medical and pharmaceutical professions. In a field study of 2500 women, Ravnikar (1987) found 20 to 30% never filled their prescriptions, 20% stopped within nine months, and 10% used the drugs on an intermittent basis. In spite of over half of the noncompliers stating concerns with cancer as their reason, the author patronizingly suggested that women may have difficulty remembering to take a daily pill and recommended the patch as a method of increasing compliance. A more recent study indicates that low compliance continues. Berman *et al.* (1996) followed 2000 women aged 46 to 63 who had received prescriptions for hormones. Within one year, 38% had stopped filling their prescription and 76% of the remaining took less than the prescribed dose. A year later, the figures were 59% and 90%, respectively.

Initially, the medical profession responded to this lack of compliance by assuming that women were uninformed as to the benefits of hormone therapy – the implication being that if women were *properly* informed, they would readily accept their physician's recommendations (Ettinger, 1988; Hahn, 1989; Nachtigall, 1990; Ryan *et al.*, 1992). The goal became to educate women on their need for hormone therapy. Although the rhetoric has emphasized the importance of shared decision-making for physician and patient, the preferred outcome is clearly obedience rather than consensus. Women who comply are described as "more knowledgeable about the benefits of ERT...they have done some research and/or received appropriate counseling" (Thompson, 1995, p. 191), and as "generally well informed about its risks and benefits and have good rapport with their physician" (Lobo, 1995a, p. 981), and "When a patient is adequately informed, it has been my experience that she will choose to take ERT" (Gambrell *et al.*, 1993, p. 10).

Hammond (1996) recommends using bone density measurements – not with the primary goal of obtaining information on osteoporosis but to encourage compliance with hormone therapy: "if a patient elects to use estrogen, I usually do not obtain density studies....If she should not take estrogen or desires not to, then I will do bone density studies to help inform her of her present and future risks" (p. 10S). The use of bone density screening for this purpose was actually the focus of a study by Ryan *et al.* (1992). They provided bone density information and then assessed compliance with hormone therapy. They found that 40% of the women with low bone density were not taking hormones eight months later. They concluded, "until improved compliance [with hormone therapy] has been demonstrated screening cannot be widely recommended" (p. 325). This conclusion is not based on a risk–benefit assessment of health – surely if a woman were to utilize bone density information to improve her diet or increase exercise, the women's overall health would improve. Rather, the conclusion is based on risk–benefit assessment of profits – the cost of the screening versus the sales of pharmaceuticals.

Charles *et al.* (1997) have outlined various methods of shared decision-making in the medical context: (1) Paternalistic – the physician either authoritatively tells the patient what to do or provides the patient with particular information carefully selected to support the physician's recommendations; (2) Informed – the physician aids the patient in obtaining knowledge so that the patient can decide; (3) Professional-as-agent model – the physician chooses what she/he believes the patient would choose if properly informed. Although the medical literature labels the process as "informed decision-making" which seems closest to (2), what is actually described is closer to (3). The typical decision-making process for hormone therapy corresponds to what Glick and Fiske (1997) call "benevolent sexism." This is characterized by the powerful (the expert physician) believing their knowledge to be superior and feeling an obligation to the less powerful (the patient) to protect and provide.

Indeed, since women are at greater risk to die from breast cancer than from cardiovascular disease prior to age 75 and since most women, today, who are encouraged to take hormone therapy are under the age of 75, their decision not to take hormones is not only understandable but, perhaps, wise. Risk–benefit analysts describe a phenomenon called "discounting," which refers to the temporal discrepancy between the benefit and the risk as influencing the decision-making process. The example provided by Tolley *et al.* (1994) involves children who have a huge discount rate in deciding whether or not to smoke; the decision is to forego an immediate pleasure in order to reduce the probability of heart disease or cancer 50 years later. In the context of deciding whether one will take hormone therapy, women who believe that hormones might protect them from cardiovascular disease 25 years hence but might increase their risk of breast cancer or thrombosis today, may apply a discount rate to their decision that is both expected and informed.

In contrast to assuming that noncompliant women are ignorant or uninformed, Janine O'Leary Cobb (1993), publisher of a newsletter on menopause, has received over 7000 letters from readers and concludes that "the reluctance to use hormone therapy is nearly always based on knowledge, not ignorance" (p. 1). Women who are knowledgeable concerning women's health and who see hormone therapy as the latest in a series of misogynist developments in medicine – estrogen therapy, DES, oral contraceptives, IUDs and breast implants – may, using appropriate caution, reject hormone therapy. What do these earlier "treatments" have in common that might inform women about hormone therapy? They were marketed and approved on the basis of inadequate research (Seaman and Seaman, 1977). They were later found to have life-threatening side-effects, and, most relevant, they were developed, not to treat illness, but to enhance the patriarchal view of femininity – big breasts, fertility, spontaneous sex, and "feminine forever."

With hormone therapy, women who continue to be noncompliant after being "properly informed" are then in danger of being labeled paranoid, irrational, or sentimental. In 1988, Ettinger documented various side effects, in addition to uterine cancer, of estrogen therapy. He reported that estrogen users, compared to nonusers, experienced a 5 to 7 times increase in abnormal uterine bleeding and that 25% of estrogen users eventually required a hysterectomy. He then states that women "need special reassurance to overcome *irrational* fears" (p. 34S, emphasis added). Lobo (1995b) coined the term *cancer phobia* to describe women who refused hormone therapy because they were concerned about breast cancer. Perhaps the ultimate example of interpreting noncompliance with medical advice as a deficiency in the woman patient comes from Studd (1989). He recommends prophylactic oophorectomy (castration) – only for women who have adequately fulfilled their reproductive role – in order to prevent the possibility of ovarian cancer. He apparently finds his arguments for castration in women so convincing, he concludes: "the only worthwhile argument against prophylactic oophorectomy…[is] a sentimental desire to keep her ovaries" (p. 508).

Particularly troubling are reports of clear mis-use of hormone therapy. Prescribing guidelines recommend an estrogen-only regimen for women who have had their uterus removed since these women need not be concerned with the heightened risk of uterine cancer, whereas women who have not had their uterus removed require an estrogen-plus-progesterone regimen. In a large population-based study on the use of hormone therapy in the UK, Moorhead *et al.* (1997) found that 41% of women taking hormones who had had their uterus removed were prescribed the combined regimen, and 31% of those who had a uterus had received at least one prescription of estrogen alone. In the US, Rosenberg *et al.* (1998) noted similar practices in a large study on hormone therapy in Black women. Eight percent of those without a uterus were prescribed estrogen-plus-progesterone while 16% of those with a uterus had used estrogen alone. Those women with a uterus who are following an estrogen-only prescription are at a heightened risk for developing uterine cancer; those without a uterus who are prescribed estrogen-plus-progesterone are unnecessarily exposed to the negative side-effects of depression and cardiovascular problems associated with progesterone.

The contradictory information, the lack of consensus among professionals, and the historical, precedent-setting medical tragedies have created a setting in which women's reluctance to take powerful drugs for an extended time is appropriate and, indeed, wise. Yet, women patients who ask for "more information" or who are reluctant to accept a physician's recommendation are treated in a manner similar to those who complain about sex discrimination or sexual harassment – they are labeled as misguided, uninformed and/or paranoid. Andrews (1995) states: "Women may not be as informed or as knowledgeable about menopause as they think they are" (p. 1). Indeed, women may be more knowledgeable about menopause than their physicians are!

Hormone therapy for men

A recent article in *Scientific American* (Hoberman and Yesalis, 1995) traced the history of testosterone treatment in men. In the early twentieth century, men were treated for a variety of problems, including sexual difficulties, with extracts from animal testicles. The authors characterize this practice as having been based in "primitive beliefs" and absurd according to current standards and knowledge. Yet, today women are encouraged to swallow the urine of pregnant mares in order to retain their femininity and physical well-being. Both women and men produce less of their respective hormones as they age, both experience similar changes in sexuality, and both appear to experience similar health problems. Why is it recommended that middle-age and elderly women take hormone supplements while it is not recommended that men of similar age take androgens? Oakley (1993) notes that the medicalization of life affects men also but only women are infantilized by the patronizing professional health care system. And, perhaps, a patriarchal medical establishment is, by definition, unlikely to pathologize men's lives.

Advocates of hormone therapy in women have claimed that testosterone decreases very slowly or not at all in men, while women experience an abrupt loss of estrogen (e.g., Boldt, 1997). Neither is accurate. Menopause is characterized by changes in sex hormones similar to those experienced by men at mid-age. Natural menopause is a slow process; gradual hormonal changes occur throughout adulthood. In contrast, women who are castrated experience an abrupt change in hormonal profile. Weksler (1995) noted that 80% of men aged over 60 had testosterone levels less than two standard deviations below that of healthy, young men. This decrease is similar in rate and magnitude to that of estrogen in naturally menopausal women. The author further notes that testosterone supplements have been found to be associated with increases in prostate specific antigen (a marker of the likelihood of prostate cancer) and a deteriorated lipid profile. There are differing opinions as to how compliant men would be if prescribed hormone therapy: "if a therapy that *seemed* to reduce the incidence of heart disease by 50% were available to men they would be encouraged to take it" (Findlay *et al.*, 1994, p. 214, emphasis added). Conversely, "If a drug which had the potential to reduce heart disease in men were available and considered for national use but was known to cause testicular cancer, doctors would refuse to prescribe it and their patients would refuse to use it" (Voda, 1993, p. 187). Contrast the medical recommendation that all postmenopausal women take hormones for the rest of their lives to the conclusion reached at a conference on hormone supplements for aging men: We "fear that without more reliable data from well-controlled clinical trials, the unscrupulous are likely to exploit the massive market of aging male baby boomers who would pay anything for an antidote to aging, proven or otherwise" (Skolnick, 1992, p. 2486). Obviously, women are acceptable victims of such exploitation!

Interestingly, the "properly informed, knowledgeable" woman is not only expected blindly to comply with medical advice, but is also responsible for her husband's compliance with medical advice as well. In a unique example of misogynist science, Boldt (1997) published an article titled "Menopause: the men's version." Throughout the article, the author addresses his remarks to the wives of middle-aged men, rather than to the men experiencing difficulties. The wives are advised to convince their husbands to seek medical treatment.

Research issues

In 1981, John McKinlay authored a paper describing the unfortunate but typical stages through which many medical innovations pass. Although McKinlay's focus is primarily on medical procedures, such as coronary bypass surgery, his analysis can be applied to pharmaceutical therapies as well – in this case, hormone therapy. His analysis emphasizes the inappropriate reliance on case studies, anecdotal reports, and observational studies while lamenting the rare use of randomized controlled trials. He takes the reader through the various stages of development and marketing from "promising report" to "professional adoption," and from "public acceptance" to "standard procedure." It is at this latter point (standard procedure) that observational studies are often published since, if the therapy has been adopted as standard procedure, then sufficient numbers of persons using the therapy are available to study. Soon the sheer volume of observational studies tends to impress professionals and the public regardless of the scientific merit.

> Although they may suggest areas that are worthy of properly designed studies that may eventually yield such evidence, clinical experience or opinions can never be a substitute for scientific evidence, no matter how distinguished the observer or how numerous the observations.
>
> (McKinlay, 1981, p. 383)

McKinlay notes that the randomized controlled trial is the only accepted scientific method of establishing the effectiveness of a treatment modality. With regard to the use of hormone therapy to treat or prevent cardiovascular disorders, this stage is just beginning in the form of the Women's Health Initiative (WHI). This study is *beginning* after at least one decade of extensive use of hormones to treat cardiovascular disease. As McKinlay points out, these studies should have been done at the first stage rather than after the therapy has already become standard procedure. Because the research on hormone therapy has not conformed to a logical or practical progression, McKinlay's stages 6 and 7 are already apparent in the scholarly literature. Stage 6 is "professional denunciation" – essentially defensive reactions by the promoters of the treatment to any new information that indicates a lack of effectiveness or severe side-effects. McKinlay notes that this often takes the form of "advisory groups." In the context of hormone therapy, conferences for these advisory groups are funded by pharmaceutical companies; the "experts" get together to discuss the pros and cons and then publish a consensus statement of their agreement. (For an example, see *Obstetrics and Gynecology*, 1996, supplement 2.) And, finally, stage 7, "erosion or discreditation," occurs when the lack of efficacy becomes too obvious and too difficult to ignore; the recommendations then become qualified. For example, rather than recommending that all women past menopause take hormones, the recommendation might be restricted to those women past menopause with increased cardiovascular risk.

CONCLUSIONS

Research on menopause and hormone therapy are of obvious importance to women, particularly to older women. However, the focus on menopause as the only phenomenon of relevance to the physical and psychological health of mid- and old-age women is absurd. Labeling those in a society who lack power as biologically inferior is so traditional, historical, and ingrained that the ideological context is not recognized. Feminists have argued for the last two decades that women deserve equal consideration with regard to research and funding priorities. The response in the US has been to increase spending on women but to continue the traditional focus on their reproductive organs (Auerbach and Figert, 1995). Why does the first large-scale, US government-funded study on women's health focus on menopause? The WHI (Women's Health Initiative) has been promoted as a study of the impact of lifestyle variables on health; yet, hormone therapy, the only drug tested, is not a lifestyle variable. The WHI is advertised as a study of prevention, but the age range is 50 to 79 – a bit too late for prevention. The WHI is advertised as a study of heart disease in women, yet it does not assess the impact of aspirin, for example, nor is there a focus on smoking or exercise.

Supporters of the WHI make assumptions that have no, little, or contradictory empirical support. According to Matthews *et al.* (1997a), the WHI is needed because the data on diets and hormone therapy on which physicians are basing their treatment recommendations are from a decade ago and may no longer be applicable. This problem will continue to exist. The clinical trials of the WHI are designed to provide information on the long-term (10 years) effects of hormone therapy. Before the trials even began, the targeted hormone therapy was already outdated. The WHI is testing sequential, oral hormone therapy while the newer forms that are currently being prescribed include combined and continuous regimens as well as alternate routes, such as implants and patches. Clearly, the effectiveness and safety vary with dose, type, and route, so the information for which we are waiting 10 years will probably be of little use. The only way to avoid this problem is to base drug-prescribing practices on valid information of effectiveness and safety. Randomized, controlled trials of hormone therapy should have been done prior to use rather than after. Since this is the stated criterion for approval by the US Federal Drug Administration, this agency, as well as the British National Formulary, does not list the treatment or prevention of cardiovascular disease as an indication for hormone therapy.

My opinion of hormone therapy in menopausal and postmenopausal women is that these drugs have been dispensed to the public prior to sufficient testing and are, therefore, currently not proven to be effective or safe. Although castration does indeed cause a hormone deficiency and, at least logically, could be considered an indication for hormone supplements, there is no evidence that natural menopause is dangerous or associated with deteriorating health. Women considering the risks and benefits of hormone therapy, "need to understand the unresolved issues in therapy...to some extent all postmenopausal users are part of an experimental therapy, often without the benefits of the surveillance found in actual research studies" (Fogel and Woods, 1995, p. 95). The expensive and expansive WHI is designed to determine the long-term benefits and risks of hormone therapy. However, the money and effort might have been better spent on determining basic health factors in aging women. For example, much of the research on hormone therapy focuses on the consequent changes in the lipid profile but focuses on those components of demonstrated relevance for men which are not identical to those for women (see Chapter 6). Basic research on women's health is missing and should be concluded prior to recommending drugs of questionable efficacy for widespread use. In a study of the rates of hormone therapy prescriptions by US primary care physicians, Stafford *et al.* (1997) concluded, "Low rates of estrogen therapy by nonobstetrician-gynecologists and substantial practice variations suggest *missed opportunities* for hormone replacement therapy" (p. 381, emphasis added). I would label these missed opportunities as wise decisions: "it may be easier to accept that valuable therapy was withheld, because its value was not yet known, than to discover that harm was done by poorly studied therapy" (Hemminki *et al.*, 1993, p. 171).

5

SEXUALITY

Sexual pleasure is not more reducible to sexual physiology than is
pleasure in listening to music reducible to auditory physiology.
(Szasz, 1980, p. 37)

people should be able to inquire into, learn about, and practice or
reject sex as freely and with the same impunities as they can
inquire into, learn about, and practice or reject religion.
(Szasz, 1980, p. 163)

THE SOCIAL CONSTRUCTION OF SEXUALITY

Sexuality in mid- and old-age women represents the epitome of a construct that
has been created out of social and political beliefs and values with little basis in
reality (Foucault, 1978; Hite, 1987).

The history of sexuality is not the mere evolution of the means of regulation of one and the same libido, but a process of social invention,
construction, and reconstruction of social meanings, that is a history of
creation and recreation of new social and psychological realities.
(Kon, 1987, p. 260)

Historically, the social construction of sexuality was driven by religion. Today,
the social construction of sexuality is driven by pervasive patriarchal values and
beliefs and by the power, status, and prestige we accord "science" and medicine.

The social construction of sexuality becomes obvious when considering
historical development or changes in the definition of healthy sexuality. Speaking
about a woman recently married, a nineteenth-century novelist comments:

They awake to find they have been living in a Fool's Paradise – a little
upholstered corner with stained glass windows and rose-coloured light.
They find that suddenly they are expected to place in the centre of their

108

life everything that up to that moment they have scarcely been allowed even to know about; they find they must obediently veer round, with the amiable adaptability of a well-oiled weather-cock. Every instinct, every prejudice must be thrown over. All the effects of their training must be instantly overcome.

(Caird, 1989 [1894], p. 250)

Thus, the woman in the quotation is expected to find sexual activity distasteful and morally reprehensible prior to marriage, but, after the ceremony, to be willing and even eager to engage in sexual activity. However, in the nineteenth century, only young women were expected to approach sex with enthusiasm – interest in sex after mid-life was thought to be a sign of illness. Edward Tilt wrote:

My experience teaches me that a marked increase of sexual impulse at the change of life is a morbid impulse. ...Whenever sexual impulse is first felt at the change of life, some morbid ovario-uterine condition will be found to explain it....It, therefore, is most imprudent for women to marry at this epoch without having obtained the sanction of a medical man.

(quoted in Smith-Rosenberg, 1985, p. 192)

As we advance into the twentieth century, aging women's sexuality is, again, reconstructed to conform to prevailing ideology: " 'Most women after the menopause, if they're reasonably healthy and happy, do not experience a diminution in sex drive,' says Dr. Ramey, the senior physiologist at Georgetown University" (Sheehy, 1992, p. 82) and "We have every reason to believe that staying in training sexually also will help to improve the quality of life in later years" (Pfeiffer, 1978, p. 31).

Szasz (1980) points out that: "For more than two hundred years...the leaders of Western science and thought maintained that masturbation caused a host of diseases and was itself a disease" (p. xi). He quotes Benjamin Rush, a leading physician in the early nineteenth century and the father of American Psychiatry: "Masturbation...produces seminal weakness, impotence, dysury, tabes dorsalis, pulmonary consumption, dyspepsia, dimness of sight, vertigo, epilepsy, hypochondriasis, loss of memory, managlia, fatuity, and death" (p. 17). Today, masturbation has quite the opposite reputation. Indeed, Masters and Johnson (1970) coined a new disease called "masturbatory orgasmic inadequacy." This disorder is meant to categorize the woman (and only women have this disorder) who is orgasmic during coitus but not during masturbation. "In the past, people in the Christian West believed that women should have as many children and as few orgasms as possible; now they believe just the opposite" (Szasz, 1980, p. 17). The differing definitions of appropriate sexual behavior have little to do with health, science, or medicine but much to do with cultural beliefs and values.

Advocates of positivism and the scientific method have suggested that today's perspective on sexuality is, indeed, more factual, more truthful, than that of a century ago; that science has lifted the repression traditionally associated with sexuality, that the openness with which sexuality is discussed and observed is healthy. Our cultural myth dictates that science works by collecting more and more information – each bit of information causes a slight modification in the "truth" so that, as more and more facts are gathered, we get closer and closer to "truth." We might, therefore, assume that extensive scientific research is responsible for this dramatic difference between the nineteenth- and twentieth-century views of sexuality. However, consistent with patriarchal values, the sexuality of aging women has never been a research interest unless the goal was to promote hormone therapy. Three of the 1700 pages of the Kinsey *et al.* (1953) reports were devoted to sexuality in older people; a computer search for research articles concerned with sexuality and menopause in the medical literature published between 1988 and 1992 yielded eight entries; a similar search of the psychological literature between 1986 and 1992 yielded 1424 entries on sexuality, four of which were concerned with menopause.

Although there is essentially no "scientific research" to support the changing views on sexuality and age, the social context has changed, changed significantly, and changed in such a way as to be consistent with the current views. This is precisely what is meant by the statement: "Sexuality is socially constructed." The definition of sex, the ages between which one should engage in sex, the gender of the partners, the appropriate order of events, the appropriate timing – all information that physicians readily provide in the guise of "scientific truth" – are essentially determined by the morals, values, beliefs, and politics of the current culture.

> Today, it is dogmatically asserted – by the medical profession and the official opinion-makers of our society – that it is healthy or normal for people to enjoy sex, that the lack of such enjoyment is the symptom of a sexual disorder, that such disorders can be relieved by appropriate medical interventions, and that they ought, whenever possible, to be so treated. This view, though it pretends to be scientific, is, in fact, moral or religious: it is an expression of the medical ideology we have substituted for traditional religious creeds.
>
> (Szasz, 1980, p. 165)

Today's view of sexuality, and in particular older women's sexuality, is not only socially constructed but the construction is sanctioned and perpetuated by today's priests – the scientists. It has been noted with pride, as if it were an advancement for humankind, that today's religion is science; we have replaced belief in religion and devotion to priests with belief in science and devotion to physicians. We have simply replaced one set of experts and one set of rules with different, but not necessarily more valid, experts and rules. The consequences of religious control of sexuality may have been repression but the consequences of scientific/medical control are that sex is reduced to the content of science – biology, the methods of science – unitary, linear causal models, and the interpretations of science – there is one and only one healthy way to be sexual. And the consequences, not surprisingly, are ideologically consistent with patriarchy: the definition of healthy sexuality for aging woman is to have sexual intercourse with her husband; her refusal to do so is interpreted as a hormonal deficiency, and the solution is to modify her biology.

Individuals in Western societies pride themselves on being "sexually free"; we no longer allow religion to dictate our sexuality – marital sex, the missionary position, and monogamy no longer necessarily restrict our behavior. Science takes credit for this liberation; by locating sex in the jurisdiction of medicine, "objective" study is possible. Szasz (1980), however, argues that medical control of sex:

> has resulted in countless people being sexually categorized, condemned, and controlled by means of pseudomedical ideas and interventions. Can anyone really believe that the lexicon of "sadism" and "masochism," of "vaginismus," "frigidity," and "impotence," of the countless "perversions," and of "castration anxiety" and "penis envy" has freed people? (p. 123)

Most scientific research and statements are based upon certain assumptions that are typically not tested but presumed to be true. For example, a scientist may conduct a study to evaluate the effectiveness of hormone medication on the sexual problems of middle-aged women. This appears perfectly reasonable until we realize that there is no evidence that middle-aged women *have* sexual problems. Gupta (1990) notes: "Sex and sexual needs are just another physiologic necessity of human beings even in late life" (p. 197). There is no evidence that sex in later life, or at any time of life, is a necessity – people who do not engage in sexual activity do not get sick, nor do they die. They may be unhappy because they wish to have sex and do not have a partner, but this is a social problem and not a biological or a medical problem and certainly does not apply to all older persons.

Today's priests decree that sex is good and sex is healthy; thus, a person who prefers not to be sexually active or not to be sexually active in the manner or with the frequency or with the gender dictated by the norm is deemed sick. In order to study sexuality in the elderly, the obvious source of information is the elderly. Yet their views are often dismissed and any lack of interest in sexual activity is attributed to underlying psychological problems: "The most vociferous opponents of elderly sexuality can be elderly persons themselves who have a compelling need to defend their own antisexual stance. For persons with lifelong sexual conflict or disinterest, age provides a plausible alibi to release themselves from anxiety-provoking sexual situations" (Sviland, 1978, p. 99); or to being or feeling ugly: "Women in their 50's and 60's who discontinue sex abstain primarily for sociological and psychological reasons, not biological factors, since they do not seek partner replacements unless they are unusually attractive and secure" (Sviland, 1978, p. 102). The potential for stigmatization is obvious: given these cultural values, mid- and old-age women are either heterosexually active or they are unattractive and psychologically disturbed.

Defining certain sexual acts as acceptable and desirable, others as sick, by defining some as sick who have sex (homosexuals), others as sick if they don't have sex (hypoactive sexual desire), we are attempting to control a human behavior in a manner similar to religious doctrines. Medicine does have a role in sex – to treat sexually transmitted diseases and to treat diseases of the reproductive tract. Psychology does have a role in sex – to treat those who are perpetrators and victims of sexual situations that are instances of power abuse and to treat those who express a desire to change some aspect of their sexual experiences. However, helping a woman restore health to her vagina or helping a woman through the aftermath of a traumatic sexual experience does not then give the expert the right to tell her how, when, how often and with whom she may have a sexual experience.

SEXUALITY AND AGING WOMEN (AND MEN)

The stereotype of the aging woman common in Western cultures has taken two forms. The first is the grandmotherly matron, somewhat overweight, who occupies her time knitting and cooking; and the second is the irritable, depressed crone who occupies her time meddling in others' lives and gossiping. Both stereotypes presuppose the absence of sexuality – the grandmother fulfilled her sexual role in the form of maternity and no longer desires sex, nor do others find her sexually appealing; the crone has always been and continues to be sexually dissatisfied and unfulfilled – feelings compounded by the realization that it is "too late." It is generally believed that stereotypes have some root in reality.

In 1953, Kinsey *et al.* reported that, in their sample of 127 postmenopausal women who had been sexually active prior to menopause, 39% reported no change in sexual activities and responses, 13% stated their responses had increased while 48% believed their responses had decreased. Kinsey and colleagues noted that, for those women who reported diminished sexual activity, the change was essentially due to their partners' declining interest in sex. With regard to a second sample of 123 women who had had their ovaries removed, there was no reported modification of sexual responsiveness or capacity for orgasm that could be attributed to the surgery. Similar findings were reported by Runciman (1978): 15% of their sample of women expressed increased sexual interest as they grew older while those who ceased being sexual indicated that the cause was their partner's lack of responsiveness.

Later surveys confirmed the considerable variability in the direction and size of the changes in sexual activity of women as they proceed through middle age.

Leiblum and Swartzman (1986) questioned 39 perimenopausal and 64 post-menopausal women; most agreed that sex remained good and 62% maintained that sexual interest and comfort increased following menopause. Similarly, in a mail survey to 967 women, Kahn and Holt (1987) concluded that,

> While some women say there is also reduced intensity of their sexual response, others say it is better than ever. Those who enjoyed satisfying sexual experiences before menopause continue to do so, some with heightened responses because of the absence of fear of pregnancy and the lack of interruption by children. (p. 167)

Hunter (1990) found some evidence for reduced sexual activity in post-menopausal women as did Hallstrom and Samuelsoon (1990), who found 29% of women aged 60 reporting the absence of sexual desire. However, the authors of both of these recent surveys noted that sexual activity in mid- and old-age women was more highly correlated with factors other than menopausal status, most notably the availability of a partner, insufficient emotional support from spouse, alcoholism in spouse, and psychological problems.

The survey data on sexuality in aging women are fairly consistent in suggesting little or no *predictable* change in sexuality as a consequence of or co-incident with advancing years. Some advantages of survey data, as opposed to laboratory data, are that persons are questioned about their actual life experiences as opposed to being tested for their "potential" sexuality in an artificial setting; and those persons surveyed tend to be selected randomly from a nonclinical population, thus allowing the researchers to make reasonable generalizations to large segments of the population and to estimate more realistically the incidence of sexual problems than one could expect to obtain from a clinical sample who are studied precisely because they have problems.

In studying topics easily compromised by sexist, agist, and classist politics, it is often instructive to compare discourses among various groups differing in their vulnerability to political oppression. In this context, the discourses on sexual behavior of aging women and aging men are compared. The cultural stereotype of sexuality in the aging man is one of continuity, virility, and potency – a form of arrogance emerging from patriarchal society and being fertilized by a cultural preoccupation with sexual activity. To some extent, this stereotype derives from a confusion between fertility and potency: men are, theoretically, capable of producing viable sperm until they die; many assume therefore, that potency continues as well. Indeed this very confusion contributes to the stereotype of the asexual, menopausal woman: she is no longer fertile, therefore, she is not sexual.

In fact, after the age of 50, a diminished sexual potency in men is common and is probably due, at least in part, to declining androgen levels (Davidson, 1980). That this stereotype of continued virility and potency places unreasonable or impossible expectations on aging men is beginning to be recognized and criticized by professionals:

There is not a functional parameter of aging that falls off more steeply than sexual performance. Nevertheless, there seems to be a tendency to classify very old males who are still performing as an achievable norm rather than an unusual example of sexual robustness. Perhaps, it would be more in accord with the facts to regard them as obsessive, unable to give up a sex habit, and unlike the rest of their contemporaries.

(Rossman, 1978, p. 71)

And on moral grounds: "When a justice of the Supreme Court is praised for his 'productivity' in siring a child at an advanced age, it occurs to no one at all to condemn him for creating an orphan – a novel version of an old theme, seduction and abandonment." (Datan and Rodeheaver, 1983, pp. 285– 6)

Thus, the stereotype of the placid, asexual aging woman and the charming, virile aging man both appear to be based on false images. That this is being recognized and the stereotypes dismissed is evident in the professional literature. Kinsey *et al.* (1953) was one of the first to attribute the aging woman's decline in sexuality to men's declining interest in social–sexual activities. In two studies (Runciman, 1978; Weg, 1983), middle-aged women who experienced diminished sexuality attributed their lack of activity to disinterested partners; in both studies, the partners, when questioned, agreed with this attribution.

The converse has, of course, been proposed, i.e., that men's declining potency is caused by unsympathetic, demanding, unresponsive women. In a survey of over a thousand women and over 500 men, Bungay *et al.* (1980) found both men and women to report an increased difficulty with sexual intercourse with age. These authors interpreted these data as "discomfort experienced by the woman leads to complaints about discomfort in the man as well" (p. 183). Similarly, Brenner (1988) suggests that an impaired sexual response in the male partner of a middle-aged woman may result from atrophic vaginal changes (obviously not *his* vaginal changes).

Sarrel (1982) is perhaps the most extreme in this view. He begins with the assumption that, in general, men's sexual problems are women's fault: "One guideline in sex therapy is that secondary erectile difficulty is often related to something the female partner is doing which has a negative effect on the male" (p. 234). In his sample of 50 older, married couples, Sarrel reported that 22 of the men felt rejected and angry because of their wives' lack of vaginal lubrication. The consequence was that these men tried harder to evoke a sexual response, became goal-oriented, and developed performance anxiety (i.e., erectile dysfunction). Sarrel reported that one man worked so hard to arouse his wife that he had a coronary thrombosis. Sarrel recommends that the woman take hormone therapy in order to treat the couple's problems. Advising that women take potentially dangerous drugs so that their male partners can have erections is a bit extreme, even for patriarchy!

Sexual stereotypes, if believed to be the norm, create unreasonable demands, guilt, and 'sick' labels from physicians and psychologists. Although I have presented a case for the falsity of these beliefs, exaggerating the implications from the work discussed above and, in essence, creating new stereotypes of the sex-hungry middle-aged woman and the impotent, frail, aging man would be equally harmful, unjust, and untrue. In fact, the available information (of which there is amazingly little) indicates that women and men experience highly similar changes in sexuality as they age. According to Weg (1983), changes in female and male sexuality with aging include: (1) declining levels of estrogen/declining levels of testosterone; (2) loss of tissue in vulva, cervix, uterus, ovaries, and vagina/testes smaller and more flaccid; (3) diminished vasocongestion of the genital tissues during sexual arousal and increased time required for lubrication/diminished vasocongestion of scrotal tissue, less testicular elevation, and increased time required for erection; (4) duration of orgasm is reduced and the number of uterine and vaginal contractions are reduced/duration of orgasm is reduced and the contractions required to expel the seminal fluid are fewer; and (5) resolution is more rapid and the multiorgasmic capacity is retained/resolution is more rapid and the refractory period considerably longer.

Thus, the changes in sexuality with aging are remarkably similar for women and men. There seems little or no empirical justification for one sex to blame the other for their declining sexuality. Although empirically or theoretically separating the effects of menopause from those of aging is difficult if not impossible, this information implicates aging as the primary source of changed sexuality in middle-aged and elderly women since the changes are similar to those of aging men who do not experience menopause. In essence, there is no reason to expect that our reproductive organs, our levels of energy and activity, our manner of communication and expressing intimacy should remain unaltered as all other aspects of our lives change as we grow older.

INFLUENCES ON SEXUALITY IN MIDDLE-AGED AND ELDERLY WOMEN

The patriarchal habit of defining women according to their reproductive status has had the unfortunate consequence of transforming a middle-aged woman who exists in a context of work, family, friends, and health to a "menopausal status." This has limited the research on sexuality in middle-aged women to that in which the design and interpretation are based on hormones as the primary determinant of sexuality. Given the information presented above, we can conclude that there are no clear and predictable changes in sexuality associated with menopause. This is not to say that sexuality remains unchanged throughout one's adult life – only that the *cause* of change is not obvious or universal. Possible sources of variability in the sexuality of mid- and old-age women are discussed below.

Biology

The stereotype of the asexual, postmenopausal woman and the emphasis on menopause as the most crucial developmental milestone for aging women derives from the myth – common to both lay persons and professionals – that throughout a woman's life, she is directed, determined, and governed by hormones, particularly estrogen. If we believe the stereotype to be true, then we believe that estrogen regulates a woman's psychological, emotional, physical and sexual states, and if we assume (incorrectly) that production of estrogen ceases with menopause (as many believe), then menopause must result in diverse and dramatic consequences. There are several difficulties with this model. First, estrogen decreases as a woman progresses through menopause, but all women, even those who have experienced castration, continue to produce some estrogen, although not necessarily from reproductive tissue, throughout their lives (Gannon, 1990). Second, there is considerable evidence to suggest that women in general, and women's sexuality in particular, are not strongly influenced by hormones. This is discussed below.

Research on the relationship between sexuality and the hormonal fluctuations associated with the menstrual cycle spans several decades. A review of the literature prior to 1980 was published in 1981 and summarized the 32 studies that had reported significant findings relating sexual arousability and menstrual cycle (Schreiner-Engel et al., 1981). Of the studies reviewed, sexual arousal peaked at ovulation in 8 studies, premenstrually in 17 studies, postmenstrually in 18 studies, and during menstruation in 4 studies. In their own study, they evaluated 30 women at three points in their cycles; the phases were confirmed by hormonal analysis, and the dependent variables included both subjective (self-report) and physiological measures of arousal. Sexual arousal and hormonal levels were found to be unrelated. A recent report by Meuwissen and Over (1992) reported the results of three studies: there were no menstrual cycle phase effects for subjective or physiological sexual arousal nor for processes believed to mediate sexual arousal including mood state, recency of sexual experience, and vividness of imagery. There seems little doubt that the predictable hormonal fluctuations associated with the menstrual cycle do not exert a meaningful influence on the sexuality of menstruating women.

Similarly, if estrogen regulated sexual responsiveness, sexual desire, and sexual activity, all postmenopausal women would experience predictable and similar changes in these various aspects of sexuality and the size of the decrement would be determined by available estrogen. Yet, the survey data contradicts the estrogen theory of sexuality: there is considerable variability in the change (or lack of change) in sexuality accompanying and following menopause and, indeed, a sizeable percentage of women report increased sexuality. Stereotypes, however, are buried deep and historically in culture and, in spite of evidence to the contrary, continue to be viewed as factual if they support and reinforce societal values. Thus, in spite of clear evidence to the contrary, many professionals continue to assume that the decreasing estrogen levels associated with menopause necessarily result in a diminished sexuality in postmenopausal women. This belief is expressed by their overwhelming support for treating menopausal and postmenopausal women with hormone therapy.

The decreasing estrogen levels that accompany the menopausal transition are apparently responsible for a decrease, in many women, in vaginal lubrication during sexual arousal. "It is a physiological fact that there is a reduced lubrication in the vagina after the menopause. Many women experience discomfort – even pain and bleeding during intercourse – when the walls of the vagina become thinner and drier" (Kahn and Holt, 1987, p. 167). But as with most human behavior, the cause-and-effect relationship is neither simple nor straightforward. According to Hunter (1990), less than half of postmenopausal women reported dryness during intercourse while a quarter of pre- and perimenopausal women reported this as a problem. And according to Reitz (1977), although some postmenopausal women experienced an increased dryness, most of these women reported that the dryness was occasional and the extent varied considerably.

Estrogen levels are undoubtedly *one* determinant of vaginal lubrication since the lubrication is more likely to be a problem after menopause than before and since lubrication is increased with estrogen supplements. However, another determinant of lubrication appears to be the frequency and regularity of sexual arousal: "Women who engaged in regular masturbation as opposed to haphazard masturbation reported increased lubrication with a partner and the disappearance of vaginal pain due to dryness" (Reitz, 1977, p. 146) and "The fact is that we can maintain and improve our ability to lubricate through any type of arousing sexual activity" (Boston Women's Health Book Collective, 1984, p. 452). The idea that infrequent or absent sexual activity may cause a woman to lubricate less or less quickly during sexual arousal is consistent with other information reported by middle-aged and elderly women: (1) the best predictor of sexuality in later life is sexuality in early life, i.e., those who have been sexually active are likely to remain so (Weg, 1983; Pfeiffer, 1978); and (2) "boredom and habit are a common [problem]....Women who embark on a new relationship in their fifties and sixties tend to enjoy more lively and active sex lives than those approaching their thirtieth wedding anniversary" (Hunter, 1990, p. 42). Thus, in spite of scientists' preference for one cause and one effect, this is yet another example of a human behavior that does not fit a unitary, linear model of causality. Both vaginal lubrication and sexual activity are multiply determined and the relationship between them appears to be interactive rather than causal.

Insufficient vaginal lubrication is easily remedied. For those women who wish a more direct and safer solution than hormone therapy, there are new products available for this purpose. Replens is a nonhormonal, drug-free, bioadhesive vaginal moisturizer and has been compared with estrogen therapy in the treatment of vaginal dryness. Nachtigall (1994) reported that both estrogen therapy and Replens therapy exhibited "statistically significant increases in vaginal moisture, vaginal fluid volume, and vaginal elasticity with a return of the premenopausal pH state" (p. 178). Such simple and obvious solutions reinforce the idea that it is not vaginal dryness that is primarily responsible for the decrease in sexuality that accompanies aging in some women at some times.

Numerous studies evaluating the impact of hormone supplements on sexual parameters have been published. In 1990, Walling *et al.* reviewed studies testing the effects of hormone therapy on sexual outcomes in postmenopausal women. Their review can be summarized as follows: (1) estrogen supplements were superior to placebo for problems with vaginal lubrication, but estrogen was not effective in increasing sexual frequency, satisfaction, or desire; (2) estrogen combined with progesterone was associated with no improvement in any measure of sexuality; and (3) several studies that evaluated estrogen combined with androgens found these drugs to effectively treat "loss of desire" and dysparneuia but none of these studies utilized placebo-control groups so essentially cannot be construed as evidence for effectiveness. No study has tested the effectiveness of hormone therapy separately for castrated and naturally menopausal women. In one uncontrolled, nonrandomized study, Kaplan (1993) tested only castrated women and found testosterone supplements to significantly improve various sexual parameters in a group of castrated women who reported an unproblematic sex life prior to surgery. In contrast, Campbell and Udry (1994) found no change in sexual motivation and behavior when giving testosterone supplements to naturally menopausal women. In general, the current consensus – a consensus not based on a particularly large or high-quality research literature – is that women who experience a natural menopause may or may not complain of problems, may or may not report enhanced pleasure from sex. However, women who have been castrated may experience sexual difficulties, and these difficulties might be alleviated by adding testosterone to the estrogen replacement regimen (Sands and Studd, 1995; Pearce *et al.*, 1995).

Both women and men produce less of their respective hormones as they age and experience similar changes in sexuality. Why is it recommended that middle-aged and elderly women take estrogen supplements in order to remain sexually active while men of similar age are not advised to take androgens? The interpretation of these changes is yet another manifestation of "biology is destiny" – for women. It has never been argued (at least by men in power) that men are unqualified to be president because of their raging testosterone. The stereotype continues that men are "objective" – they are above their biology – whereas women's high emotions and lack of logic are a consequence of their biology. Patriarchy has a clear investment in maintaining women as pure biological entities governed primarily by their hormones. The myths surrounding menstruation and menopause serve to disqualify women as competition in the workplace and reinforce their status as semi-invalids. Such stereotypes render women passive and dependent – characteristics that sap oppressed groups of the motivation to work for social and political change. Patriarchy, in order to survive as such, must keep women as separate, as other and the easiest way to achieve this is to emphasize the most obvious differences – those that are biological. Not only are women defined throughout their reproductive years as sources of sexual gratification and as mothers, but at menopause, when they are finally relieved of these social demands, they are told they have a deficiency disease, and are encouraged to take hormone supplements in order to retain their beauty and sexuality – although there is no evidence that these have been lost or that hormone supplements can cure any such loss.

Psychological factors

Anxiety has been considered of major etiological significance in the context of many psychological theories of sexual dysfunction. The idea that anxiety inhibits sexual arousal is consistent with Wolpe's (1958) theory of reciprocal inhibition, i.e., that anxiety and sexual arousal are mutually inhibiting, and with Masters and Johnson's (1970) descriptions of "performance anxiety" and "fear of rejection." Assuming a relationship between anxiety and sexual arousal is intuitively appealing in that it is consistent with many philosophical precepts of human nature as well as our scientific understanding of the autonomic nervous system. The initial stages of sexual arousal are governed by the parasympathetic system, and this is the dominant system during rest and relaxation. According to this logic, one must be relaxed in order to become sexually aroused. With regard to sexuality in middle and old age, it is commonly believed, but has not been empirically demonstrated, that as persons age, they become increasingly anxious about their physical appearance and their sexual performance and this anxiety may inhibit sexual arousal (Masters and Johnson, 1970).

Although having achieved a certain degree of popular acceptance, there is actually little empirical support for this proposed role of anxiety. The considerable research on the relationship between anxiety and sexual arousal, although facilitated by the development of genital measures of sexual arousal, such as the vaginal photoplethysmograph, has yielded surprisingly inconsistent results. In a review of the relevant literature, Heiman and Hatch (1981) concluded that it is just as likely that anxiety follows and is caused by sexual dysfunction as it is that sexual dysfunction follows and is caused by anxiety. In either case, more important than the anxiety in understanding and treating the dysfunction, are the developmental conditions responsible for the anxiety, such as relationship variables. In a later review, Barlow (1986) concluded that the relationship between sexual arousal and anxiety is complex, that the relationship varies with how sexually "functional" the individual is, and that, more often than not, anxiety had been found to *enhance*, rather than *diminish*, sexual arousal, at least in the laboratory. The picture is even more complicated when considering that almost all of the research on sexuality, in general, and sexuality and anxiety, in particular, has consisted of studying persons between the ages of 20 and 40. Consequently, most scholarly works on sexuality in the aged are not based on careful observation and experimentation but on opinion, stereotype, and inappropriate generalizations.

Another "emotion" which has been linked to sexual arousal is anger, which

119

may exert an inhibitory effect on sexual arousal. Heiman and Hatch (1981) note that the research results have been inconsistent, perhaps because researchers fail to evaluate the role of anger in the context in which the sexual activity occurs. Most of the research on anger and sexual arousal has focused specifically on anger directed at the partner. While this may be important, other sources and contexts of anger may also be relevant.

In patriarchal cultures, women may well feel anger – a diffuse, intense, chronic, and cumulative anger – when they recognize and acknowledge their economic, social, political, and sexual oppression. If emerging at or before middle age, such anger is likely to focus, at least in part, on sexuality as this is one of the deepest sources of oppression. A woman at the age of 50 may discover there was no medical reason for her to have had her uterus and ovaries removed 5 years ago, *or* her husband of 30 years may leave her for a fling with a younger woman, *or*, she may realize there are no male parallels to the dangers of oral contraceptives, DES, breast implants, IUDs, or hormone therapy, *or* she may be told by her gynecologist that she has a deficiency disease and, in order to continue being a woman, she should take potentially dangerous drugs for the rest of her life, *or* she may agree with the feminist author MacKinnon:

> Dominance eroticized defines the imperatives of masculinity, submission eroticized defines femininity. So many of the distinctive features of women's status as second class – the restriction and constraint and contortion, the servility and the display, the self-mutilation and requisite presentation of self as a beautiful thing, the enforced passivity, the humiliation – are made into the content of sex for women.
>
> (MacKinnon (1987, p. 69)

This anger, although not necessarily directed at a particular individual, could conceivably impact a woman's relationship with all men and her attitudes towards heterosexual sexual activity. Anger from this source may become more likely and more intense as one ages, as one cares less about being the perfect sex playmate, as one learns more and experiences more, and as one recognizes that patriarchal values are responsible for some of her most intense disappointments and frustrations. Perhaps, the behavior of the menopausal woman whom Wilson (1966) describes: "She thrashes about wildly, often venting a special vindictiveness upon her husband and family. Eventually she subsides into an uneasy apathy that is indeed a form of death within life" (p. 97) has more to do with consciousness-raising than with hormones.

Social factors

Numerous studies of sexuality in older women have pointed to the importance of the partner and the relationship context. Hunter (1990) and Reitz (1977) noted that a poor partner relationship characterized by boredom, lack of communication, and negative feelings towards the partner tends to inhibit sexual expression and sexual desire. In a study of 1867 women in their sixties, Lindgren *et al.* (1993) found the major reason for the lack of sexual activity was the absence of a partner. In a later study (Helstrom *et al.*, 1995) examining the influence of hysterectomy on sexuality, the authors found the crucial factor to be the partner relationship; interestingly, they reported that having no partner was associated with a lesser risk for postoperative dissatisfaction than having a poor partner relationship.

Data from the Massachusetts Male Aging Study, a community based survey of noninstitutionalized men between 40 and 70 years old (Feldman *et al.*, 1994), indicate that the combined prevalence of minimal, moderate and complete impotence was 52%. The most important determinant of impotence was age; the prevalence of complete impotence increased from 5 to 15% over this 30-year age span. Although male impotence as relevant to women's sexuality is limited to heterosexual women, the woman is often the one blamed for men's erectile difficulties. Sarrel (1990) describes a study of 50 heterosexual couples who reported developing sexual problems at the time of menopause. The men claimed:

> a variety of inhibitory feelings: 22 rejection and anger, 12 a fear of hurting their partner, and six performance anxiety. Eighteen men reported physical difficulties with sex: eight reported an inability to penetrate…and ten reported being unable to sustain erection for the prolonged stimulation time required by the woman before intercourse. (p. 29S)

According to Dr. Sarrel, of the 38 men who had problems with erection, the problem was corrected in 28 when the woman was treated with hormones. In addition to estrogen therapy, Sarrel recommends androgen supplements for those for whom the estrogen does not alleviate the problem – he does not say if the man or woman should take the androgens. Placing the responsibility for men's sexual performance on women is taken a bit further in a recent popular article (Boldt, 1997): the author places responsibility on the wife for getting her impotent husband to the doctor.

Goldstein and Teng (1991) concluded that the frequency of intercourse in middle-aged and elderly women is more a measure of the partner's ability to have an erection than the woman's interest or desire. Both this comment and Sarrel's research imply that the physical, emotional, and psychological characteristics of the woman and her preferences are viewed as trivial in comparison with her partner's ability to perform. Historically and currently, "Those who are sexually privileged (males) have their sexual needs met, those who are not (females) must adapt to whatever standard is currently in vogue" (Richgels, 1992, p. 128). And, when aged women express concern about their sexuality, they are not taken seriously. Barber (1996), in discussing the medical aspects of sexuality in aging women, comments: "Often, the patients complain that they have lost their pubic hair or that it has become gray and they are ashamed. They should be reassured that the eyesight of their partner may be poor and he may not notice this change" (p. 971).

Individual preference

By assuming there needs to be a *reason* not to be sexual – an unsupportive partner or a restrictive society – we are implying that the only natural, healthy course is to be sexual, and, in most sub-cultures, heterosexual and social. Szasz (1980) proposes that one's sexuality is a personal choice; if one's sexual behavior is criminal, then a legal problem exists but never a medical one. Indeed, "Calling unwanted behavior a disease is...the first step that leads to the acceptance of various interventions – from psychological therapies to penile prostheses – as bona fide treatment" (p. 83). The possibility that a woman might choose to abstain from sex, regardless of the interest and performance level of her partner, has not been considered. There is some indication that, as women age, they become less interested in sexual activity. In situations where modifications in sexual activity are common, such as heart disease, diabetes and cancer, women appear less distressed by their loss of interest than do men (Goldstein and Teng, 1991). Furthermore, these same authors noted that in surveys of elders, the frequency of intercourse was similar for men and women but the frequency of masturbation declined much more rapidly in women than in men – less than 1% of women over 71 had masturbated in the previous 6 months.

Apparently, many middle-aged and elderly women *choose* not to be sexually active. Can a woman choose to abstain from sex without being diagnosed as suffering from a physical or psychological illness? Many authors, while claiming "scientific objectivity," stereotype, label, or outright blame by subtly implying that not to be sexually active is "sick." Runciman states:

> If a woman has been plagued with a nonorgasmic response or by a lack of regular, recurrent sexually satisfying coital activity during her active reproductive years, there is reason to believe that the advent of the post-menopausal years may serve to decrease the sex drive and to make the idea of any sexual expression increasingly repugnant. This individual, of course, uses the excuse of advancing years to avoid the personal embarrassment of inadequate sexual performance or the frustrations of unresolved sexual tensions....applies particularly to those who have always felt that sex was something they 'had to go through.' Many unconsciously welcome the advancing years to abandon the function that has been unpleasant since childhood.
>
> (Runciman (1978, p. 86)

The implication is clear – that if a woman chooses to not engage in sexual activity during middle and old age, she must have unnatural attitudes towards sexuality, be sexually inadequate, or have faked a previously positive attitude toward sexual activity. Corby and Azrit (1983) offer ever more damning interpretations by suggesting that the lack of sexual interest in older women may be a defense mechanism or due to not being able to find a man.

MacKinnon not only accepts the choice not to be sexual as "not sick" but accepts that a refusal to be sexual is a healthy response, perhaps the only healthy response, for the woman who is truly aware of crimes against women committed with permission, if not enthusiasm, by proponents of the patriarchy:

> The assumption that in matters sexual women really want what men want from us, makes male force against women in sex invisible. It makes rape sex. Women's sexual "reluctance, dislike, and frigidity," women's puritanism and prudery in the face of this sex, is "the silent rebellion of women against the force of the penis," – an ineffective rebellion, but a rebellion nonetheless.
>
> (MacKinnon, 1987, p. 79)

Current sexual mores and the medicalization of women's reproductive development interact to deny legitimacy for freely chosen sexual abstinence. Surely, the freedom of sexual expression (or the freedom to abstain from sexual expression) is so basic a human right as to be a prerequisite for economic, political, and social equality for women.

CONCLUSIONS

Mid- and old-age in women are not, contrary to popular belief, universally associated with diminished sexual activity; some women report a decrease, others an increase, but the majority report no change. This conclusion is consistent with literature focusing on the relationship between hormones and sexuality – that sexuality and hormones are *not* related to a statistically or clinically significant degree is apparent from the lack of covariation between phases of the menstrual cycle and sexuality, from the lack of a universal impact of menopause on sexuality, and from the ineffectiveness of hormone supplements to influence sexual satisfaction, frequency, or desire. There are, however, in middle and old age, relationship and family transformations, professional concerns and challenges, physical illnesses, normal aging, and a continual resetting of priorities that could, and probably do, impact a woman's sexuality. The development and growth that characterizes the progression through adulthood include changes in roles, work, stressors, relationships, emotionality, leisure activity, family involvement – in virtually all areas of life. There is no reason to expect sexuality to be exempt from these developmental processes.

The proscriptions and prescriptions regarding sexuality are primarily a product of the social, political, and moral environment. This is particularly true for the middle-aged or elderly woman for whom even the suspect logic of biological imperatives has no meaning. In the nineteenth century, menopause was seen as a sign that sexuality was at an end; women who felt healthy, vigorous, and sexy enough to marry were labeled "sick" and advised to see their physician. Today, menopausal women who prefer not to be sexual are advised to see their physician for help in restoring their lost sexuality. What has not changed is that women's personal choices and preferences were and are not taken seriously, and that their normal biological development and growth has been pathologized.

Regardless of time and place, aging and menopause have meant an increased freedom to women (Gannon, 1985; Smith-Rosenberg, 1985) – if only freedom from pregnancy and childbearing. In the nineteenth century, social roles restricted women to such an extent that this freedom was, perhaps, not apparent or threatening to the social order. However, in the recent twentieth century, with an emphasis on health and fitness and with greater social and professional opportunities available to women, the mid- and old-age woman, still healthy and vigorous, may strive for greater personal independence and compete with men in the workplace. Science and medicine may be serving the needs of the patriarchy by encouraging women to stay at home, stay dependent, and stay in bed. We cannot, of course, ignore the "coincidence" that menopausal women were informed that "sex is healthy" about the time that it became possible for them to spend their money on hormones advertised to restore beauty, youth, charm, and sexuality (Wilson, 1966).

In concluding this chapter, I would like to mention that a discussion of aging and sexuality is, perhaps, relevant to far fewer women than we might expect. The economic, social, and medical problems of many of the elderly preclude a serious consideration or interest in sex. The Boston Women's Health Book Collective (1984) clarify the significance of some of the immediate concerns of the elderly:

> poor medical care, due to high cost, lack of insurance coverage, inadequate medical understanding of aging and maldistribution of doctors....Money worries due to being on a small, limited income....Inadequate income also makes it harder to take care of our bodies in simple but crucial daily ways. It is difficult, for instance, to get enough exercise if we don't feel safe on the streets or have little access to indoor exercise facilities. A worsening economic situation and drastic cuts in social programs make it more difficult each month for thousands of older women to get adequate calories, let alone vitamins and special diets. Some already subsist partly on pet food. Many are starving....Four million American women between fifty-five and sixty-five have no health insurance. (p. 453)

The position in the hierarchy of needs occupied by the expression and enjoyment of sexuality should not be of concern to physicians or psychologists nor should they dictate "proper" or "healthy" sexual behavior. Some elderly women will place great emphasis on sexuality, others will choose to abstain – in either case, we need not assume their choices or their reasons are poor ones. And, for many elderly women, those who are struggling to survive, sexuality is simply irrelevant.

6

CARDIOVASCULAR HEALTH

Women are less likely than men to be routinely tested for cardio-vascular symptoms and more likely to suffer unrecognized heart attacks....Women who come to the doctor with severe symptoms are not as likely as men with lesser symptoms to be given coronary arteriography, catheterization, or bypass surgery....When women do have coronary artery bypass surgery, they are more likely to be given sedatives for anxiety and agitation rather than narcotic anal-gesics for postoperative pain.

(Lorber, 1997, p. 44)

Studies of women and cardiovascular technologies must proceed with an appreciation of women's connection with the medical establishment and the history of economic and political power that have created and sustained a gender-biased research and practice arena.

(Beery, 1995, p. 434)

There are clear and persistent gender differences in the incidence of coronary heart disease (CHD). Rates of CHD are three to four times higher in men than in women in the middle decades of life and roughly twice as high in the elderly. Men experience eight times more myocardial infarctions (MIs) than do women, although this disparity diminishes with age. Similar gender differences have been found for Caucasians (Mendelson and Hendel, 1995), African Americans (Cannistra *et al.*, 1995), and Native Americans (Howard *et al.*, 1995). The cause of these well-documented differences between women and men in CHD have been assumed to be biologic, usually hormonal. However, there are several tantalizing bits of information that argue against this. Godsland *et al.* (1987) point out that, in societies where CHD is rare, there are no gender differences in cholesterol levels; these authors interpret this to mean that the gender differences in cholesterol levels found in our society, are due to gender differences in diet, exercise, and stress level. Also, in contradiction to a biological interpretation, Strickland (1988) reports that, in the US, the wives of men who develop CHD are twice as likely to suffer from CHD than women whose husbands are free of the disease. Unless CHD is contagious, this suggests powerful environmental influences. Rather than hormones, "the leading causes of death in this country are linked to dysfunctional life styles and behaviors" (Strickland, 1988, p. 387).

The decline in the last several decades in CHD mortality in the US has been steeper for men than for women and steeper for Caucasians than for African Americans (Mosca *et al.*, 1997). Among men, this has resulted in, for the first time, African American men being at greater risk than Caucasian men. Caucasian women have historically had a lower rate of CHD – about 50% – than African American women and this continues to be the case (Liao and Cooper, 1995; Mendelson and Hendel, 1995). Racial differences in risk factors have been cited as the cause for the racial differences in CHD: Cannistra *et al.* (1995) reported that African American women, compared to Caucasian women, had higher rates of hypertension, diabetes, obesity, elevated cholesterol, and smoking. African American women have almost twice the rate of obesity that Caucasian women have (Shumaker and Smith, 1995). Finally, Kuller (1995) proposed that a higher prevalence of left-ventricular hypertrophy among African Americans may explain some of the difference.

In many industrialized countries race and socioeconomic status (SES) are confounded; in the United States, SES is lower, in general, for African Americans than for European Americans. Cannistra *et al.* (1995) reported that 57% of the African American women in their study were insured through Medicaid or attended the program free of charge, compared with 15% of Caucasian women. One consequence of SES is quality of medical care, particularly in the United States, where a national health service does not exist, and those without financial resources do not have access to medical care. Liao and Cooper (1995) pointed out that African Americans are treated with bypass surgery and angiography half as often as European Americans and that African Americans are more likely to die outside the hospital. Indeed, CHD in women tends to be more prevalent among those with lower levels of education and economic status (Shumaker and Smith, 1995). Thus, racial differences in the incidence of CHD may be due, at least in part, to differences in SES.

Beginning in the early 1960s and continuing today, many countries have allocated public resources to educate the public on risk factors and risk-reduction strategies. In the US, the success of such a policy was evaluated by J.W. Davis *et al.* (1995). They measured changes between 1980 and 1990 in knowledge of and interest in risk modification in a large sample of men and women across the age span. They found a 38% increase in knowledge of risk factors and a 14% increase in knowledge of risk-reduction strategies. However, when grouped according to educational level, those with more education had greater *knowledge* of both but were similar to those with less education on *desire* to decrease risk. An important finding for planning future public policy was that those with less than twelve years of education had already, at a young age, developed disproportionately high prevalences of CHD risk factors. Those with higher levels of education were also higher on other indicators of SES such as level of health care, availability of health care, and literacy. Compared to the large quantity of CHD research devoted to risk factors such as hypertension and high cholesterol level, the amount of time, effort, and resources focused on SES factors associated with CHD have been minimal. SES is obviously an umbrella term that encompasses factors other than financial resources, such as access to healthy food, knowledge of healthy food, safe places for working and exercising, and access to good medical care. Perhaps, there is a political motivation behind the neglect and denial of the salience of economic factors on health. If CHD were found to be largely caused by poor economic conditions, governments might be pressured to develop more equitable economic policies.

DETERMINANTS OF CARDIOVASCULAR DISEASE

The cardiovascular system consists of the heart and the circulatory system, the latter including arterial and venal blood vessels. The purpose of the cardiovascular system is to transport nutrients to the cells of the body and eliminate cellular waste products. The heart is divided into four chambers that provide a pathway and pumping system for blood flow. Deoxygenated blood returns from the body to the right atrium; the right atrium pumps the blood to the right ventricle which, in turn, pumps the blood to the lungs. In the lungs, blood gives up carbon dioxide, picks up oxygen, and then returns to the heart by way of the left atrium. The left atrium pumps the blood to the left ventricle. The pressure of the heart beat pumps the blood from the left ventricle through the arterial system, supplying oxygen to all the cells of the body. After an exchange of oxygen and carbon dioxide in the cells, the blood returns to the heart via the veins. Structurally, the heart is a muscle, the myocardium; the coronary arteries supply blood to the heart muscle. "Heart disease" and "coronary heart disease" (CHD) are general terms that include a variety of specific diagnoses referencing different functions and structures of the heart and circulation system. The leading cause of death for both women and men in most Western, industrialized societies is heart disease. Disease, deterioration, or abnormal function in the heart or in the blood vessels may cause cardiovascular problems.

Atherosclerosis is a cause or an exacerbating factor of many forms of heart disease. The extent and development of atherosclerosis is determined primarily by genetics and high levels of cholesterol in the blood. Cholesterol causes plaque to adhere to the vessel walls; this causes a narrowing of the blood vessel which, in turn, impedes blood flow. If severe and if this occurs in the coronary arteries, this condition is known as ischemic heart disease. Under conditions of physical or psychological stress, the heart requires an increased blood supply; if the coronary arteries are partially blocked with plaque, they may be inadequate to carry the additional load, depriving the myocardium of needed oxygen. This often causes chest pain known as angina pectoris. Ischemic heart disease may be complicated by the development of thrombi. A thrombus is an aggregation of

127

blood platelets, fibrin, and clotting factors; a thrombus may attach to the interior wall of a blood vessel and combine with plaque to further occlude the artery. If blockage occurs in a coronary artery, MI and death may result. If the thrombus breaks away from the wall of the vessel, it may be carried in the blood stream as an "embolus," and eventually cause a blockage elsewhere. This condition is referred to as a thromboembolism; emboli lodging in the pulmonary vessels supplying the lungs or the coronary arteries can be fatal. An embolus occurring in the brain vasculature is one cause of cerebrovascular accident or stroke. (Further information on thrombosis may be found in Chapter 4.)

Mortality rates for heart disease have declined by 50% over the past 40 years in both men and women. This decrease is usually attributed to improved health habits such as smoking cessation and decreases in dietary animal fat (Schaefer *et al.*, 1995). A nation-wide, cross-sectional survey in the United States from 1960 to 1991 revealed a consistent and progressive decline in serum total cholesterol levels in all age-sex groups (Johnson *et al.*, 1993). The authors note that the observed trend in serum cholesterol levels coincided with a similar decline in coronary heart disease mortality. They attribute these changes to the success of public health programs. Other cultural and societal trends have undoubtedly also contributed to the diminishing mortality from CHD, such as increased exercise participation, anti-smoking campaigns, and recognition of the risks of caffeine, nicotine, and alcohol.

Lipid metabolism

Lipids refer to a group of chemical compounds that circulate throughout the body in the blood stream; they include triglycerides, phosopholipids, and cholesterol. Cholesterol is the most well-known lipid due to its salience to cardiovascular disease. In the United States, one can hardly read a magazine or newspaper, watch television, or have a conversation at a party without discovering a new and better way to reduce cholesterol. The terms "cholesterol," "blood lipids," "lipids," and "lipoproteins" tend to be used interchangeably. Total cholesterol (TC) is made up of three primary components. Low-density lipoproteins (LDLs) comprise about 60 to 70% of the total; these lipids, the "bad" cholesterol, are the ones that can build up in the arteries and contribute to atherosclerosis. High-density lipoproteins (HDLs) comprise about 20 to 30% of the total; these so-called "good" lipids carry the cholesterol back to the liver for processing or removal from the body and, therefore, prevent accumulation and build up on the artery walls. Finally, there are very-low-density lipoproteins (VLDLs), comprised primarily of triglycerides; the precise action of these is controversial. In general, CHD risk increases as total cholesterol, LDL and triglyceride levels increase and as HDL levels decrease. According to current recommendations, total cholesterol levels of less than 200mg/dl are desirable, between 200 and 239 mg are considered borderline, and over 240 mg/dl are high and potentially dangerous. LDL levels of less than 130 mg/dl are desirable,

130 to 159 are borderline, and over 160 mg/dl are considered high risk for CHD. Levels of HDL over 35 mg/dl and triglycerides below 250 mg/dl are considered healthy. These recommendations should be used cautiously by women, however, since, until recently, almost all of the research on lipids and CHD has only focused on men.

Recognizing that women have been ignored in research on cardiovascular disease, researchers have recently focused on women. Initial findings suggest gender differences in those components of the lipid profile that are predictive of cardiovascular morbidity and mortality. While total cholesterol and LDL levels appear to be of particular importance to men's risk, HDL and triglyceride levels are particularly important predictors of cardiovascular risk in women (Mosca *et al.*, 1997). Meilahn *et al.* (1995) concluded that high triglycerides are a better predictor of CHD in women than in men, and that women do not seem to be as affected by elevated LDL levels as are men, as long as HDL levels are high. Cooper and Whitehead (1995) note that, in contrast to men, elevated triglycerides are an independent risk factor for mortality in women, whereas total cholesterol is not. In a recent prospective observational study of 1462 women followed for 20 years, Bengtsson *et al.* (1993) reported that serum triglyceride concentrations, but not total cholesterol, posed a clear threat to mortality. Data consistent with these results have been reported by Samsioe and Mattsson (1990) and Utian (1990), and similar conclusions have been reached in several reviews of this research literature (Bergmann *et al.*, 1997; Corti *et al.*, 1995). A position paper by the American Dietetic Association (1995) states: "In women…low levels of high-density lipoprotein cholesterol…are more predictive of cardiovascular disease than are high levels of LDL-C, especially if levels of plasma triglycerides are also high" (p. 323). The emerging consensus appears to be that the lipid profile of particular danger to women consists of high levels of triglycerides and low levels of HDL.

A variety of risk factors have been shown to be associated with an artherogenic lipid profile, although the results among studies have not been entirely consistent. The more common predictors of a poor lipid profile include obesity, high waist-to-hip ratio, older age, sedentary lifestyle, and smoking (Krummel *et al.*, 1993; Kuller *et al.*, 1995; Pasquali, *et al.*, 1997). Examining risk factors associated with specific components of the lipid profile in a large sample of women aged 45 to 65 years, Schrott *et al.* (1994) noted that HDL levels did not vary with age but were associated with leisure time exercise, income, alcohol intake, smoking and education level; triglycerides were associated with smoking, leisure time exercise, fat mass, fat distribution and education. Several researchers (Kuller *et al.*, 1995; Pasquali *et al.*, 1997; Sowers, 1998) as well as the American Dietetic Association (1995) emphasized the importance of diabetes or abnormal insulin metabolism: "Diabetes mellitus is a powerful and independent risk factor for cardiovascular disease….Women with diabetes have twice the risk of heart disease than men with diabetes. In the Framingham study, diabetes mellitus was associated with a fivefold risk of cardiovascular disease among women"

(American Dietetic Association, 1995, p. 364). Not surprisingly, diabetes is found to have some of the same risk factors as high cholesterol levels such as obesity and older age.

Prevention of CHD through public health efforts aimed at lowering cholesterol has been somewhat successful (Schrott *et al.*, 1997). Recently, however, there has been an increasing number of concerns raised about potential adverse consequences of *low* cholesterol. Muldoon *et al.* (1990) quantitatively reviewed six randomized, controlled trials on the effectiveness of lowering cholesterol by drugs, diet, or both in men with raised cholesterol levels. The outcome measure was death. Cholesterol lowering was, as expected, associated with a lowered incidence of death from cardiovascular disease, *but not total mortality*. There was no consistent relationship between cholesterol lowering and cancer, but they did find a significant increase in deaths from accidents, suicide, or violence in those receiving treatment to lower cholesterol levels. Jacobs *et al.* (1992) reviewed 19 cohort studies from different countries. For men, a "U"-shaped curve fits the relationship – high mortality was associated with high total cholesterol and with low cholesterol, while reduced mortality was associated with moderate levels of cholesterol. In contrast, for women, there was no association between total cholesterol and total mortality.

Several follow-up studies have been done in order to provide enlightenment of these rather surprising findings. Golier *et al.* (1995) found that those with a lifetime history of serious suicide attempts were likely to have low serum cholesterol, but this was true only for men. In one of the few studies to examine the individual components of cholesterol, Lindberg *et al.* (1994) reported that, in men, depression was associated with low total cholesterol and low LDL, whereas, in women, low triglycerides were associated with increased depression. Although the potential dangers of low or lowered cholesterol levels appear to have empirical support, researchers have yet to delineate the pathway or pathways involved and to examine or understand the gender differences thoroughly. Furthermore, as Hillbrand and Spitz (1997) have argued, we need to distinguish between an individual who has constitutionally low cholesterol and one who has lowered a previously high level of cholesterol. Of particular importance to this discussion is recognizing that research on men cannot be assumed to be valid for women.

Low HDL, high levels of triglycerides and diabetes appear to be particularly important risk factors for CHD in women. Although a variety of recommendations have been published regarding the benefits of lifestyle changes and medical treatments, the research on risk factors has not established cause-and-effect relationships. Causal relationships are often inferred on the basis of our personal view of the world, cultural values and practices, and idiosyncratic "common sense." For example, there has been consistent evidence (see Chapter 3) that regular exercise of moderate intensity is associated with high HDL, that persons with sedentary lifestyles have low levels of HDL, and that initiating an exercise program of moderate intensity is associated with increasing levels of HDL. One might reasonably conclude that increasing the intensity of activity *causes* HDL levels to increase. However, Williams *et al.* (1982) randomly assigned sedentary persons to exercise and no-exercise (control) groups. The authors not only measured the lipid outcomes but also monitored compliance with the exercise program. As expected, exercise improved the lipid profile. Interestingly, those with initially high HDL and lower triglycerides were more compliant and were more easily encouraged to increase the intensity of their training. These results indicate possible *interactive* pathways in which initial lipid levels influence the likelihood of exercising and exercising improves the lipid profile. Unfortunately, these data suggest that those who are more likely to benefit from increasing their activity level are those less likely to do so.

Blood pressure

Blood pressure is the force exerted by blood against the blood vessel wall. The standard method of measuring blood pressure is the height of a column of mercury pushed by the pressure of the blood; this is typically expressed as mmHg. Each time the heart beats, the left ventricle pumps blood into the aorta. The pressure in the aorta fluctuates between systolic blood pressure – the peak blood pressure occurring in response to the heart ejecting blood – and diastolic blood pressure – the lowest blood pressure occurring when the heart is resting between beats. In the normal young adult, systolic averages 120 mmHg and diastolic 80 mmHG. Hypertension (high blood pressure) has traditionally been defined as a diastolic blood pressure greater than 90 mmHg. Hypertension is a risk factor for CHD because of the increased work load on the heart and the damage to the arteries from excessive pressure. The increased pressure causes the left ventricle to enlarge in response to the extra work load; high pressure in the arteries is one cause of atherosclerosis developing in the coronary arteries, as well as in the arteries of the rest of the body. In addition to the risks associated with atherosclerosis described above, additional problems develop as a consequence of high blood pressure and include increased risk of cerebral hemorrhage or stroke and progressive damage to the kidneys (Guyton, 1982). According to Perlman *et al.* (1989), high blood pressure is, perhaps, the strongest predictor of heart disease in women.

Hypertension tends to be associated with the same risk factors as high cholesterol and these include increasing age, poor diet, smoking, obesity, and sedentary lifestyle. In a recent study, Gardner and Poehlman (1995) proposed that the apparent age-related increases in blood pressure may be more related to the cumulative effects of an unhealthy lifestyle than to age. They evaluated the association between age and blood pressure while statistically controlling for various risk factors. In men, the association between age and blood pressure was primarily related to an increase in body fat, whereas, in women, the primary factor was the distribution of fat. After statistically controlling for these risk factors, only in women older than 62 did the association between age and blood pressure remain significant. Since the common mid-life increases in fat mass and distribution of fat are determined, at least partially, by exercise and diet, these data suggest life habits as a major determinant of hypertension.

Aging, menopause, and castration

Aging has been defined as a gradual reduction in reserve capacity in all physiological systems over time (Albert and Cattell, 1994). Accordingly, the risk of cardiovascular problems and disorders increases with age in all persons. These age-related changes have been well documented for the cardiovascular system as well as for many of the risk factors associated with cardiovascular disorders, such as high blood pressure and plaque accumulation in the blood vessels. These trends over the life span may be due simply to "wear and tear," to the cumulative effects of poor health habits, to the physical and psychological stress characteristic of the culture, and/or to the impact of environmental pollutants found in the air, food, and water.

The association between CHD and age is further defined by gender. Women's risk of CHD trails that of men by approximately 10 years (Pagley and Goldberg, 1995) and remains lower than that of men throughout life. The difference in CHD between men and women tends to decrease in middle age. This "narrowing of the gap" at middle age has been the focus of intense discussion in recent years. Many gynecologists have endorsed the view that the cardiovascular advantage in young women is due to a protective effect of estrogen, and the "narrowing of the gap" at middle age reflects the loss of this protection with menopause due to diminished estrogen production (e.g., Whitehead, 1988). Cardiologists, on the other hand, attribute the decreasing gender differences in CHD with age to changes in testosterone levels in men as they progress through middle age. Godsland *et al.* (1987) have proposed that the primary reason for the early and dramatic gender difference in CHD is the detrimental influence of testosterone: as men age, their level of testosterone declines and their age-related rate of increase in cardiovascular disease diminishes accordingly. As can be seen in Figure 6.1, the slope of the age-related increases in cardiovascular disease remains essentially the same for women as they progress through middle age and menopause. If menopause and/or estrogen were a major contributor, one would expect to see a steeper slope (an increased rate of change) around the time of menopause. According to Newnham and Silberberg (1997): "The absence of a change in slope of the CHD incidence curve at the time of menopause belies the proposed importance of oestrogen deficiency" (p. 5). In contrast, the slope of the line tracking men's risk for CHD across the life span becomes more gradual around mid-life. This supports the cardiologists' interpretation that men's age-related risk diminishes as their testosterone level diminishes. Perhaps male puberty is more to blame for cardiovascular problems than is female menopause.

Attributing the diminishing gender differences in CHD during middle age to men's diminished testosterone levels rather than to women's diminished estrogen levels is consistent with data on the relationship between androgens, including

132

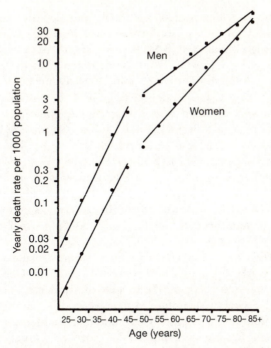

Figure 6.1 Death rates from ischemic heart disease (plotted logarithmically) in men and women according to age

Source: From R.F. Heller and H.S. Jacobs (1978) Coronary heart disease in relation to age, sex, and the menopause, British Medical Journal, 1: 472. Reprinted with permission of BMJ Publishing Group.

testosterone, and lipids: "Both endogenous and exogenous androgens have a suppressive effect on HDL cholesterol in males" (Bagatell and Bremner, 1995, p. 255). Furthermore, in women, higher serum testosterone levels have been found to be significantly associated with lower HDL levels (Haffner *et al.*, 1995). Additional support for the detrimental effects of androgens on the cardiovascular system are studies finding supplemental androgens to be associated with increased risk of cardiovascular disorders (e.g., Walsh, 1992). Indeed, Wild (1995) has proposed a syndrome that identifies a subset of women with cardiovascular risk parallel to that of men and characterized by excessive androgens. He outlines a variety of manifestations of this syndrome, including dysfunctional insulin action, lowered HDL, heightened triglycerides, diabetes, central body obesity, and polycystic ovaries, as well as the more commonly recognized effects of androgen excess in women such as hirsutism, anovulation, and infertility.

Fat mass, or the percentage of body mass composed of fat, tends to increase with age. Frequently this gain has been attributed, in women, to menopause (e.g., Tremollieres *et al.*, 1996). However, since men exhibit similar changes in body composition as they age, the cause of the weight gain is more likely due to age and/or the tendency for persons to decrease their level of physical activity as they progress through middle age (B.M. Posner *et al.*, 1995). Some authors have proposed that weight gain, *per se*, is not as detrimental to the cardiovascular system in women as is the distribution of adipose tissue. A central distribution of body fat, or a high waist-to-hip ratio, is referred to as an "android" fat distribution since this shape is common in overweight men. While there is no doubt about the ill effects of obesity for CHD, waist-to-hip ratio as an independent risk factor for cardiovascular disease is controversial. Some (e.g., Kuller *et al.*, 1995) have argued that fat distribution is a direct consequence of weight. In other words, persons who are obese also have a high waist-to-hip ratio; if weight and fat distribution are highly correlated, then either or both could be responsible for the increased CHD risk. In contrast, others (Bengtsson *et al.*, 1993) have interpreted the data to indicate that weight distribution is more important than weight, *per se*.

Although CHD clearly increases with age, natural menopause does not appear to impact cardiovascular risk (e.g., Barrett-Connor and Goodman-Gruen, 1995; Newnham and Silberberg, 1997). In spite of considerable empirical data to the contrary, the scholarly literature in gynecology has, with few exceptions, endorsed the opinion that menopause causes increased cardiovascular risk. This misconception seems to have several methodological and theoretical sources: (1) the common research and clinical practice of equating the physiology and health of naturally menopausal and castrated women; (2) the difficulty of practically and statistically separating the effects of menopause from those of aging; and (3) the motivations for conceptualizing menopause as a deficiency disease. These will be addressed individually below.

The research literature on menopause has consistently failed to distinguish natural menopause from castration (see Chapter 4). Until quite recently, scientists believed that the ovaries ceased functioning with menopause and that, endocrinologically, natural menopause and castration were equivalent. Consequently, a common research practice has been to combine castrated and naturally menopausal women in the study of menopause. The resulting ambiguity has contributed to the persistent belief that menopause is associated with increased risk of cardiovascular disease. Today, we know that the ovaries continue to function and secrete hormones after menopause, albeit in a reduced capacity; the postmenopausal ovary is not "dead" but continues to contribute actively to the biochemical profile. Those scholars who have incorporated this knowledge into their research designs have documented differences between naturally menopausal and castrated women in CHD risk. Considerable data indicate a significant increase in the incidence of CHD following castration, whereas no change in CHD risk is apparent with natural menopause (Blumenthal *et al.*, 1991; Christiansen and Riis, 1990; Colditz *et al.*, 1987; Farish *et al.*, 1990; Godsland *et al.*, 1987; Kritz-Silverstein *et al.*, 1997; Lobo, 1990; Notelovitz *et al.*, 1983). The reason for these cardiovascular differences between naturally menopausal and castrated women is not apparent. One hypothesis is that castration may create an unfavorable lipid profile by lowering HDL and increasing triglycerides. As discussed above, the main lipid risk factors for CHD in women are low levels of HDL and high levels of triglycerides. Everson *et al.* (1995) reported such a pattern when comparing premenopausal women to castrated women. In contrast, neither Farish *et al.* (1990) or Pasquali *et al.* (1997) found castration to result in a decrease in HDL or an increase in triglycerides. Thus far, the basis for the increased risk of CHD associated with castration remains a mystery.

The result of combining naturally menopausal and castrated women is to underestimate the degree of cardiovascular risk associated with castration and to overestimate the risk associated with natural menopause. Until more researchers begin to recognize the importance of this distinction and to modify their research protocols accordingly, the scholarly literature will continue to reinforce the historical, but erroneous, belief that natural menopause and castration are equivalent, and that both are associated with an increased risk of CHD.

A second source of confusion with regard to CHD and menopause is the difficulty of distinguishing between the independent contributions of menopause and aging. Naturally menopausal women are, as a group, older than premenopausal women, and the traditional scientific methods offer little help in disentangling the effects of the two. To illustrate, consider a study (Stevenson *et al.*, 1993) in which the authors compared 395 premenopausal women to 147 postmenopausal women on various lipid measures; the latter group had experienced natural menopause and none were taking hormone therapy. The authors found that the postmenopausal women had significantly poorer lipid profiles than did the premenopausal women. However, the average age of the premenopausal group was 32.5 while the average age of the postmenopausal group was 54.7. The authors conclude: "These results clearly demonstrate that menopause has profound effects on lipid and lipoprotein concentrations" (p. 87). Since there is simply no way to tease apart the effects of age and menopause, the authors' attribution to menopause, rather than to age, is simply arbitrary. Women's estrogen levels diminish gradually and idiosyncratically with regard to age and menopausal status, and postmenopausal women continue to secrete small and varying amounts of estrogen. Since the hypothesis linking menopause and CHD is based upon the diminishing estrogen levels associated with the menopause, rather than menopause *per se*, more precision may be gained by studying the association between endogenous estrogen levels and indicators of CHD. Barrett-Connor and Goodman-Gruen (1995) evaluated the endocrinological profile and cardiovascular risk pattern in 651 postmenopausal women; these authors reported that estrogen levels were not associated with historical or current indices of CHD.

The detrimental impact of menopause on the cardiovascular system has become so widely accepted that this belief is a clear source of bias and has taken the form of an assumption, rather than a hypothesis, in designing and interpreting research. In a study on age and blood pressure in men and women between 17 and 81 years of age, Gardner and Poehlman (1995) found that men of all ages and women under the age of 62 did not exhibit a clear relationship between age and high blood pressure. However, in women older than 62, there was a significant association between age and systolic blood pressure. In spite of the typical age of menopause being 50 years, these authors attributed the age-related increases in blood pressure in women over 62 to menopause. Not only are such conclusions absurd and misleading, they detract resources and attention from the search for the actual causes of CHD in women.

A third source of confusion is the political, social, and economic contexts that have motivated the medical profession to conceptualize menopause as a deficiency disease. This is but a continuation of the historical relationship between the medical profession and women's bodies. Throughout most of the twentieth century, pregnancy and birth have been a "medical experience," controlled and attended by physicians. Now that women have largely reclaimed their right to a drug-free, more-or-less natural childbirth and since a healthy pregnancy has become associated with a healthy diet, exercise, and no drugs, the remaining reproductive event in women's lives has become the medical focus. By labeling menopause as a disease, any and all changes traditionally attributed to the typical aging process, have been recategorized as menopausal symptoms. Menopause has been cited as the primary cause of cardiovascular disorders, osteoporosis, incontinence, depression, wrinkles, diminished libido, to name but a few of the over one hundred unpleasant and/or dangerous changes said to be associated with menopause (Weideger, 1977). In this context, attributing women's cardiovascular problems to menopause is readily accepted and believed. Indeed, the US government has funded many of the studies in which no evidence was found to support the belief that menopause causes cardiovascular problems. Yet, a government publication contradicts these research findings: "*For reasons unknown*, estrogen helps protect women against CVD during the childbearing years....After menopause, the incidence of CVD increases with each passing year posing a greater risk" (National Institute of Health, 1995, p. 17, emphasis added).

The "discovery" of CHD as a consequence of menopause in women was partially informed by the business interests of the medical and pharmaceutical industries. In early days, hormone therapy was prescribed for hot flashes and "femininity" (Wilson, 1966). However, these indications became untenable as the dangers of hormone therapy, primarily uterine cancer, became known and publicized. The "do no harm" core of medical ethics dictates that side-effects not out-distance the treated disease for lethality. Thus, treating bothersome, but not dangerous or life-threatening symptoms, such as hot flashes and wrinkles, with a drug that could cause cancer became untenable. Only the presence of life-threatening diseases could justify the use of life-threatening treatment. Thus, osteoporosis and cardiovascular disease were "discovered" to be "caused" by menopause. Both are common afflictions of aging women and men and, previously, both had been understood to be determined by age, genetics, and lifestyle. Today, this view remains essentially the same for men, whereas, for women, both illnesses have been reconceptualized as being *caused* by menopause. Neither the transformations to sex-linked, hormonally based diseases nor the "cure" provided by hormone therapy are supported by adequate research, and are, thus, difficult to explain or understand except as motivated by profit in a misogynist culture. The labeling of menopause as a disease completes the medical control of women's reproductive lives and continues defining women according to their reproductive status. Creating illnesses and then providing cures enhances the profit of pharmaceutical companies as well as of those physicians who prescribe and, therefore, monitor the extensive and serious side-effects of the medications.

To summarize, there are clear increases in cardiovascular morbidity and mortality and in various risk factors for CHD with aging. The rate of deterioration of cardiovascular function with aging is, in part, due to modifiable, lifestyle factors; changing these may delay the typical aging effects. Natural menopause does not appear to be associated with increased cardiovascular risk or increased cardiac mortality, whereas castration places women at risk for a variety of adverse reactions including a decline in the functional capacity of the cardiovascular system. Since it seems unlikely that the postmenopausal ovary secretes sufficient hormones to account for the large difference between naturally menopausal and castrated women's physical health, researchers have suggested that the condition that created the necessity for castration may also have contributed to heart problems; a likely candidate is diabetes. Diabetes may cause abnormal uterine bleeding (Cutler, 1988), which is a common indication for castration, and diabetes is a major risk factor for cardiovascular disease in women. The importance of the distinction between natural menopause and castration may diminish in the future; the trend seems to be an increasing recognition on the part of both physicians and women that castration may pose a serious threat to health and should, if possible, be avoided.

TREATMENT, INTERVENTION, PREVENTION

The treatment and prevention of cardiovascular diseases is a primary concern to public health officials, to medical professionals, and to those who are scholars of lifestyle, such as psychologists, sociologists, nutritionists, and exercise physiologists. As such, a tremendous amount of information has accumulated. Since prevention has numerous advantages over treatment, lifestyle parameters associated with cardiovascular disorders are of major interest and are discussed below. The research supporting drug and high-technology medical procedures, such as angioplasty and bypass surgery, are beyond the scope of this book. However, literature regarding gender discrimination in the utilization of these treatments will be discussed. Finally, of particular relevance to women is the use of hormone therapy in the prevention and treatment of cardiovascular disorders.

Lifestyle factors impacting cardiovascular disease

A large number of lifestyle factors have been implicated in the development and maintenance of cardiovascular disorders. I will focus on those that are readily modifiable – exercise and diet – although mention is made also of those factors which may mediate the relationship between lifestyle and CHD, such as obesity and diabetes. Smoking is a primary risk factor for CHD, but will not be discussed here since this information is readily available. (See Chapter 3 for additional information on the benefits of modifying lifestyle.)

Exercise

The tremendous public interest in aerobic exercise has focused considerable scholarly attention on the potential benefits to the cardiovascular system. The relationship between exercise and cardiovascular disorders is typically evaluated in a cross-sectional study in which CHD risk and/or outcome measures and exercise habits are assessed, and the strength of the association is analyzed; no attempt is made to modify either CHD outcomes or exercise. Since the recent research on cholesterol risk for CHD (discussed above) indicates that the lipid components of relevance to women are HDL and triglycerides, the discussion below focuses on these components, as well as actual CHD morbidity and mortality.

Greendale *et al.* (1996) examined the association between self-reported leisure, home, and occupational physical activity and CHD risk factors in Caucasian women aged 45 to 64. HDL was significantly associated with leisure and home physical activity but not work activity. In addition, high levels of leisure physical activity were also related to lowered levels of insulin and fibrinogen. In a study similar but avoiding the unreliable nature of self-report measures, Kokkinos *et al.* (1995) assessed cardiorespiratory fitness, using a treadmill, and divided the sample into low, moderate, and high fitness. These groups were then compared on lipid levels, blood glucose levels, and anthropometric indices. Linear, or dose–response, relationships were found: level of fitness was inversely related to weight, fat mass, resting heart rate, triglycerides, LDL, and total cholesterol and directly related to HDL. In a longitudinal study, Kuller *et al.* (1995) followed women for 5 years with age at entry to the study between 42 and 50; HDL was higher in those who drank alcohol moderately and who engaged in deliberate physical activity and was lower in those with a high fat mass and who smoked. These studies are highly suggestive of the potential benefits of exercise on the cardiovascular system. None the less, family, friends, and medical personnel often assume that exercise of sufficient intensity to be beneficial is beyond the capabilities of elderly persons. In response, LaCroix *et al.* (1996) assessed walking distance per week (including intentional exercise, errands, and work) and hospitalizations for CHD events and CHD deaths. Persons were categorized according to less than 1 hour, 1 to 4 hours, and more than 4 hours of walking per week. For women, those with more than 4 hours per week of walking had significantly less CHD morbidity and mortality than the more sedentary. Interestingly, those who engaged in vigorous exercise did not gain greater benefits over those with four hours of walking. Thus, even extremely low levels of exercise (half hour of walking each day), which are within the capabilities of most elderly, are associated with beneficial effects on the cardiovascular system.

These studies are, however, observational and preclude inferring that the exercise *causes* a healthy cardiovascular system. An equally plausible interpretation of these data is that those with healthy cardiovascular systems are inclined to exercise. Scientifically, we can be more confident that exercise *causes* cardiovascular benefits by observing cardiovascular effects in persons who are changing their exercise habits in a predictable fashion. King *et al.* (1995) studied the effects of differing intensities and formats of endurance exercise on fitness and HDL cholesterol levels in healthy, but previously sedentary, persons aged 50 to 65. The exercise formats were high-intensity in a scheduled group format, high-intensity at home, and low-intensity at home. Fitness improved in all groups and was successfully maintained for the two years of the study. No group exhibited changes in HDL in the first year but, by the end of the second year, both home-based programs resulted in significant increases in HDL. These were especially pronounced in the low-intensity group, suggesting again that high-intensity exercise is not necessary to achieve cardiovascular benefits. A similar time frame was noted by Williams *et al.* (1982) who concluded that at least 9 months of exercise is required to modify lipid levels.

Studies in this area have largely evaluated aerobic exercise. Although resistance exercise (i.e., weight lifting) has been found to benefit osteoporosis, the CHD advantages are less clear. Boyden *et al.* (1993) randomly assigned young women to supervised exercise and control groups for 5 months. The exercise group, but not the control group, showed significant decreases in LDL and total cholesterol but no changes in triglycerides or HDL. Resistance exercise should not yet be dismissed as irrelevant to CHD risk factors in women since older women may respond differently, and training longer than 5 months may be required to modify HDL and triglycerides.

Several studies have compared the effects of exercise and hormone therapy on cardiovascular risk factors. Lindheim *et al.* (1994) and Binder *et al.* (1996) randomly assigned older women to exercise alone, hormone therapy alone, both, or neither. In general, both studies found that exercise and hormone therapy had similar effects on lipids with the exception that hormone therapy increased triglycerides while exercise decreased triglycerides – a finding of considerable relevance to women. In addition to the triglyceride advantage, exercise was also associated with reduced weight, increased fitness, and healthier insulin metabolism. However, a final determination of the relative benefits of exercise and hormone therapy is delayed until research is available on estrogen-plus-progesterone therapy, which is the most commonly prescribed hormone therapy today. Previous research has been limited to assessing the effects of estrogen-only therapy.

The benefits of exercise on health, in general, are reviewed by Fentem (1994). According to this author, exercise maintains function and reserve capacities, prevents disease, and ameliorates the effects of age and chronic disease. Exercise helps the cardiovascular system by slowing heart rate and lowering blood pressure – both reduce the workload of the heart. The prevalence of risk factors for CHD and stroke are strongly associated with a sedentary lifestyle. There is, of course, no way to escape aging and death but one can delay illness and disability by modifying lifestyle: "Active women have a cardioprotective effect of one decade when compared to sedentary women" (Notelovitz, 1990, p. 207).

The considerable benefits of exercise on health, in general, and the cardiovascular system, in particular, leads to the question of compliance with exercise regimens. Permanent changes in any lifestyle behavior are difficult to achieve in adults, particularly older adults, who have firmly established habits and behaviors. On the other hand, the dramatic increase in exercise participation in the last two decades in Western societies offers encouragement to public health promoters of exercise. The difficulty is to facilitate such changes in those who most need them – the obese, the diabetic, and the sedentary. Research studying ways and means of accomplishing this task is clearly needed. Eaton *et al.* (1993) reported that, for women, "short-term success with exercise and weight loss, exercise recommendations for their children, and work outside the home predicted adoption or maintenance of increased physical activity" (p. 209). King *et al.* (1995) compared adherence rates among three different types of exercise regimens and concluded that high-intensity–low-frequency, home-based regimens were complied with better than low-intensity–high-frequency home-based and high-intensity, group-based regimens. Low adherence to exercise programs may, in part, be due to an unenthusiastic promotion by the medical profession. Block *et al.* (1987) discouraged physicians from recommending the prophylactic use of exercise until more research had been done to determine the frequency, intensity, and type of the most beneficial exercise. Although more research is welcome, waiting is absurd. Given the clear and multisystem benefits of exercise, most needed is the development of creative methods designed to increase rates of initiation and maintenance.

The rates of initiating and maintaining exercise regimens vary according to race and gender. Konstam and Houser (1994) found that half of the eligible male coronary patients enrolled in a structured cardiac rehabilitation program, whereas only 10% of the women did so. In a study by Cannistra *et al.* (1995), 51% of the African American women, compared to 64% of the European American women, completed a 12-month cardiac rehabilitation program. The most obvious explanation for these findings is that cardiac rehabilitation programs have been designed and structured for middle-class White men. An appropriate exercise program for a woman who has sole responsibility for three small children, financial constraints precluding adequate child care, and a high likelihood of assault while exercising or while traveling to an exercise facility requires creativity and commitment. An appropriate exercise program for a 70-

year-old woman who has been sedentary throughout her life requires powerful reinforcement. Clearly, the programs designed for middle-class men are inadequate to meet the needs of women.

In spite of the lack of wide-spread endorsement by the medical community, the popular press has been wonderfully relentless in promoting exercise. In a recent article in the magazine *Prevention*, Eller and Goldstein (1997) have applied the concept of matching personality and career to matching personality and exercise mode; they propose that long-term adherence to a regular exercise program is improved if one selects the "right" exercise. A personality test is provided, and the scores allow placing oneself in one of five personality categories; the reader can then find the type of exercise that his/her personality type would most likely find pleasant. Although the "personality test" has not been validated by traditional psychometric methods, and the accuracy of the "match" between exercise and personality has not been studied empirically, the idea that the "best" exercise varies among individuals in a potentially predictable manner is intriguing and, from a public health point of view, deserving of considerable attention. Readers with a history of failing to maintain exercise programs may find encouragement.

Diet

The importance of diet in the development and exacerbation of cardiovascular disorders has been repeatedly documented. A complete discussion of this topic would be repetitious of numerous popular books and scholarly publications. There have been brief trends and fads concerning healthy diets, and many people have been discouraged by the contradictory and changing information conveyed by medical personnel and the media. None the less, the importance of lowering fat, particularly saturated fat, in the diet has been a consistent recommendation for several decades. There is some reason for concern (discussed above) if an individual has or achieves extremely low cholesterol, but this does not negate the considerable evidence that lowering dietary fat has cardiovascular benefits in persons with high serum cholesterol levels.

As with exercise, a major source of concern is compliance with dietary recommendations. In a meta-analysis of 17 randomized, controlled trials of dietary behavior interventions, Brunner *et al.* (1997) concluded, "Dietary advice from health care or health promotion personnel appears to be effective in achieving modest dietary change and accompanying cardiovascular risk reduction" (p. 1415). Participants in the Framingham Study (B.M. Posner *et al.*, 1995), who have been studied for over three decades, have been quite successful in modifying their dietary cholesterol: 35% of the men and 60% of the women decreased consumption of high-fat animal products. In addition, 63% of the women and 56% of the men reported having changed their eating habits in order to be healthier. McCann *et al.* (1996) assessed persons' readiness to adopt a cholesterol-lowering diet in a large sample of men and women who had high serum cholesterol and poor dietary habits. Women, particularly older women, were more likely to volunteer for the diet intervention than were men. Agreeing to participate in a diet-altering intervention is, of course, quite different from adhering to the dietary requirements on a long-term basis. On the other hand, adhering to dietary regimens may be easier for women than for men because of their traditionally greater knowledge of and skill preparing food. Statistics from the Framingham study (B.M. Posner *et al.*, 1995) indicate that women are more likely than men to comply with dietary recommendations and to be successful in making permanent and healthy changes in their diet. Public health programs designed to promote healthy diets are needed both for palliative treatment in older persons and for prevention of chronic illness in younger persons.

As discussed above, gender differences in lipid components of relevance to CHD risk have been documented. Since most of the CHD research has been limited to men participants, the dietary recommendations derived from this research may be applicable only to men. Denke (1994) recommended a low-cholesterol diet as the first step in treating high cholesterol in women with the hope of obviating the need for drug therapy. The dietary recommendations were developed with the goal of impacting LDL levels – those lipids of importance to men. This diet did not achieve a positive outcome for women since it resulted in small and nonsignificant *decreases* in HDL. With the accumulation of more data on women's cardiovascular systems, dietary recommendations may appropriately become gender-specific.

Medical issues of particular interest to women

Gender discrimination in cardiovascular treatment

Although a discussion of drug treatment and high-technology cardiovascular treatment procedures is beyond the scope of this book, I have included this section on gender discrimination since awareness of this problem may enable women to be better informed consumers.

In the last decade, women's high risk for myocardial infarction and their high probability of dying from their first heart attack have been documented and acknowledged. An assumption shared by health professionals and the public has been that women are treated for cardiovascular problems as skillfully and as aggressively as are men – an assumption that has proved to be inaccurate. If the medical profession had responded to the recognition that women are at high risk for CHD by simply extending the standard of care developed for men to women with CHD, problems would have ensued, since the diagnostic and treatment procedures had been developed on men. But, at the very least, this would have offered a beginning while conducting the necessary research to develop a knowledge base with which to design treatment protocols for women. Instead, cardiovascular problems in women have become a menopause problem – a familiar scenario. In the nineteenth century, tuberculosis was a lung disease in men and a uterine disease in women (French, 1992); today, cardiovascular disease is a cardiovascular problem in men and a hormonal disease in women. We have simply progressed from one myth to another myth and, in the mean-time, women still do not receive adequate treatment for cardiovascular disorders.

A gender bias in CHD treatment has been well-documented in the United States (for a more complete discussion, the reader is referred to Beery, 1995). Compared to men, women had to wait longer to see a physician and to have an initial electrocardiogram when presenting with chest pain in an emergency room, and, among those with acute myocardial ischemia, 56% of the women and 83% of the men were admitted to intensive care (Heston and Lewis, 1992). Green and Ruffin (1994) studied the medical records of those evaluated for potential acute cardiac ischemia and found that men were more likely to be admitted to the hospital than were women. In a large-scale study, Travis *et al.* (1993) examined US statistics on a variety of cardiovascular procedures and treatments and analyzed the data according to geographical area and gender. The authors found significant gender differences with rates consistently higher among men for angiocardiography, catheterization, angioplasty, and bypass surgery; on average, gender accounted for 25% of the variance in the rates of diagnosis and treatment.

The medical community has responded with a variety of explanations and justifications for this apparent gender discrimination in cardiovascular treatment. The most common response is to claim that women are actually treated appro-priately while men are being overtreated (Green and Ruffin, 1994). Obviously, this does not address the reason why treatment differs on the basis of gender. Indeed, women may benefit more from cardiovascular procedures than do men. In a review of this area, Hussain *et al.* (1996) provide statistics suggesting that women are actually in greater, rather than less, need for aggressive treatment: reinfarctions occur three times more often in women than in men; women receiving standard care for thrombolytic therapy had twice the mortality than men. Yet, only 23% of the recipients of thrombolytic therapy were women. Rankin (1990) found that, compared to men, women in her sample had more shortness of breath, poorer cardiac functional status, longer intensive care unit stays and proportionately more deaths. Women were also found to recover better than men in that they were quicker to return to sexual activities, recreation activ-ities, and work and reported less depression and anxiety at a 3-month follow-up. Interestingly, the author interpreted the gender differences in the recovery data as an indication that, compared to men, women are more comfortable with the sick role, rather than concluding that women have healthier coping responses and healthier psyches. Travis *et al.* (1993) dismissed the medical justifications of such gender bias and concluded: "The basic rationale for not performing surgery on women, namely that women are not suitable candidates (older, sicker, smaller, weaker), harkens back to historical debates about the delicate nature of women and the necessary limitations on women's education and employment" (p. 277).

Cardiovascular treatment has also been found to vary with race. Goff *et al.*

(1994) examined hospital records over a 2-year period and concluded: "Age-adjusted 28-day case-fatality rates were higher among Mexican Americans than among non-Hispanic Whites and higher among women than among men hospitalized for definite or possible myocardial infarction" (p. 474). Liao and Cooper (1995), commenting on a report that Blacks are half as likely to undergo angiography and half as likely to have bypass surgery as Whites, propose that the differences are due to SES. This interpretation is supported by research data indicating that racial disparities in cardiovascular procedures are a consequence of ability to pay. In Los Angeles, Carlisle *et al.* (1997) reviewed over 100,000 hospital discharge records. Lower use of high-technology cardiovascular procedures were found for African-American and Latino patients while Asian and Pacific Islanders had rates similar to Caucasians. Racial differences were not found when the data were restricted to those patients with private insurance, suggesting that ability to pay is the source of the racial differences. Since elderly women are more likely to be poor than elderly men, this seems a possible and partial explanation for gender differences as well.

Hormone therapy

The differences in cardiovascular risk between naturally menopausal women and those who have been castrated are discussed above. Since only castrated women are at increased risk for cardiovascular disorders with menopause, logic dictates that only castrated women should be treated with hormone therapy. None the less, hormone therapy has in the past been and continues to be prescribed for the treatment of cardiovascular problems in women experiencing either form of menopause. This practice has led to difficulties in the interpretation of research on the benefits of hormone therapy. In spite of these ideological and methodological difficulties, some tentative conclusions can be drawn.

Studies of estrogen therapy limited to castrated women have yielded results that are fairly consistent in demonstrating a positive impact on the lipid profile (Kim *et al.*, 1996; Watts *et al.*, 1995). Although not all studies measured all lipids, the data indicate a tendency for estrogen treatment to be associated with a decrease in LDL and total cholesterol and an increase in HDL. Given the importance of triglycerides for the cardiovascular health of women, it was disappointing that these studies did not report this. In general, the overall impact of estrogen on the lipid profile in castrated women appears to be beneficial.

Studies limited to naturally menopausal women have been less positive. Marsh *et al.* (1994) evaluated the impact of continuous estrogen and progesterone and found decreases in LDL, HDL, and triglycerides. Sequential hormone therapy was evaluated by van der Mooren *et al.* (1997); the therapy resulted in decreases in TC and LDL and increases in HDL and triglycerides. Conrad *et al.* (1995), using a randomized, placebo-controlled design, reported rather interesting results: the hormone therapy caused significant reductions in TC and LDL but so did the placebo, and there were no differences between the impact of the placebo and that of the hormones. Although the results of these studies are not consistent, a clearer view is afforded by focusing on HDL and triglycerides – those lipids of most relevance to cardiovascular disorders in women. In this context, these studies indicate that hormone therapy does not confer clear benefits in naturally menopausal women since none of the studies found both an increase in HDL and a decrease in triglycerides. This conclusion might have been predicted since hormone therapy in naturally menopausal women must consist of both estrogen and progesterone in order to protect against uterine cancer, and progesterone has been found to have ill-effects on the cardiovascular system (Bagatell and Bremner, 1995; Voda, 1993).

There have been several studies published in which castrated and naturally menopausal women have been combined. The results are difficult to interpret unless the data are reported separately for each group; this was the case in two studies. Folsom *et al.* (1996) followed women for three years, recording their hormone use and lipid profile at regular intervals. Castrated women who received estrogen therapy were found to have lowered LDL, increased triglycerides, and increased HDL, while naturally menopausal women who received estrogen-plus-progesterone therapy yielded a similar profile but with no change in HDL. Miller *et al.* (1994) randomly assigned women to two different doses of estrogen for 4 months and then added progesterone to the regimen. In this way, they were able to assess the impact of estrogen alone and then the additional effect of adding progesterone. Estrogen caused decreases in LDL, increases in HDL, and increases in triglycerides; the addition of progesterone reversed the LDL and HDL effects but not the triglyceride change. These studies further support the previous conclusions – estrogen therapy appears to benefit the cardiovascular systems of castrated women while estrogen-plus-progesterone therapy does not appear to benefit, and may even harm, the cardiovascular systems of naturally menopausal women.

There have been a variety of epidemiological or observational studies published, and these are often cited in support of the benefits of hormone therapy on cardiovascular health (e.g., Bush *et al.*, 1987; Henderson *et al.*, 1988). In this type of study, women are not randomly assigned to take hormones or placebo. Rather, the researcher identifies women in the population who either take or do not take hormones, for whatever reason. These groups are then compared on some factor of interest such as heart attack or cardiovascular death. Although this type of study is valuable in order to assess the feasibility of conducting more rigorous studies, it is of no value as a definitive answer as to drug effectiveness. It is not possible to evaluate from these studies if hormone therapy is beneficial in protecting women from cardiovascular disease or if taking hormones is simply associated with other factors, such as exercise and smoking, that are exerting a causal influence. None the less, the controversy over the appropriate interpretation of these studies has spawned interesting information on the characteristics of those women who choose to take hormones.

In general, women who take hormone therapy are more affluent, are more highly educated, have higher-status jobs, smoke less, exercise more, are more likely to be Caucasian, are leaner, have lower blood pressure, are more likely to use vitamin and calcium supplements, and are more likely to have been castrated than those who do not take hormones (Abraham *et al.*, 1995; Barrett-Connor, 1993; Brett and Madans, 1997; Derby *et al.*, 1995; Jonas and Manolio, 1996; Nagata *et al.*, 1996). Rosenberg *et al.* (1998) noted similar correlates among African American women: hormone users were more educated, exercised more, were leaner and were less likely to have a history of diabetes, heart disease, and breast cancer. Two studies have been specifically designed to evaluate baseline characteristics of women who choose to take hormone therapy. Persson *et al.* (1997) reported that women who complied with physician recommendations for hormone therapy had fewer children, a later age at first birth, and a higher prevalence of hysterectomy or castration than those choosing not to take hormones. Moorhead *et al.* (1997) noted that a history of ischemic heart disease or diabetes was associated with a lower likelihood of taking hormones. Any differences found in observational studies comparing users and nonusers of hormone therapy may be caused by hormone therapy, any one of the above factors, or a combination of all of the above.

Gynecologists versus cardiologists

Prevention is clearly the ideal method of reducing the incidence of cardiovascular disease, and modification of lifestyle factors, such as exercise, smoking, and diet, are the most effective techniques of achieving this goal. None the less, in spite of best efforts, cardiovascular disease will remain a major cause of death because of the essential nature of the cardiovascular system to life. The misguided emphasis on menopause as a major cause of cardiovascular disease in women has disturbed traditional boundaries in medical specialties. Once, persons with suspected heart problems would consult a cardiologist, internist, or family practitioner, whereas, today, women are encouraged to consult a gynecologist. Grimes (1988) comments:

> Cardiovascular disease poses a direct threat to the health of most women in the United States. Obstetricians–gynecologists are uniquely qualified to reduce that threat, because they are the principal health care providers for women and because preventive medicine is the thrust of obstetric and gynecologist practice in the United States. (p. 1662)

There are several disturbing messages here. First, while obstetricians–gynecologists are specialists on women's reproduction, they are not specialists on women since women are considerably more than reproductive machines. Indeed, there is, perhaps, a danger here in that women may believe that by "passing" a yearly pap smear and mammogram they are healthy and devoid of physical problems. Second, the idea of obstetrics and gynecology as a medical specialty with a particular and unique focus on prevention is difficult to take seriously from a profession responsible for bringing us DES, Thalidomide, oral contraceptives, and hormone therapy while minimizing the crucial role of preventative strategies such as exercise and nutrition.

CONCLUSIONS

Cardiovascular disorders are a major cause of death in women. Since men are more likely to suffer premature cardiovascular death than are women, CHD has been viewed, until recently, by the medical profession and the public as primarily a man's illness. Consequently, the research on risk factors and treatments has studied men's physiology and biochemistry. With increased longevity, the prevalence of cardiovascular disorders in women has become more apparent and, with this recognition has come an obvious need for research on women. A major contribution thus far has been the identification of gender differences in risk factors for CHD, specifically with regard to lipids. While elevations in LDL and total cholesterol are predictive of CHD in men, elevations in triglycerides and low HDL are predictive in women. The relevance of this information for establishing appropriate treatment is obvious.

From the historical and cultural traditions of attributing the psychological and physical states of women to reproductive events and physiology has emerged the currently popular opinion that CHD is but one of many adverse consequences of menopause that is effectively treated with hormone therapy. This misconception has been reinforced by the unique role of the medical profession in Western society. According to Kaufert et al. (1994), women who have been castrated report more symptoms, see their physicians more often, are more likely to be prescribed hormones, and are more likely to comply with this recommendation. Consequently, the knowledge base of the practicing physician is largely derived from assessing and treating castrated women. Since the vulnerability for cardiovascular disease is increased with castration, these women do have a greater risk for cardiovascular problems and do benefit from hormone therapy. In contrast, alterations in risk for CHD do not vary with menopausal status or with endogenous levels of hormones in women who experience natural menopause, and hormone therapy apparently does not confer cardiovascular benefits to naturally menopausal women.

Treatment of cardiovascular disease often occurs in the context of severe illness and disability and often does not result in full recovery. Prevention is clearly preferred. Major determinants of cardiovascular disease are lifestyle factors: diet, exercise, psychological stress, smoking, and environmental pollutants. Prevention, however, requires a lifelong dedication and commitment that is often believed by professionals and the public to be beyond the willingness and capability of most. Yet, public health efforts to reduce dietary cholesterol in the US have been surprisingly successful. The lack of enthusiasm for prevention of

CHD through lifestyle changes emanates from research reports of poor compliance, but the research participants were men, and we cannot assume the results to be descriptive of women. There is some evidence to indicate that, compared to men, women may be more motivated and better able to achieve healthy lifestyle changes.

7

OSTEOPOROSIS

Nature did not make a mistake in ceasing ovarian estrogen production after the reproductive years, or by giving women smaller bones, or by limiting calcium absorption with age, or even by allowing for bones to thin. On the contrary, osteoporosis is simply a long-term negative side-effect of a very positive survival strategy; a strategy that draws calcium from the bones to the blood so that the body can live. Nature provided us with the capacity for accumulating tremendous bone mineral reserve, so that we would always have both lifelong strong bones and a constant source of minerals for transfer to the blood in times of need. We, however, have outdone ourselves in accumulating ways to deplete our bones of their precious stores of life-supporting minerals.

(Brown, 1988, p. 6)

For many aging women, osteoporosis has become the focus of intense fear and is associated with an image of inevitable disability and dependence. Although osteoporosis is a serious and potentially debilitating disease, the scholarly research, as well as the mass media, is characterized by sensationalistic interpretation of poor quality research and biological reductionism. The popular myth portrays osteoporosis as a crippling, degenerative disease caused by menopause and cured by hormone therapy. The goals of the discussion below are to dispel some of these myths, delineate the major determinants of osteoporosis, examine controversial issues, and describe methods of prevention and treatment.

THE BIOLOGY OF OSTEOPOROSIS

A brief description of typical or normal bone formation may facilitate an understanding of the pathogenesis of osteoporosis. New bone is continually formed and existing bone continually reabsorbed throughout life. At young ages, particularly the years of growth, more bone is formed than lost. Peak bone mass is reached at about age 30 to 35 years, after which time bone reabsorption exceeds bone formation. Everyone loses bone with advancing age. Peak bone mass and

149

the rate of bone loss vary among individuals; the individual with a low peak bone mass, a high rate of loss, and demonstrated susceptibility to fractures is viewed as suffering from osteoporosis. Osteoporotic fractures typically occur in the vertebrae, distal radius, and the hips. Prevention of osteoporosis may be implemented by either increasing peak bone mass or decreasing the rate of bone loss. In general, peak bone mass is determined by genetics, diet, weight-bearing load, and exercise. Rate of bone loss is determined by the same factors but can be accelerated by a variety of circumstances, such as castration and corticosteroid treatment.

Bone metabolism is a complex process and dependent on a variety of interacting systems for normal activity. Calcium is a crucial ingredient in the making of bone and a byproduct of bone absorption. Intestinal absorption of calcium from the diet is the primary source of calcium, and vitamin D is essential for adequate calcium absorption. Vitamin D is converted to its active form, 1,25-dihydroxyvitamin D, in the kidneys, a conversion that requires adequate levels of parathyroid hormone (PTH). Thus, PTH is a primary factor in the regulation of serum calcium levels. Increases in PTH, which can be triggered by falling levels of calcium, cause an accelerated rate of bone reabsorption and an increase in serum and urinary calcium. Calcitonin, a hormone secreted by the thyroid, has effects opposite to those of PTH and decreases the rate of bone remodeling. Since osteoporosis is characterized by a decrease in skeletal mass, a variety of biochemical measures have been viewed as positive indications of this disorder. These include high serum and urinary concentrations of calcium, low levels of 1,25-dihydroxyvitamin D, high levels of PTH, and low levels of calcitonin, as well as direct measures of intestinal absorption of calcium using radioactive isotopes.

The primary concerns with osteoporosis are the disabilities, deformities, and fractures that may occur when bone strength is insufficient to provide integrity to the body. The disorder has been categorized as "primary" if the cause is a normal, developmental process and as "secondary" if caused by a pathological process or agent, such as chronic corticosteroid use. Primary osteoporosis is further divided into Type 1, which is defined as resulting from the decreasing estrogen levels associated with menopause, and Type 2, which is defined as resulting from general aging. Further distinctions are made regarding the specific type of bone: cortical bone is the outer, dense shell of compact bone; trabecular bone is the inner, open, sponge-like region. In Type 1 osteoporosis, loss primarily occurs in the trabecular bone compartment. "Thinning and actual loss of horizontal connecting trabeculae leads to characteristic weakness of the cancellous regions of bone, increasing the patient's susceptibility to vertebral compression fractures, distal radial fractures, and intertrochanteric femoral fractures" (Silver and Einhorn, 1995, p. 10). In Type 2 osteoporosis, "bone loss is more global, affecting cortical and cancellous bone. This commonly affects the femoral neck, predisposing patients to fractures in this region [hip]" (Silver and Einhorn, 1995, pp. 10–11).

Similarly, a variety of measures are assumed to reflect bone health, such as bone density, bone size, bone mineral content, and absence of fractures. Given such a wide array of relevant factors, methodological variation in research on osteoporosis is considerable, and, as might be expected, the results are not entirely consistent. A variety of assessment procedures have been developed but assessment has lagged behind recognition and concern with the problem. Current assessment techniques have not been adequately evaluated in terms of relevant bone sites, identification of persons at risk, radiation exposure from some assessment techniques, and accuracy in predicting fractures. A particular difficulty in assessment stems from disagreement as to the definition of "normal." Bone loss with aging is normal and does not necessarily lead to difficulties – only when the bone loss reduces bone strength to below the fracture threshold is there reason for concern. The most popular definition of osteoporosis is a bone mineral density 2.5 standard deviations below the peak bone mass of young adults (Marcus, 1996). An alternative is to define the disorder as having a bone mass of one standard deviation below the expected bone mass for the person's age and sex (Johnell, 1995). Both of these definitions are based on the average or typical individual of a certain age and sex. As a universal definition, neither is appropriate because poor development of peak bone mass characterizes young adults in certain cultures and sub-cultures, making them a poor standard with which to judge healthy bone. If the typical lifestyle of those individuals of one's age and sex is characterized by poor diet and a sedentary activity level, then the peak bone mass and rate of bone loss of the cohort is undoubtedly predictive of osteoporosis.

The increasing attention to osteoporosis in recent years is primarily due to concern with fractures occurring in the elderly years, causing deformity and disability and even death. Although 90% of the hip fractures occur in persons older than 70 years old, the research on osteoporosis has focused on women in their fifties. This may be viewed as positive in the sense of facilitating prevention; however, the true relationship between osteoporosis and fractures remains unmeasured and questionable since the time span between interventions and outcomes (20 years) is beyond the resources of most researchers. Marcus (1996) notes that older people have substantially higher fracture risks than younger people at all levels of bone density, suggesting that there are other factors of considerable importance in predicting the likelihood of a fracture. Heaney (1998) concurs and notes bone mass may not be the strongest predictor of fractures. In reviewing 15 studies on the relationship between osteoporosis and fractures, Cummings (1985) concluded that, although those with fractures have usually been found to have less bone mass than those without fractures, the differences were not large enough to suggest it as the primary determinant. Furthermore, the seriousness of the consequences of fractures has been questioned: Browner et al. (1996) followed 9,704 women aged 65 and older for 6 years. Fractures of the hip or pelvis occurred in 361 but, according to the authors, only 9 of the 64 deaths that followed were caused or hastened by the fracture. In most cases, death was due to conditions unrelated to the fractures. Recently, researchers have begun to examine the association between incidence of fractures and the probability of falling. This is discussed further below.

THE DEMOGRAPHICS OF OSTEOPOROSIS

Current opinion on the demographics of osteoporosis is summarized by Gordon (1990): "Bone loss with aging (osteoporosis) is very largely a female problem resulting from loss of gonadal function" (p. 225). Although this view is common among medical practitioners and the public, the evidence for such a statement is of marginal quality and unresolved contradictions are frequently encountered. Consider the following: (1) if osteoporosis were solely a menopausal disorder, all older women would suffer from it, yet only 25% do so (Notelovitz, 1989); (2) African-American women, in general, have low rates of osteoporosis but do experience menopause (Han *et al.*, 1996), and men suffer from osteoporosis, yet do not experience menopause (Stanley *et al.*, 1991); (3) among the Chinese in Singapore, the rate of osteoporosis is greater for men than for women (Brown, 1988); and (4) in the last 20 years, osteoporotic fractures increased in urban areas of Scandinavia to an incidence rate that is the highest in the world (Johansson *et al.*, 1992). In general, osteoporosis is higher among Caucasians than Africans or Asians; higher rates for women are found more among Caucasians than among Africans or Asians where men are sometimes found to have higher rates than women (Stini, 1995). Clearly, osteoporosis is not adequately described as a disorder of postmenopausal women. Figure 7.1 breaks down mortality from fractures into race and gender categories; race appears to be far more relevant than gender.

Cultural values and practices provide a partial, but important, explanation for the differences in the incidence of osteoporosis between women and men in Western societies. Since all persons lose bone in middle and old age, the higher rate of osteoporosis in women compared to men is likely due to differences in peak bone mass. Bone mass peaks at about age 35 and is determined largely by lifestyle. Figure 7.2 depicts the impact of peak bone mass and rate of bone loss on fractures. Consequences of culturally imposed gender roles exert a strong influence on gender differences in peak bone mass: (1) men are less likely to be concerned about their weight and are, therefore, heavier than women; the heavier weight of men builds stronger bones; (2) our cultural gender ideals may have impacted reproductive selection by favoring tall, muscular men and small, frail women; (3) because men tend to eat more to maintain their heavier weight, they are more likely to have adequate calcium intake; and (4) traditionally, exercise has been more socially acceptable for men than for women; exercise leads to greater bone density, and the sunlight from outdoor exercise increases vitamin D. Seeman (1993) notes that men have the same risk factors for osteoporosis that have been noted for women: " risk factors for fractures include excessive alcohol

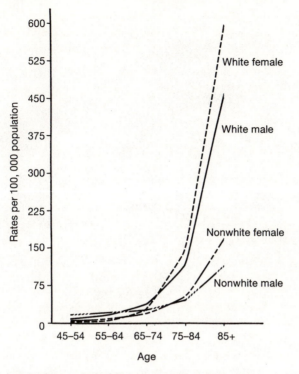

Figure 7.1 Annual death rates from falls by age, race, and sex

Source: From A.P. Iskrant (1968) The etiology of fractured hips in females. *American Journal of Public Health*, 58: 486. Reproduced with permission from the American Public Health Association.

intake, tobacco use, inactivity, leanness, low calcium intake, and reduced strength. Drug therapy, such as corticosteroids, anticonvulsants, heparin, and excessive thyroid hormone replacement, may cause bone loss" (p. 24S).

The acceptance of osteoporosis as a women's disorder due to menopause is partially based on the myth that women's sex hormones stop abruptly with menopause while men's sex hormones retain their young adult level throughout life – both statements are now known to be incorrect (see Chapter 4). In fact, both men and women exhibit gradually decreasing levels of their respective sex hormones as they age and, unless castrated, continue to produce small amounts throughout life. Wishart *et al.* (1995) evaluated men between the ages of 20 and 83 and found that testosterone (the major androgen in men) decreased and sex hormone binding globulin (SHBG) increased with age. SHBG binds sex hormones, rendering them biologically inactive so the authors also measured free androgens – those available for biological action – and found a 26% fall in free androgens between the ages of 30 and 40 and a further 16% decrease between 40 and 50, followed by a slower rate of decrease to age 80. These authors also measured bone density, which exhibited a strongly negative

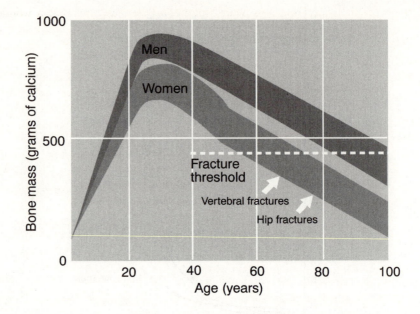

Figure 7.2 Hypothetical association between bone mass and fracture vulnerability

Source: Reprinted with permission from *Nature* (G.R. Mundy, Boning up on genes. *Nature*, 367: 216). Copyright 1994, Macmillan Magazines Limited.

association with age; they concluded, "bone loss in men appears to accelerate after age 50" (p. 144).

The accelerated bone loss noted in women after castration has also been found in men. Daniell (1997) found castrated men to have a bone mineral density of 17% less than noncastrated men of the same age. Stepan *et al.* (1989) assessed biochemical markers of bone formation in men before and after castration and concluded that the pattern and rate of bone loss were similar to that observed in women after castration. A major cultural, social, and biological difference between men and women in many Western countries is the rate of castration. Women are far more likely to have had their ovaries surgically removed than are men to have had their testicles surgically removed. Women are, therefore, more likely than men to experience a sudden and drastic reduction in hormones and consequently, more likely than men to be at risk for the bone deterioration believed to occur following castration. Gender differences in osteoporosis could also be related to the traditional gender-related activities and careers promoted by our society – that of housewife for the woman and wage earner for the man. For those who conform to these expectations, a woman's career diminishes considerably when her children leave home, usually when the woman is in her forties, and a man's career does so when he retires, usually in his sixties. Both of these events may be accompanied by a drastic reduction in physical activity leading to increased vulnerability for osteoporosis. A further source of gender differences in osteoporosis may be psychotropic medication. Halbreich *et al.* (1995) found psychiatric patients treated with antidepressants and neuroleptics had bone density below normal for their age and sex; and women are more likely to be prescribed psychotropic medication than are men.

The undeniable expectation that all women be mothers may place women at further risk. One study found a strong association between bone strength in elderly women and the number of children they had had – women who had not had children lost virtually no bone over a 10-year study period (Abdulla *et al.*, 1984). Pregnant women have higher calcium needs due to the demands of the fetus–infant and, if these needs are not met with diet or supplements, the woman's bones will be depleted of calcium in order to supply the need (Blanch *et al.*, 1994). This demand apparently has long-term negative consequences and predisposes the woman to osteoporosis as she ages. Women who were 20 to 30 years of age in the 1950s are today 60 to 70 years of age and their bones may be suffering the consequences of the gender roles of the time – little exercise, poor diet, and frequent pregnancies.

Cross-cultural differences in the incidence of osteoporosis have been noted. Beyene (1986) conducted a qualitative study of menopause in Greek and Mayan women. Both groups were agrarian and had adequate intake of calcium and high levels of physical activity; in neither group was osteoporosis noted as a problem. The vast majority of research on culture and osteoporosis, however, has consisted of comparing African Americans and European Americans. The results of various studies have been consistent in finding higher bone density at every site throughout the adult life cycle (women) (Aloia *et al.*, 1996), greater bone mass at each age and body mass category (women) (Cauley *et al.*, 1994), and lower rates of hip fracture (men) (Stanley *et al.*, 1991) among African Americans compared to European Americans. Researchers have concluded that the primary source of these differences is a difference in peak bone mass rather than a difference in the rate of loss (Han *et al.*, 1996; Gasperino *et al.*, 1995). In general, the effects of culture and race are difficult, if not impossible, to separate from social economic class. House *et al.* (1994) noted that "Earlier in the century smoking, high fat diets, and lack of exercise were more prevalent in high education and income groups, but as their impact on health has grown, they have become more prevalent at lower socioeconomic levels" (p. 230). The potential impact of this trend may be a decreasing rate of osteoporosis among the affluent and an increasing rate among the poor.

LIFESTYLE

Diet

Diet is a crucial factor in the development and maintenance of the bone structure. In the study of dietary relevance to osteoporosis, calcium has been the primary focus. According to Stini (1995), our ancestors consumed a diet that was extremely high in calcium; in response, natural selection favored the development of relatively inefficient intestinal absorption of calcium – a necessary adaptation because calcium in excessive quantities can be fatal. Today, we consume considerably less calcium than our ancestors did but our digestive system has not evolved in parallel; the consequence is that calcium deficiency is common. Adaptation has provided some "fine tuning" by improving calcium absorption efficiency in times of particular need such as adolescent growth, pregnancy, and lactation. The obvious intervention in cases of suspected osteoporosis is to increase the dietary and/or supplemental intake of calcium.

The majority of women in the United States consume less than 50% of recommended calcium, and recommended intake may be an underestimate of ideal intake. The results of early research on the effectiveness of calcium supplements in treating osteoporosis were inconsistent – some studies found calcium to be effective, others did not. There were several problems with this early research that probably contributed to the inconsistencies. First, if current theory is correct, calcium is effective in reducing age-related osteoporosis, but not menopause-related osteoporosis. Consequently, if calcium is tested on women within 5 years of menopause, the calcium would have minimal impact, and researchers would conclude that calcium is not an effective treatment. However, if the women were more than 5 years past menopause, the calcium would likely have a significant impact and the researchers would conclude that calcium is an effective treatment. These complexities are convincingly addressed by Heaney (1993) who reviewed 43 studies assessing the association between calcium intake and bone health. Twenty-six studies found calcium intake associated, in some way, with bone mass, loss, or fracture; 16 did not. These inconsistent results have been used to argue that calcium is not an effective method of intervening with osteoporosis. Heaney, on the other hand, analyzed possible causes of the inconsistencies. First, he noted that observational studies should not be considered as evidence since they are based on self-reported and historical information. The accuracy of recalling information, such as size of servings in the diet 5 years ago, is highly questionable. In controlled trials, this continues to be a minor problem since all self-report data are subject to bias but, as Heaney points out, the researcher is at least fairly sure that the experimental group did, indeed, consume more calcium than the control group. Nineteen of the 43 studies were controlled; in 16 of these calcium was found to be effective in decreasing or stopping bone loss.

The second problem Heaney addressed was the influence of menopausal status. As discussed above, in the first five years of menopause, bone loss is accelerated as levels of estrogen diminish; during these years, calcium may not be highly effective in improving bone. According to Heaney, of the 19 controlled studies, 12 excluded women in the early years after menopause, and all 12 of these studies found calcium to significantly improve various indices of bone health. Rather than simply dismissing the potential benefits of calcium, Heaney (1993) provided a promising and logical interpretation of the relevant research. He recommends 1500 mg/day and notes that it is never too late to start; he cites European studies which suggest the reductions in fracture rates can be noted in as little as 18 months. Others (Reid *et al.*, 1995) have estimated, on the basis of short-term studies, that 30 years of continuous post-menopausal use of calcium supplements could yield a cumulative benefit of 10%, sufficient to reduce fracture risk by 50%.

Other components of the diet have been evaluated for their influence on osteoporosis but these are assumed to be influential because they impact the absorption and/or the utilization of calcium. Sojka (1995) argues that magnesium supplementation must accompany calcium to ensure proper calcium metabolism. Strause *et al.* (1994) reported that supplementing with zinc, manganese and copper improves the impact of calcium on the bone structure. Vitamin D is a major factor in the metabolic pathway of bone remodeling. According to Gallagher (1996), age and/or menopause results in increased bone reabsorption. The result of increased bone reabsorption is a slight increase in serum calcium which, in turn, suppresses PTH secretion. The lowered PTH levels cause decreases in 1,25-dihydroxyvitamin D (vitamin D) leading to reduced calcium absorption. Chapuy *et al.* (1992) found that supplementation with vitamin D and calcium reduced the risk of hip fractures and other nonvertebral fractures in elderly women. Furthermore, vitamin D alone (without additional calcium) was found to increase bone density at the femoral neck in women over 70 years of age during a two-year period (Ooms *et al.*, 1995).

In addition to the developmental changes in the metabolic pathways of vitamin D, people may get less vitamin D as they age because a major source of vitamin D is sunlight; those who are disabled, confined, or ill may lose this source of vitamin D. Gloth *et al.* (1995) measured various indices of vitamin D metabolism comparing healthy elders and homebound elders. The homebound exhibited greater vitamin D deficiency than the healthy elders. Dawson-Hughes led two studies (Dawson-Hughes *et al.*, 1991; Dawson-Hughes *et al.*, 1995) in which the seasonal variation in sunlight on vitamin D supplementation was evaluated. In the first study, all participants received calcium supplementation while vitamin D and placebo were randomized. All demonstrated increased bone mass between June/July to December/January and decreased bone mass between December/January to June/July; those who received the vitamin D had less bone loss. In the later study, all 247 women received 500 mg supplemental calcium while half received 100 IU of supplemental vitamin D and half received 700 IU. The changes in spinal and whole-body densities were not different between groups but, after two years, the high vitamin D group had lost less mass from the femoral neck than the low vitamin D group. Interestingly, 70% of the benefit occurred in winter/spring and 30% in summer/fall.

Conversely, some dietary components may interfere with or harm calcium absorption. Barrett-Connor *et al.* (1994) collected lifetime dietary histories from elderly women. The authors found opposing and interactive effects of caffeinated coffee and milk consumption: lifetime coffee intake of two cups per day was associated with decreased bone density but only in women who had not drunk milk on a daily basis. The consequences of meat protein on bone loss with aging has been the focus of several studies. According to Marsh *et al.* (1988), omnivorous diets have a considerably higher sulfur content than vegetarian diets. Sulfur causes an increased acidity in the urine, requiring the body's calcium to be used as a buffer and, as a result, more calcium is excreted and lost. These authors found that those elderly who had the least bone mineral density were the vegans (vegetarian without dairy products) and those that ate meat, whereas vegetarians who included dairy products in their diet had the highest bone density. In a rare cross-cultural study, Abelow *et al.* (1992) analyzed the amount of calcium and animal protein in the diet and the fracture rate in 16 countries. A strong positive relationship was found when female fracture rates were regressed against estimates of dietary animal protein. This is a promising area of research, particularly in a world where animal abuse is widespread and the human population is outstripping the land's ability to produce food; the use of valuable land to raise animals for consumption is an inefficient use of resources.

The ideal cure for osteoporosis is prevention. Data from men indicate that some bone loss in middle and old age does not necessarily render an individual vulnerable to fractures. The essential reason for the lower rate of fractures among men compared to women and among African Americans compared to European Americans is assumed to be differences in peak bone mass. With sufficient peak bone mass, normal hormone-related bone loss and normal age-related bone loss in both men and women do not reduce skeletal integrity below the fracture threshold and are not a major source of fractures, disability, or death (see Figure 7.2). Peak bone mass is determined by genetics and by early lifestyle factors. Two studies (Soroko *et al.*, 1994; Murphy *et al.*, 1994) have assessed lifetime milk consumption and bone mineral density in mid- and old-age women. In the former study, greater bone mineral density was noted in those women who reported regular milk consumption between the ages of 20 and 50; in the latter study, the factor exerting the greatest influence was milk consumption before the age of 25. In a cross-sectional study of young adult women, Kanders *et al.* (1988) concluded that the bone mineral density of young women is dependent on nutritional status; they recommend 800 to 1000 mg/day of calcium for optimum bone health. These authors comment that, if these results are substantiated in longitudinal studies and if the benefits of calcium persist into the elderly years, then the average age of osteoporotic fractures might be delayed for 10 years by simple modifications of diet and activity. Although "modification of diet and activity" may sound simple, most individuals recognize and are familiar with the difficulty in permanently altering lifetime habits. (See Chapter 3 for more on diet.)

Exercise

Historical trends in fitness may partially explain the recent increase in osteoporosis. Stones and Kozma (1996) note that, in the UK, fitness decreased between 1939 and 1969; this is probably due to the lower levels of exercising for some decades after World War II. Interestingly, the discovery of ancient bones in a church crypt led investigators to conclude that the bones of elderly women buried between 1729 and 1852 were in better shape than the bones of modern women of the same age. The differences were attributed to previously greater levels of physical exercise (O'Leary Cobb, 1993). Women who are in their seventies and eighties today were in their twenties and thirties in the mid-1940s. Low rates of exercise may have prevented adequate development of peak bone mass, predisposing these women to osteoporosis later in life.

Perhaps the most effective and safest method of reducing the risk of osteoporosis is exercise. "Physical activity is consistently identified as one of the most significant health interventions in the lives of the elderly" (O'Brien and Vertinsky, 1991, p. 349). The beneficial effects of weight-bearing exercise on bone density and size, as well as the detrimental effects of immobility have been known for decades; they are certainly known by anyone who has broken a bone and been dismayed at the emaciated limb that emerges from the cast. Notelovitz (1989) estimated that bedridden persons initially lose 4% of their bone mass per month; he recommends 4 hours of walking to prevent the bone loss associated with 20 hours of bed rest. Why hasn't this common knowledge been used, until only recently, to justify exercise as treatment and prevention for osteoporosis? Perhaps, we were accustomed to seeing elderly people immobile or, perhaps, it was assumed that, to be effective, the exercise had to be strenuous and prolonged and beyond the capabilities of elderly persons.

Observational studies have documented a strong association between exercise and bone integrity. In one research study, Lane *et al.* (1986) found runners, aged 50 to 72, to have a 40% higher bone density than sedentary persons of the same age and weight; another (Sazy and Horstmann, 1991) reported cross-country runners aged 50 to 59 to have 20% greater bone mineral density than nonexercisers of a similar age and weight. Other studies have demonstrated significant effects with considerably less strenuous exercise. Healthy elderly women who walked at least a mile a day and whose current exercise level reflected lifelong exercise habits had greater bone density than those who exercised less (Krall and Dawson-Hughes, 1994). In a large longitudinal study of both women and men, Greendale *et al.* (1995) evaluated lifetime leisure time physical activity and current bone density. While no association was found for the radius, wrist, and spine, a strong relationship was noted between bone mass for all hip measurements and current exercise.

The results from observational studies are strengthened by numerous experimental trials. Dalsky *et al.* (1988) recruited 35 women, aged 55 to 70, who had been sedentary. Seventeen of these began an exercise program for an hour three times a week of walking and jogging with stair climbing added as they became more fit. At the end of 9 months, the exercisers had increased their bone mineral content by 5.2% while the controls lost 1.4%. In another study (Notelovitz, 1989), aerobic exercise, in the form of treadmill and stationary biking, was compared to muscle strengthening and no exercise; controls lost 9.9% of their bone mineral content, strengthening subjects lost 3.8%, biking lost 0.5%; in contrast, treadmill subjects gained .4%. Ayalon *et al.* (1987) developed dynamic bone loading exercises for elderly women who already suffered from osteoporosis. After one year, bone density of controls declined, whereas that of exercisers increased by 3.8%. Finally, Preisinger *et al.* (1996) randomly assigned elderly women with back problems to either exercise or no exercise groups. The exercise group was further divided into those who complied with the exercise regimen and those who did not. The compliant exercisers had significantly more bone density and less subjective back pain after four years.

While the vast majority of studies on exercise and bone health are studies of bone loss, a few have examined the impact of exercise on peak bone mass. Kanders *et al.* (1988) examined calcium intake, exercise, and bone mass in healthy women aged 25 to 34 years. Vertebral bone mass was significantly related to exercise and calcium intake. The authors concluded that with adequate calcium and exercise, the premenopausal woman could increase the bone density of her spine by as much as 10 to 15%; this would delay the age of threshold for vertebral crush fractures for 10 years. Although this is but a small sample of the large literature that has grown in the last decade on the relationship between bone health and exercise, the results across studies tend to be consistent. O'Brien (1996) presents the results of a meta-analysis of six trials suggesting that exercise reduced the risk of hip fractures by 50%. A similar conclusion was reached in a review by Notelovitz (1990) who emphasized that, while hormone therapy may slow bone loss, only exercise has been found to actually increase bone in elderly women. According to Thorngren (1995), the first line of treatment and prevention for osteoporosis in the Scandinavian countries is diet and exercise with hormones being recommended only for high-risk persons.

Some scholars have claimed that exercise may cause bone *loss* in younger women. This misconception derives from early studies finding alterations in reproductive functioning in young women who were competitive athletes and who trained excessively. Amenorrhea and low levels of estrogen have been noted in exercising young women but these results are limited to those who engage in extremely high levels of exercise participation and who report high levels of physical and psychological stress associated with competition (Clapp and Little, 1995). Furthermore, women who experience very early menopause and those who have been castrated tend to exhibit abnormally high rates of bone loss (Kritz-Silverstein and Barrett-Connor, 1993). Despite the highly questionable relevance, this information has been cited as a reason to discourage exercise for elderly women. None the less, amenorrhea and abnormal menopause should not be confused with the relatively harmless experience of missing a menstrual period or two. The exercise recommendation for elderly women to combat bone loss and the exercise recommendation for younger women to build peak bone mass are not recommendations for excessively strenuous, stressful, or competitive exercise, but for moderate and relaxing exercise. There are few similarities between a 20-year-old woman training 4 hours a day for the Olympics and a 70-year-old woman walking for 30 minutes a day.

The exercise required for bone building need not be strenuous, but it does need to be weight-bearing. If the bone is stressed regularly by lifting or supporting weight, the bone will respond by becoming stronger. Aerobic exercise, such as walking, jogging, and dancing, are weight-bearing and strengthen primarily the lower half of the body. Ideally, those at risk for osteoporosis should engage in an exercise program that builds bone throughout the body, such as combining aerobics with weight-lifting. Furthermore, if the body is deficient in calcium and only the lower body is exercised, the calcium may be redistributed to the area most in need, leaving the unexercised bones worse off than before. Sazy and Horstmann (1991) make the following recommendations:

> Exercises that produce increases in bone density of cortical and trabecular bone in the upper and lower extremities include calisthenics, aerobics, running, jogging, and weight lifting. The exercises should be performed either daily or at least three times weekly. Individual exercise capacity is a function of age, recent exercise habits, clinical status, and mind set. Postmenopausal women can benefit by weight-bearing/resistance exercises if performed every other day for more than 30 minutes a session....Benefits include prevention and treatment of coronary artery disease and type II diabetes, psychological well being, and maintenance of musculoskeletal composition. (p. 365)

Most researchers of exercise and bone health have evaluated aerobic exercise; few have studied strength training. Nelson *et al.* (1994) found high-intensity strength training exercises to be an effective and feasible means to maintain bone density. However, the most important benefits of strength training may not be the impact on bone density but rather the impact on falling; this is discussed below.

A major issue in establishing the validity and practicality of exercise as a form of treatment and prevention for osteoporosis is compliance. Although there has been sufficient media coverage of the benefits of exercise to convince anyone of its benefits, more than half of US women are sedentary. Among adults who begin an exercise program, approximately 50% of men and women quit within

161

six months (Marcus *et al.*, 1995a). In contrast, Notelovitz (1990) comments that compliance is generally good because of the reinforcement value; that is, exercise increases mobility and provides social interaction. Given the low rates of compliance, this seems an overly optimistic view and one that may apply more to the elderly than to the young who are the target for prevention strategies. The reasons for a sedentary lifestyle in young women are, perhaps, more complicated; they include full responsibility for young children, parks and streets not being safe for women, embarrassment of being clumsy in public, inadequate transportation, lack of money for proper clothing and equipment, and little personal control over their time and behavior (Marcus *et al.*, 1995a).

Shephard (1993) makes an interesting comment concerning exercise: time spent exercising almost equals the extension of the life span provided by exercise so if a person does not like to exercise, it may not be worth it. Although logical, Shephard's comment assumes the goal to be life extension, whereas the more likely consequence of exercise is functional extension or what Fries (1989) refers to as the "compression of morbidity" – a delay in disability. Furthermore, public health efforts designed to increase the convenience and pleasure of exercise may be found, when systematically evaluated, to be successful. For example, many malls allow persons to use the long indoor corridors as a walking course before and after business hours; in the US, old railway lines are being converted to trails for hiking, jogging, and biking. Considerably more can be done in order to facilitate exercise participation that is both pleasant and reinforcing: work sites could allow flexible work hours, availability of showering and changing facilities onsite, incentives, availability of child care, safety, and convenient strategies for incorporating walking and bicycling into commuting (Marcus *et al.*, 1995a). Clearly, a key to exercise participation is secondary reinforcement. Persons who maintain a regular exercise schedule typically gain something other than health and weight benefits. Secondary reinforcements are unique to the individual: highly social persons may join an aerobics class, whereas solitary persons may take up jogging alone in the country. (See Chapter 3 for more on exercise.)

Other lifestyle factors

Lifestyle factors, other than diet and exercise, that have been found to be associated with fractures include excessive alcohol intake, tobacco use, and medical treatment with corticosteroids, anticonvulsants, heparin, and thyroid replacement (Seeman, 1993). In an unusual study, bone density was evaluated in 41 pairs of women twins, aged 27 to 73, discordant for tobacco use (Hopper and Seeman, 1994). The authors concluded that women who smoke one pack of cigarettes a day throughout adulthood will, by the age of natural menopause, have an average deficit of 5 to 10% in bone density. In contrast, the relationship between bone density and alcohol intake appears to be nonlinear. Felson *et al.* (1995), reporting data from the Framingham Study, found no association with alcohol intakes less than 7 ounces per week. However, in older women who consumed more than 7 ounces per week, alcohol intake was associated with higher bone density. As one might expect, there is an upper limit. Moniz (1994), in reviewing this literature, concluded that the impact of alcohol intakes on bone is curvilinear – between 7 and 27 ounces per week appears to benefit bone health, whereas intakes greater than 28 ounces per week are predictive of bone loss in older women.

FALLS

Osteoporosis is of primary concern in older women's health because of its potential for increasing the risk of fractures. Of, perhaps, equal importance in determining fracture risk is the probability of falling. In a review of the research in this area, Johnell (1995) noted that increased body sway – a measure of balance predictive of falling – was associated with an increased risk of fractures; this effect was independent of bone mineral density. He further commented that the relative risk for fractures associated with a one standard deviation increase in sway was similar to that found for one standard deviation decrease in bone mineral density. In spite of the obvious importance of falls in the health of the elderly, this topic has received little research attention compared to that devoted to bone density; this is somewhat paradoxical since preventing falls is probably easier than preventing bone loss. The lack of interest in falling research may, in part, be due to the results of several early studies finding hormone therapy to be ineffective in preventing falls, precluding major funding opportunities for research by the pharmaceutical companies.

A major predictor of falling is muscle strength. Marcus (1995) comments that the falls most likely to result in fracture are those that occur during transfers (such as changing from sitting to standing), and muscle strength is a primary determinant of these falls. Preisinger et al. (1995) examined the effects of menopause or hormone therapy on muscle strength and concluded that neither later onset of menopause nor hormone therapy had a noticeable influence on muscle strength. Hammar et al. (1996) assessed the effects of hormone therapy on postural balance and found a statistically significant improvement in the two most difficult tasks; however, only 19 women were tested, they all had normal postural balance prior to the study, and no control group was used. Finally, Armstrong et al. (1996) assessed balance, sway, leg strength, walking speed, and falls at intervals over one year in women who had incurred a fracture in the previous three months. Half of the 116 women took hormone therapy while all of the women received calcium supplements. The hormone therapy did not increase muscle performance, improve balance, or reduce falls over the year of the study; in fact, there was some indication that hormone therapy had a nega-tive influence on muscle strength. The authors also tested for covariation with endogenous hormone levels and concluded that the hormonal fluctuations asso-ciated with natural menopause were not related to measures of balance and strength. Thus, it appears that neither muscle strength nor the probability of falling is influenced by menopause or by hormone therapy.

Although systematic, experimental data are lacking, there are a variety of risk factors assumed to be associated with falling which include the following: poor vision, cognitive impairment, alcohol use, low weight and muscle mass, low muscle strength, tobacco use, sedentary lifestyle, low dietary calcium, low physical activity, use of sedatives and tranquilizers, use of psychotropics, abnormality of balance and gait, and foot problems (Meunier, 1993; Peris and Guanabens, 1996; Seeman, 1993; Simoneau and Leibowitz, 1996). Some of these risk factors may be associated with gender differences in fractures. Causes underlying the 50% prevalence of falls in men compared to women (Seeman, 1993) include that women are more likely than are men to have low weight, low muscle mass, and low muscle strength, and to be sedentary. According to Belgrave (1993), women are five times more likely than are men to be on tranquilizers. Finally, Meunier (1993) recommends that those who provide services to the elderly attend to the living environment and aid the individual in eliminating slippery surfaces, stairs, and obstacles and to assure adequate lighting.

MENOPAUSE, CASTRATION, AND HORMONE THERAPY

Since bone loss is a natural part of aging and since menopause occurs in aging women, distinguishing the effects of menopause from those of aging on the osteoporotic process has been difficult. Recent data (Heaney, 1990; Nordin *et al.*, 1990) indicate that bone loss occurs with age and with diminishing levels of sex hormones to a similar degree in men and women. In women, at menopause, the rate of bone loss increases transiently for approximately 5 years and then returns to the lower age-related rate of loss. Since the menopause-related bone loss is assumed to be due to diminishing levels of hormones associated with menopause, hormone therapy has been recommended in order to prevent this loss.

Castration in both women and men appears to have adverse consequences on bone health. Melton and Riggs (1983) presented data suggesting that castrated women are at a higher risk for osteoporosis than are naturally menopausal women. This is consistent with data on men indicating accelerated bone loss following castration. If castration, in either gender, occurs early and interferes with the development of peak bone mass, the bone density in old age is compromised to an even greater extent. Indeed, the differences in fracture rate and osteoporosis between men and women in Western societies and the reason osteoporosis is called a "women's problem" could well be due to the differences between men and women in the incidence of castration – 25% for women (Cutler, 1988), practically nonexistent for men.

Clear interpretation of the research data on menopause and osteoporosis is jeopardized because of considerable methodological difficulties. Most researchers equate castration with natural menopause and study groups consisting of women with either form of menopause. If castrated women have considerably more loss than naturally menopausal women, which seems to be the case, then the data that are published – the average loss – will be an underestimate of the bone loss in castrated women and an overestimate of bone loss in naturally menopausal women. Conclusions as to the effectiveness of hormone therapy are also questionable because of poor research design. Hormones are more likely to be effective during the first 5 years of menopause. Lifestyle interventions are more likely to be effective in women who are at least 5 years past menopause. Yet, these factors – castration versus natural menopause and years since menopause – are often ignored in the research design and analysis; this has yielded ambiguous and contradictory information.

Researchers who have limited their participants to castrated women have found clear, unambiguous benefits of estrogen therapy. Field *et al.* (1993) evaluated three dosages of transdermal estrogen for two years in women who had recently been castrated; a significant dose–response effect was found. Similarly, Watts *et al.* (1995) compared 2-year trials of estrogens and estrogen-plus-androgen on bone mineral density in castrated women; both regimens improved bone health.

In women who experience natural menopause, hormone therapy has been found to be ineffective in preventing age-related bone loss but to slow or stop the menopause-related bone loss if treatment is initiated concurrently with the onset of menopause. However, the menopause-related loss is not prevented but simply delayed and will occur when the woman ceases hormone therapy (Nordin *et al.*, 1990; Fogelman, 1991). Since the average age of the onset of menopause is 50 years and the age of greatest vulnerability to fractures is 70 years, it would seem that prolonged or lifelong hormone therapy would be necessary to impact the rate of fractures. Yet, the research does not support this conclusion. Felson *et al.* (1993) examined data from the Framingham Study cohort to determine the effects of early hormone therapy on bone mass in elderly women and the ideal duration of such therapy. They reached several conclusions: (1) at any age, only women who had taken hormones for more than 7 years had significantly higher bone density than nonusers; and (2) hormone therapy for more than 7 years offered a minimal (3.2%) benefit after the age of 75. The authors concluded that their data were consistent with that of other studies and indicated that the effect of hormone therapy on bone mass is negligible at the age of highest risk for fractures. Similar results were reported by Cauley *et al.* (1995) who assessed both bone mass and fracture risk. They found a benefit on bone mass for current users but only if they had initiated therapy within 5 years of menopause: "Previous use of estrogen for more than 10 years or use begun soon after menopause had no substantial effect on the risk for fractures" (p. 9).

Although screening for osteoporosis by measuring bone mineral density has been recommended, the goal of screening appears to be the promotion of hormone use rather than to inform women of potentially important health risks. Rizzoli and Bonjour (1997) offer a decision flow chart for selecting women who should be screened. The authors suggest that women who are ready and willing to take hormone therapy not be screened while those who express ambivalence be screened. Garton *et al.* (1994) evaluated middle-aged women's attitudes toward hormone therapy and osteoporosis prevention. Although few expressed a willingness to take hormones, 96% indicated that they would consider taking hormones if their bone scan indicated a high risk of osteoporosis. The authors' goal of compliance with recommendations to take hormone therapy is clear in their conclusion: "long-term compliance might be enhanced by disclosure of fracture risk" (p. 7). Ryan *et al.* (1992) assessed compliance with recommendations for hormone therapy following screening for osteoporosis. Screening did lead to increased usage of hormone therapy among women at most risk for osteoporosis. However, even with screening, 40% of women with low bone density did not comply with hormone recommendations. The authors concluded "until improved compliance has been demonstrated screening cannot be widely recommended" (p. 325). The authors of none of these studies considered that women may benefit from osteoporosis screening by changing their diet and exercising if they were found to be at high risk; their only concern was whether or not screening would increase a woman's willingness to take hormones.

Raffle (1993) nicely summarizes these issues in an editorial in the *British Medical Journal*:

> No trials have assessed the effectiveness of bone mass screening in preventing osteoporotic fractures. Decisions about its value are therefore based on indirect evidence....None [of the screening advocates] seriously considered the requirement for screening to benefit those screened....[There] seems no prospect that screening for osteoporosis will meet the basic requirements for a screening programme – namely, that those offered screening must be better off as a result, that overall the screening programme must do more good than harm....Published work on screening for osteoporosis is based largely on experience in the United States, where widespread growth of screening has been driven by commercial factors and not by public health policy. (p. 654)

The issues surrounding screening are applicable to all areas of medicine in the United States where there is considerable ambiguity and confusion among both professionals and lay persons about priorities in medicine and health. The rhetoric is one of concern and health, whereas the practice seems driven by economics. These issues are less salient in countries in which medical care is provided to all, regardless of ability to pay.

To summarize, both aging and menopause seem to be responsible for bone loss in elderly women. The menopause-related bone loss begins at the time of menopause and continues for approximately 5 years. The age-related bone loss begins around age 35 and continues throughout life. If women who have experienced natural menopause begin hormone therapy at the time of their menopause, they will slow the menopause-related bone loss as long as they continue to take the hormones. Since menopause occurs around 50 and the average hip fracture age is about 70, a woman would have to take hormones for 20 years in order to achieve this benefit. Yet, even then, the little information available indicates that any benefit of hormones on bone density does not necessarily translate to a reduction in fracture risk at an elderly age.

PREVENTION AND TREATMENT

While hormone therapy does not impact age-related bone loss, lifestyle factors do; diet and exercise can prevent and even reverse age-related bone loss (Dawson-Hughes, 1991; Gerber and Rey, 1991; Nordin *et al.*, 1990; Rikli and McManis, 1990; Sidney *et al.*, 1977). More importantly, diet and exercise are the keys to prevention. Given this information, one might ask why the recognition of osteoporosis as a problem did not spur a widespread campaign through schools, organizations, and the media to encourage and facilitate healthy, bone-building diets and exercise in young persons? Why did the success of public health efforts to reduce dietary cholesterol not encourage similar dietary changes aimed at preventing osteoporosis? Perhaps, lifestyle improvements are not stressed as the means to prevention and treatment because osteoporosis has been popularized as a woman's problem – as a menopause problem. None the less, despite the medical emphasis on menopause and hormones, public health efforts are being targeted at increasing awareness of the importance of healthy food, exercise, and fitness and of the considerable adverse, long-term health consequences of castration.

In addition to hormone therapy and lifestyle modifications discussed above, a variety of drugs have been developed to treat established osteoporosis. Each is discussed briefly. The reader should note that the development of these drugs is a recent endeavor and that recommendations based on effectiveness and safety are likely to change as new research is published.

Bisphosphonates (etidronate, pamidronate, alendronate) encourage bone formation by decreasing bone turnover and inhibiting bone reabsorption. Bisphosphonates are specific to bone tissue, have minimal side-effects, and are associated with no known risk of cancer. Eighty to 85% of patients improve if therapy is provided for at least 5 to 7 years. Etidronate and alendronate have been approved in the US for the treatment of osteoporosis (Hodsman *et al.*, 1996). Of primary concern in the treatment of osteoporosis is the maintenance of benefits after drug withdrawal. Orr-Walker *et al.* (1997), reporting the results of a controlled, randomized trial, note that the rate of bone gained with bisphosphonates slows over time, and that bone loss is rapid when the drug is withdrawn. Similar conclusions were reached by Fairney *et al.* (1998) who tested cyclical etidronate plus calcium for three years of treatment and one year of treatment withdrawal. In contrast, Stock *et al.* (1997) found the increases in bone density associated with alendronate treatment diminished only slightly in the two years after discontinuing the drug. Dose–response relationships – strong support for causal inferences – were noted by McClung *et al.* (1998) after testing a placebo versus 1, 5, 10, or 20 mg of alendronate. In this study and an earlier one by Tucci *et al.* (1996), safety and tolerability of these drugs were found to be good.

Fluoride has a long history in the treatment of osteoporosis. It has been approved by government health agencies in Europe but, in the United States, there has been controversy about its effectiveness and safety and it has not been approved. The weight-bearing skeleton is the primary site of action, particularly the spine. Fluoride acts by stimulating bone formation, and the benefits continue linearly up to at least 6 years. The most recent studies show significant reduction in fractures with minimal side-effects using slow-release sodium fluoride (Murray and Ste-Marie, 1996).

Calcitonin is produced in humans by the thyroid gland and is involved in calcium metabolism. It suppresses the activity of osteoclasts, decreasing bone reabsorption. The traditional route of treatment is injection but, more recently, an intranasal mode of delivery has been developed, which makes this treatment more accessible. Calcitonin has been found to reduce acute pain associated with osteoporotic fractures, particularly back pain from crush fractures common in spinal osteoporosis. Calcitonin also reduces bone loss and increases bone density in those with osteoporosis. However, information is currently lacking regarding the safety and effectiveness of long-term use. Observational studies indicate that calcitonin may be effective in reducing fractures. Side-effects are minimal and dose-related; side-effects are considerably less with the intranasal form than the injectable form, accounting for the greater compliance with the former than the latter (Siminoski and Josse, 1996). Calcitonin has been used, with partial success, to treat the accelerated bone loss following castration in men (Stepan *et al.*, 1989). Calcitonin provides the added benefit of analgesia but there is rapid reversal of bone health when the treatment is stopped (Notelovitz, 1996).

These pharmaceutical treatments for osteoporosis and fracture prevention have not received adequate research attention. Most of the research funds have been devoted to studies on hormone therapy, and many physicians assume hormones to be the treatment of choice. As the adverse side-effects of hormone therapy become more widely known and acknowledged, interest in these drugs will probably increase. However, the newer drug treatments for osteoporosis have not yet been subjected to studies of long-term risks and benefits; they may not, in fact, be safer than hormone therapy. Cost is an obvious cause for concern with any treatment or intervention. Calcium and hormone therapy are relatively low cost compared to calcitonin and bisphosphonates, although the price of the latter would be expected to decrease if the demand increased.

CONCLUSIONS

Osteoporosis is not a disorder associated with menopause in women but a disorder affecting persons of all ages, both genders, and all races whose lifestyles preclude healthy bone. Medical and sexual politics create the ideological milieu in which physicians prescribe hormone therapy, with its attendant risks of endometrial and breast cancer, rather than focus on lifestyle interventions that confer numerous *positive* side-effects in all areas of middle-aged and elderly persons' lives. Although the current focus is on rate of bone loss during middle and old age, a significant determinant of fracture vulnerability is peak bone mass at approximately age 35. High peak bone mass increases the probability that one will maintain sufficient bone integrity to remain above the fracture threshold in old age. Men's peak bone mass averages 25% higher than that of women (Albanese *et al.*, 1975), and this difference has been attributed to women's traditionally lower participation in sports and exercise, their lower body mass, and their smaller muscle mass. With the dramatic increase in women's participation in all forms of exercise in the last two decades, the increased appreciation for health and fitness, and the increasing reluctance of women to have prophylactic castrations, the problem of osteoporotic fractures in elderly women may soon be eliminated, or, at least, drastically reduced.

8

CONCLUDING REMARKS

women do between two-thirds and three-quarters of the work in the world. They also produce 45 percent of the world's food. But they are still granted only 10 percent of the world's income and 1 percent of the world's property.

(French, 1992, p. 30)

a woman must have money and a room of her own.

(Woolf, 1957[1929], p. 4)

The dream of researchers in the health and social sciences is to discover the essential cause, the final common denominator, the primary and overriding source that explains the individual variability in well-being. Unfortunately, the more we know, the more we are forced to acknowledge the impossibility of this quest. None the less, my attention has been repeatedly drawn to a factor that comes close to achieving this level of salience – access to or the personal control of resources sufficient to enable a life beyond mere survival. Such resources allow the basic necessities of well-being: knowledge of health risks and health strategies through education, environments free of violence and pollution, nutritious food, quality health care, and experiences of personal control and self-efficacy. And, I would argue, differential access to such resources is the basis for gender, ethnic, and racial variability in well-being. In Western cultures, these resources are most closely approximated by social and economic class.

In the past several decades, population-based research has evaluated the impact of a wide range of biological, behavioral, environmental, and other potential risk factors on adverse health outcomes. When one sorts through this vast collection of studies, the relationship of low socioeconomic status and poor health rises to the top of the findings over and over again, across different disease outcomes, in different age groups, and in different areas of the world. The strength and consistency of this relationship has been remarkable.

(Guralnik and Leveille, 1997, p. 728)

I conclude with a discussion of socioeconomic status (SES) and its impact and influence on psychological and physical well-being in mid- and old-age women.

There is considerable evidence documenting a strong influence of SES on health, disability, and mortality. Most recently, Hemingway *et al.* (1997) assessed the association between SES and eight health outcomes in over 8,000 British civil servants aged 39 to 63. Significant age-adjusted gradients were found across SES groups for physical, social, and psychological outcomes for women and for men and for those with and without documented disease. Similarly, Marmot *et al.* (1997) combined three large samples, one from Britain and two from the US; each sample exhibited similar SES gradients for adult women and men in physical and mental morbidity and in psychological well-being. The authors concluded that the association between health and SES is not limited to poor health among the poor but that there is a linear gradient documenting this association at all levels of SES.

The prevalence of specific diseases and risk factors for women, averaged within social class, is charted in Table 8.1; the association between social class and health is obvious. Various explanations for high psychological and physical morbidity and mortality among those with few material resources have been proposed: (1) work environments are characterized by low control, low variety and skill use, high pace, low supports, and low satisfaction (Marmot *et al.*, 1997); (2) accessible medical care is of poor quality (Kuller, 1995); (3) high mortality leads to the stress and loneliness of early widowhood (Arbuckle and deVries, 1995); (4) diets are high in meat, fats, sugars, preserves, potatoes, and cereals that

Table 8.1 Observed prevalence of disease and risk factors within social class, in women of all ages

	Social class					
	I	*II*	*IINM*[a]	*IIM*[b]	*IV*	*V*
Ischemic heart disease	1.8	3.4	5.2	4.4	5.9	7.2
Stroke	0.5	0.9	2.3	1.5	2.0	2.5
Mean blood pressure	130/72	132/72	136/73	134/73	136/73	141/75
Cholesterol >6.5 mmol/l	26	29	35	33	33	36
Smoking >20 cigarettes/day	24	24	23	28	30	30
Obesity (body mass index >30)	11.8	14.3	15	19.7	21.9	22.6
Physically inactive	15	15	17	24	22	22

Source: Adapted from W.P.T. James, A. Ralph, and S. Leather (1997) The contribution of nutrition to inequalities in health. *British Medical Journal*, 314: 1546. Reprinted by permission of BMJ Publishing Group.
Notes:
[a] NM = non-manual;
[b] M = manual;
Values are percentage of population; blood pressure is given as mean values.

translate into inadequate consumption of calcium, iron, magnesium, folate, and vitamin C (James *et al.*, 1997); (5) there are few or no resources to inspire the motivation to quit smoking, exercise, reduce stress, and eliminate toxic and unhygienic environments (Samuelsson *et al.*, 1994); (6) the lack of educational opportunities leads to insufficient knowledge of cardiovascular risk factors and strategies to decrease risk (S. Davis *et al.*, 1995); and (7) the poor have little control over their personal lives and the environment (Rodin, 1989).

Age exerts a clear influence on the relationship between health and SES; indeed, the association increases with age. Most of the risk factors for poor health (smoking, obesity, poor medical care, poor diet, environmental pollution, sedentary lifestyle) have cumulative effects so that the longer someone is at risk, the greater the probability of morbidity; these risk factors are more prevalent in the poorer classes than in the affluent classes. House *et al.* (1994) concluded that those persons in the upper SES strata approach the ideal of relatively low levels of morbidity and high levels of function until late in life while low SES persons suffer increasingly from illness and disability as they progress through middle age to old age.

Currently, the rate of disability among the aged is relatively high: after age 85, over 20% of women require assistance to walk across the room, 69% need help with housework, and 25% require assistance to climb stairs (O'Brien and Vertinsky, 1991). Penning and Strain (1994) reported that over 50% of their sample, average age 75 years, experienced some disability with women reporting more than men. Clark (1997) compared African Americans to European Americans on rates of disability in 1982, 1984, and 1989; in all examined years, the rates for African Americans significantly and substantially exceeded the rates for European Americans and the differences increased with time. The most powerful predictor of functional capacity in old age was SES. The association between race and disability and gender and disability could well be mediated by SES since both African Americans and women are at greater risk for experiencing poverty – both as a continuation of earlier SES status and/or as a consequence of a work history that precludes adequate income in old age (Maddox *et al.*, 1994). Consequently, while at all ages those with higher SES have superior health compared to those at the lower end, with age, the differences become more pronounced and dramatic.

Research documenting SES influences on health is often "disguised" as studies of racial and/or gender differences. Kuller (1995) noted the ever-widening gap in CHD mortality between Caucasians and African Americans. The overall decline in CHD mortality in the last several decades, usually attributed to healthier lifestyles, has occurred primarily among the wealthy and educated. Kington and Smith (1997) reported racial differences in functional status associated with chronic disease in a large US sample of persons aged 51 to 61. Among those with chronic diseases, African Americans and Hispanics reported worse function than Caucasians. This difference was eliminated by controlling for SES; in other words, for persons of similar SES, there were no racial differences in health measures. Many researchers and politicians have ignored SES differences among races and ethnicities and between genders, and have attributed health differences to biological differences, reinforcing the basic tenet of patriarchy – biological determinism. The poor health, functional incapacities, and psychological distress of women and minorities can then be used as a justification for economic and political discrimination:

> The nonsense propagated by ideologues of biological determinism…is meant to legitimate the structures of inequality in our society by putting a biological gloss on them and by propagating the continual confusion between what may be influenced by genes and what may be changed by social and environmental alterations.
>
> (Lewontin, 1992, pp. 36–7)

If poor health can be conveniently blamed on genes, and if a lack of opportunity in education and occupation can be conveniently blamed on poor health, then solving health problems does not require changing the economic structure or government policy, and the status quo is, once again, validated and reinforced.

The "feminization of poverty" has been an essential claim of the women's movement for decades; this trend clearly continues and escalates with age with elderly women's income at 57% of elderly men's (Belgrave, 1993). Hardy and Hazelrigg (1993, 1995) note the clear trend from 1959 to the present of increased poverty among women; single mothers and older women account for most of the trend. These authors published statistics on the rates of poverty for women and men between the ages of 65 and 74 years in seven countries. In all countries surveyed with the exception of the Netherlands and Sweden (two countries with strong government policies designed to equalize income levels), a greater percentage of women than of men lived in poverty. The US had the highest rate of overall poverty and the largest discrepancy between women (38.4%) and men (14.7%). The authors suggest that the high rates of poverty among elderly women are due to women's typical working conditions characterized by low wages, low job security, and lack of fringe benefits. To these Keith (1993) adds that women, compared to men, have more work interruptions due to family responsibilities, are more likely to experience sex discrimination, are more likely to work part time, and have fewer pension benefits. Keith also identifies social reasons for women's poverty such as that women who marry tend to marry men older than themselves and women live longer, resulting in the high probability that those married women who had depended upon their husband's financial support will fall into poverty with widowhood. The gender differences in poverty among the elderly tend to be additive to those of race and ethnicity with the highest rates of poverty found among minority women and the lowest rates among White men (Hardy and Hazelrigg, 1995). Twenty-seven percent of single older women live below the poverty level; the rate rises to 66% if they are Black (Schulz, 1997).

Access to quality health care is a major predictor of physical and psychological well-being throughout the life span. Access is determined, to a great extent, by financial resources, and the delivery of health care is compromised by racial and gender discrimination. Although health care is more equally distributed in socialist countries than in capitalist ones and more in countries with government-funded health systems, barriers to quality health care remain a problem for persons of low SES regardless of the health care structure. Persons of low SES are less likely to take time from work to visit a health care worker, have less access to efficient transportation, and have less access to child care while lacking the education and environment conducive to healthy exercise and diet. Difficult access to medical care in childhood and young adulthood is likely to continue with the effects of poor care accumulating to yield high levels of morbidity, disability, and mortality in old age. One would expect that since 75% of those without medical insurance in the US are under 35 and are women (Travis *et al.*, 1995), elderly women will not only suffer the consequences of long-term neglect but will also continue to have considerable difficulty accessing medical care. Van de Mheen *et al.* (1997) examined population data in the Netherlands and concluded: "Educational level of the mother, occupation of the father and financial situation of the family are the most important childhood characteristics in the explanation of socio-economic health differences in adult life" (p. 13). To break the cycle that culminates in elderly women living in poverty and poor health, solutions must address these concerns across the life span.

There is evidence for both racial and gender differences in access to medical care and in the quality of the medical care that is available; these differences are, at least partially, explained by SES. (See Chapter 6 for a discussion of gender discrimination in medical treatments of CHD.) Perhaps, the most dramatic racial differences have been found in the medical response to cardiovascular symptoms. Liao and Cooper (1995) reported that African Americans were half as likely to undergo angiography and half as likely to have bypass surgery as European Americans. Carlisle *et al.* (1997) examined disparities in the use of cardiovascular procedures in the US among African Americans, Latinos, Asians, and Whites. Compared to White patients, lower procedure use was found among African Americans and Latinos. Further analyses revealed that these discrepancies were present for persons in all types of health insurance categories except for those with private insurance. Assuming private insurance to be available to the more wealthy, the racial differences were likely the result of SES.

The medical community has been slow to admit the possibility of prejudice and bias as an explanation of the differences in access to quality medical care. In the US, National Public Radio's Brenda Wilson (1997) noted that Blacks were 32% less likely to undergo bypass surgery than were Whites and questioned two cardiologists about possible explanations. Dr. Eric Peterson commented that, perhaps, Blacks were receiving appropriate treatment if their physical condition indicated that they had little to gain from such procedures. But, in fact, Wilson reported, the opposite was found: the racial differences were greatest among those who stood to benefit the most from such procedures. Peterson then speculated that if Blacks were properly informed as to the risks and benefits associated with such treatment, they would consent to the treatment, implying that the aggressive procedures are, indeed, recommended by the physician but are refused by the patient – yet one more instance of "blaming the victim." Later in the program, Dr. Louis Culler stated:

> Physicians see these patients who are poor as having a poor prognosis, rightfully or wrongfully, because of their associated diseases, and decide that bypass surgery is not as indicated as [for] a white patient or an upper class white patient who basically is out there playing tennis or golf, takes care of himself, has normal blood pressure or controls his blood pressure.
>
> (Wilson, 1997, p. 2)

If the poor do, indeed, have a low likelihood of recovery, the reason could well be due to the consequences of a lifetime of poverty – poor diet, unsafe areas of residence and work, hostile work environments, poor air and water quality, and, ironically, low access to health care. Denying medical care to children, young adults, and pregnant women who lack adequate financial resources eventually creates an underclass of elderly with poor prognosis for most disorders and illnesses.

In spite of widespread publicity in the US regarding the difficulty persons lacking financial means encounter in accessing medical care and noting the millions of persons with no medical insurance whose only access to medical care is through emergency services, the medical community refuses to acknowledge their role in maintaining the present health care system. Various rationalizations place the blame for inadequate medical care on the patient and fail to acknowledge the likely influence of racial, ethnic, and gender discrimination and, in the US, the questionable distinction of being the only Western society without some form of national health care. Carlisle *et al.* (1997) suggest that African Americans receive poor medical care because of a language barrier between the patient and the physician; yet, language does not seem to be a barrier to quality health care when the patient is a wealthy foreign official.

Brangman (1995) criticizes the health care system as being culturally insensitive, yet, ironically, does so in a culturally insensitive manner. She suggests one reason for the poor medical care provided African Americans is their primitive and ignorant preference for home remedies – an explanation that is both convenient and arrogant since folk remedies may be the only help available to those who lack financial resources, and, when researched, are often found to be effective. This author further proposes that African Americans do not *seek* medical care because they are suspicious of physicians. Indeed, they have good cause for their suspicions:

there has been a long history of abuse and neglect in medical research of minorities, including African Americans....Past calamities, such as the Tuskegee studies of syphilis using maltreated African American men, have created a less than credible reputation for researchers among many racial and ethnic minority communities.

(Rousseau and McCool, 1996, p. 242)

Gamble (1997) notes that the Tuskegee studies are only a small portion of the long history of medical and scientific abuse of powerless minorities. In her documentation of historical abuses, she notes an example as recent as 1989. The severity of these past and continuing abuses dictates a clear obligation on the part of the medical community to, at the very least, serve disenfranchised groups in a manner dictated by the recipients' needs, rather than the providers' convenience and profits.

Unequal distributions of resources, knowledge, and control are demanded by the ideologies, politics and economics of most Western societies. The consequences are illness, disease, and disability among those without power and financial resources – women, the elderly, and ethnic minorities. The system is safeguarded from criticism by the overriding ideology of biological determinism. Attributing difference to biology takes the blame away from industry and business who exploit the poor and governments who fail to provide for the poor and places the fault on the individual. Kington *et al.* (1997) examined the relationship between health status and reproductive history among women over the age of 50. They concluded: "Women with high parity status, a history of an infant's death, and an early first pregnancy may be at greater risk of poor health in later life" (p. 33). Although these conditions are widely recognized as SES correlates, the authors interpreted their results as biological rather than financial or social. Similarly, Cannistra *et al.* (1995) noted that Black women have higher mortality after myocardial infarction than do White women. In studying this further, they found that Black women were less likely to complete a cardiac rehabilitation program than were White women and concluded that the Black women lacked adequate motivation. The authors did not seriously consider the source of the racial differences to be the inability to pay for transportation or child care or the opportunity to take time away from work.

Two studies investigated the high rates of CHD among Native Americans (Campos-Outcalt *et al.*, 1995; Howard *et al.*, 1995). Both studies focused on the prevalence of medical CHD risk factors in these populations but neither mentioned that these medical risks are logical outcomes of cultural risks – the poverty, isolation, and alienation that Native Americans are forced to endure. "Understanding the contribution of health behaviours and psychosocial characteristics to socioeconomic health inequalities requires an acknowledgment of how they are moulded over time by the SES conditions imposed at each stage of the lifecourse" (Lynch *et al.*, 1997, p. 817). McDonough *et al.* (1997) noted that although income was a strong predictor of mortality, persistent low income was particularly consequential.

176

Intellectual and practical "blindness" to the importance of SES continues to be apparent. The US government has recently funded the Women's Health Initiative – a longitudinal study designed to study women over 50. Although publicized as including an examination of racial differences, an independent assessment of the project concluded that the small sample sizes of minority groups preclude the appropriate analyses (Thaul and Hotra, 1993). Researchers in the project (Matthews *et al.*, 1997a) acknowledge the impact of poverty on health but virtually eliminate the poor from the study by not providing compensation or transportation in exchange for participation. One component of the study will test psychological mediators between SES and health outcomes. Although intellectually interesting, the outcomes are predictable and are unlikely to be used to improve the health of the poor any more than the knowledge we have already gained has brought relief.

The priorities of research and delivery of health care are often consistent with expediency and profit rather than the result of concern for the health of the population:

> The goal of improved population health will be similarly elusive while medical care is commodified and exploited for commercial gain in the marketplace. Recognition of the powerful forces that polarize our world and commitment to reversing them are essential for the achievement of human rights for all, for the improvement of public health, and for the peaceful progress required to protect the "rational self-interest" of the most privileged people on earth against the escalation of war, disease, and other destructive forces arising from widespread poverty and ecological degradation.
>
> (Benetar, 1998, p. 295)

To illustrate, consider the tremendous government and industrial investment in high-technology reproduction. At present, in the US, women who are infertile, but otherwise healthy, and who request the expensive, complex, and potentially dangerous procedures of *in vitro* fertilization (IVF) are often reimbursed by insurance, whereas many pregnant women who are poor do not have access to basic prenatal care. The incredible profits realized from high-technology reproduction have motivated Western physicians to export the technology to developing countries. In a recent article, Okonofua (1996) offers several criticisms of a proposal to introduce IVF clinics to Nigeria: (1) a preferred way to address infertility is through prevention by improving living conditions, eliminating practices such as female genital mutilation, and increasing access to family planning and safe abortion for women; (2) the author questions "how the government can justify such a programme in view of its high cost and the fact that there are other more serious health problems in the country requiring more immediate attention" (p. 958); (3) equity of access in a country with glaring inequity in health matters is an impossibility; and (4) other programs, ones more essential to health, are currently underfunded, such as family planning, maternal and prenatal health clinics, and the guarantee of safe and healthy living conditions. The author concludes: "the direct and indirect costs of reproductive technology will increase the per capita health care expenditures without significantly improving the health of the population" (p. 962). With the exception of female genital mutilation, each of these describes reality in most Western societies.

The overwhelming complexity of studying and solving health problems is readily apparent when considering the obstacles of addressing informative research questions. A true scientific experiment requires manipulating a variable and observing the consequences of that manipulation. However, cultural variables cannot be systematically isolated and manipulated: we cannot provide middle-class incomes to persons living in poverty or rid cultures of prejudice and evaluate the outcome. Although the scientific method is often believed to be the one and only route to truth, the true scientific experiment does not lend itself to addressing the most pressing issues in health. The information required to determine the impact of culture on physical and psychological well-being is complex, interactive, difficult to measure, and frequently eludes obvious interpretation within the context of popular theories and perspectives. Organizing relevant information within a coherent and logically consistent structure is a daunting task. Not only do scholars across disciplines have highly divergent, even contradictory, opinions but also, within disciplines, scholars lack agreement on the most fundamental of issues. None the less, data emerging from numerous disciplines, including sociology, anthropology, psychology, medicine, economics, and political science, support the tenet that the dominant ideology of a culture dictates gender, age, and race appropriate behavior, emotions, occupations, beliefs, lifestyles, and roles; these, in turn, determine access to resources and, ultimately, health and well-being.

The methodologies and priorities of the physical and social sciences require dramatic transformation in order adequately and successfully to address current and future health concerns of mid- and old-age women. Rather than emphasize palliative management of adverse outcomes from a lifetime of poverty, prejudice, and toxic environments, research programs need to address methods of modifying or eliminating these sources of physical and psychological disturbance: a depressed, middle-aged African American is better served by eliminating racism than by developing better anti-depressants; an elderly woman suffering the consequences of a lifetime of poor nutrition is better served by providing an adequate pension than by developing a new form of hormone therapy; infertile women are better served by broadening the cultural definition of "womanhood" than by developing techniques that induce temporary fertility but are potentially harmful to health and are only available to the affluent. We do not require a "true experiment" to know that racism, gender discrimination, class exploitation, ageism, and homophobia are major sources of distress and poor health. We need to do something about it!

REFERENCES

Abdulla, H.I., Hart, D.M., Lindsay, R., and Aitken, M. (1984) Determinants of bone mass and bone loss response to oestrogen therapy in oophorectomized women. Presented at the Fourth International Congress on the Menopause, Orlando, Florida.

Abe, T., Furuhashi, N., Yamaya, Y., Wada, Y., Hoshiai, A., and Suzuki, M. (1977) Correlation between climacteric symptoms and serum levels of estradiol, progesterone, follicle-stimulating hormone, and luteinizing hormone. *American Journal of Obstetrics and Gynecology*, 129: 65–67.

Abelow, B.J., Holford, T.H., and Insogna, K.L. (1992) Cross-cultural association between dietary animal protein and hip fracture: A hypothesis. *Calcified Tissue International*, 50: 14–18.

Aber, C.S. (1992) Spousal death, a threat to women's health: Paid work as a "resistance resource." *Image: Journal of Nursing Scholarship*, 24: 95–99.

Abraham, S., Perz, J., Clarkson, R., and Llewellyn-Jones, D. (1995) Australian women's perceptions of hormone replacement therapy over 10 years. *Maturitas*, 21: 91–95.

Abrams, W.B. and Berkow, R. (eds) *The Merck Manual of Geriatrics*. Rahway NJ: Merck, Sharp, and Dohme Research Laboratories.

Abramson, L.Y., Seligman, M.E.P., and Teasdale, J. (1978) Learned helplessness in humans: Critique and reformulation. *Journal of Abnormal Psychology*, 87: 49–74.

Adelmann, P. (1993) Psychological well-being and homemaker vs. retiree identity among older women. *Sex Roles*, 29: 195–212.

Akkad, A.A., Habiba, M.A., Ismail, N., Abrams, K., and Al-Azzawi, F. (1995) Abnormal uterine bleeding on hormone replacement: The importance of intrauterine structural abnormalities. *Obstetrics and Gynecology*, 86: 330–334.

Aksel, S., Schomberg, D.W., Tyrey, L., and Hammond, C.B. (1976) Vasomotor symptoms, serum estrogens and gonadotropin levels in surgical menopause. *American Journal of Obstetrics and Gynecology*, 126: 165–169.

Albanese, A., Edelson, A.H., Lorenze, E.J., Woodhull, M.L., and Wein, E. (1975) Problems with bone health in the elderly. *New York State Journal of Medicine*, 35: 326–346.

Albee, G.W. (1982) The politics of nature and nurture. *American Journal of Community Psychology*, 10: 1–36.

Albert, S.M. and Cattell, M.G. (1994) *Old Age in Global Perspective: Cross-cultural and Cross-national Views*. New York: G.K. Hall.

Albertazzi, P., Pansini, F., Bonaccorsi, G., Zanatti, L., Forini, E., and DeAloysio, D. (1998) The effect of dietary soy supplementation on hot flushes. *Obstetrics and Gynecology*, 91: 6–11.

Aloia, J.F., Vaswani, A., Russo, L., Sheehan, M., and Flaster, E. (1995) The influence of menopause and hormonal replacement therapy on body cell mass and body fat mass. *American Journal of Obstetrics and Gynecology*, 172: 896–900.

Aloia, J.F., Vaswai, A., Yeh, J.K., and Flaster E. (1996) Risk for osteoporosis in Black women. *Calcified Tissue International*, 59: 415–423.

American Dietetic Association (1995) Position of The American Dietetic Association and The Canadian Dietetic Association: Women's health and nutrition. *Journal of the American Dietetic Association*, 95: 362–366.

Amos, P.T. and Harrell, S. (1981) Introduction: an anthropological perspective on aging. In P.T. Amoss and S. Harrell (eds) *Other Ways of Growing Old*. Stanford: Stanford University Press (pp. 1–24).

Andrews, W.C. (1995) The transitional years and beyond. *Obstetrics and Gynecology*, 85: 1–5.

Arber, S. and Lahelma, E. (1993) Inequalities in women's and men's ill-health: Britain and Finland compared. *Social Science and Medicine*, 37: 1055–1068.

Arbuckle, N.W. and deVries, B. (1995) The long-term effects of later life spousal and parental bereavement on personal functioning. *The Gerontologist*, 35: 637–647.

Archer, D.F. (1982) Biochemical findings and medical management of menopause. In A.M. Voda, M. Dinnerstein, and S.R. O'Connell (eds) *Changing Perspectives on Menopause*. Austin: University of Texas Press.

Arling, B. (1976) The elderly widow and her family, neighbors, and friends. *Journal of Marriage and the Family*, 38: 757–768.

Armstrong, A.L., Oborne, J., Coupland, C.A.C., MacPherson, M.B., Bassey, E.J., and Wallace, W.A. (1996) Effects of hormone replacement therapy on muscle performance and balance in post-menopausal women. *Clinical Science*, 91: 685–690.

Aschoff, J. (1980) The circadian rhythm in man. In D.T. Krieger and J.C. Hughes (eds) *Neuroendocrinology*. Sunderland MA: Sinauer.

—— (1982) Circadian rhythms in man. In J. Brady (ed.) *Biological Timekeeping*. Cambridge: Cambridge University Press.

Auerbach, J.D. and Figert, A.E. (1995) Women's health research: public policy and sociology. *Journal of Health and Social Behavior*, extra: 115–131.

Avis, N.E. and McKinlay, S.M. (1991) A longitudinal analysis of women's attitudes toward the menopause: Results from the Massachusetts Women's Health Study. *Maturitas*, 13: 65–79.

Ayalon, J., Simkin, A., Leichter, I., Raifmann, S. (1987) Dynamic bone loading exercises for postmenopausal women: Effect on the density of the distal radius. *Archives of Physical Medicine Rehabilitation*, 68: 280–283.

Aycock, N.R. and Jollie, W.P. (1979) Ultrastructural effects of estrogen replacement on postmenopausal endometrium. *American Journal of Obstetrics and Gynecology*, 135: 461–466.

Badawy, S.Z.Z., Elliott, L.J., Elbadawi, A., and Marshall, L.D. (1979) Plasma levels of oestrone and oestradiol-17B in postmenopausal women. *British Journal of Obstetrics and Gynaecology*, 86: 56–63.

Bagatell, C.J. and Bremner, W.J. (1995) Androgen and progestagen effects on plasma lipids. *Progress in Cardiovascular Disorders*, 38: 255–271.

Balducci, L., Lyman, G.H., and Schapira, D.V. (1994) Trends in prevention and treatment of breast cancer in the older woman. In B.J. Vellas, J.L. Albarede, and P.J. Garry (eds) *Facts and Research in Gerontology*. New York: Springer (pp. 179–182).

Ballinger, C.B. (1975) Psychiatric morbidity and the menopause: Screening of general population sample. *British Medical Journal*, 3: 344–346.

—— (1976) Subjective sleep disturbance at menopause. *Journal of Psychosomatic Research*, 20: 509–513.

Bandura, A. (1977) Self-efficacy: Toward a unifying theory of behavioral change. *Psychological Review*, 84: 191–215.

Barber, H.R.K. (1996) Sexuality and the art of arousal in the geriatric woman. *Clinical Obstetrics and Gynecology*, 39: 970–973.

Barlow, D. (1986) Causes of sexual dysfunction: The role of anxiety and cognitive interference. *Journal of Consulting and Clinical Psychology*, 54: 140–148.

Barrett-Connor, E. (1993) Estrogen and estrogen–progestogen replacement: Therapy and cardiovascular diseases. *American Journal of Medicine*, 95: 40S–43S.

Barrett-Connor, E. and Goodman-Gruen, D. (1995) Prospective study of endogenous sex hormones and fatal cardiovascular disease in postmenopausal women. *British Medical Journal*, 311: 1193–1196.

Barrett-Connor, E. and Kritz-Silverstein, D. (1993) Estrogen replacement therapy and cognitive function in older women. *Journal of the American Medical Association*, 269: 2637–2641.

Barrett-Connor, E., Chang, J.C., and Edelstein, S.L. (1994) Coffee-associated osteoporosis offset by daily milk consumption. *Journal of the American Medical Association*, 271: 280–283.

Bart, P. (1969) Why women's status changes in middle age: the turns of the social ferris wheel. *Sociological Symposium*, Fall: 1–14.

Batista, M.C., Cartledge, T., Zellmer, A., Merino, M., Axiotis, C., Bremner, W.J., and Nieman, L.K. (1995) Effects of aging on menstrual cycle hormones and endometrial maturation. *Fertility and Sterility*, 64: 492–499.

Bauer, D.C., Grady, D., Pressman, A., and the Study of Osteoporotic Fractures Research Group (1994) Skin thickness, estrogen use, and bone mass in older women. *Menopause: The Journal of the North American Menopause Society*, 1: 131–136.

Beekman, A.T.F., Kriegsman, D.M.W., Deeg, D.J.H., and van Tilburg, W. (1995) The association of physical health and depressive symptoms in the older population: age and sex differences. *Social Psychiatry and Psychiatric Epidemiology*, 30: 32–38.

Beery, T.A. (1995) Diagnosis and treatment of cardiac disease: Gender bias in the diagnosis and treatment of coronary artery disease. *Heart and Lung*, 24: 427–435.

Belgrave, L.L. (1993) Discrimination against older women in health care. *Journal of Women and Aging*, 5: 181–189.

Bem, S.L. (1993) *The Lenses of Gender*. New Haven: Yale University Press.

Benetar, S.R. (1998) Global disparities in health and human rights: A critical commentary. *American Journal of Public Health*, 88: 295–300.

Bengtsson, C., Bjorkelund, C., Lapidus, L., and Lisser L. (1993) Associations of serum lipid concentrations and obesity with mortality in women: 20 year follow up of participants in prospective population study in Gothenburg, Sweden. *British Medical Journal*, 307: 1385–1388.

Bergkvist, L., Adami, H-O, Persson, J., Hoover, R., and Schairer, C. (1989) The risk of breast cancer after estrogen and estrogen–progestin replacement. *New England Journal of Medicine*, 321: 293–297.

Bergmann, S., Siegert, G., Wahrburg, U., Schulte, H., Assmann, G., Jaross, W., and DRECAN Team (1997) Influence of menopause and lifestyle factors on high density lipoproteins in middle-aged women. *Menopause: Journal of the North American Menopause Society*, 4: 52–61.

Berman, R.S., Epstein, R.S., and Lydick, E.G. (1996) Compliance of women in taking estrogen replacement therapy. *Journal of Women's Health*, 5: 213–220.

Best, N.R., Rees, M.P., Barlow, D.H., and Cowen, P.J. (1992) Effect of estradiol implant on noradrenergic function and mood in menopausal subjects. *Psychoneuroendocrinology*, 17: 87–93.

Beyene, Y. (1986) Cultural significance and physiological manifestations of menopause: A biocultural analysis. *Culture, Medicine, and Psychiatry*, 10: 47–71.

Binder, E.F., Birge, S.J., and Kohrt, W.M. (1996) Effects of endurance exercise and hormone replacement therapy on serum lipids in older women. *Journal of the American Geriatric Society*, 44: 231–236.

Bishop, M. (1996) Estrogen and minor depression in older women. *Newsletter from Institute of Aging* (University of Pennsylvania), 6: 1, 5.

Blake, E.J., Adel, T., and Santoro, N. (1997) Relationships between insulin-like growth hormone factor-I and estradiol in reproductive aging. *Fertility and Sterility*, 67: 697–701.

Blanch, J., Pacifici, R., and Chines, A. (1994) Pregnancy-associated osteoporosis: report of two cases with long-term bone density follow-up. *British Journal of Rheumatology*, 33: 269–272.

Blanchard-Fields, F. (1989) Controllability and adaptive coping in the elderly: an adult developmental perspective. In P.S. Fry (ed.) *Psychological Perspectives of Helplessness and Control in the Elderly*. New York: North-Holland (pp. 43–61).

Blazer, D., Burchett, B., Service, C., and George, L.K. (1991) The association of age and depression among the elderly: an epidemiological exploration. *Journal of Gerontology*, 46: M210–M215.

Blier, R. (1984) *Science and Gender*. New York: Pergamon.

Block, J.E., Smith, R., Black, D., and Genant, H.K. (1987) Does exercise prevent osteoporosis? *Journal of the American Medical Association*, 257: 3115–3117.

Blumenthal, J.A., Emery, C.F., Madden, D.J., Schniebolk, S., Walsh-Riddle, M., George, L.K., McKee, D.C., Higginbotham, M.B., Cobb, F.R., and Coleman, R.D. (1991) Long-term effects of exercise on psychological functioning in older men and women. *Journal of Gerontology*, 46: 352–361.

Boldt, E. (1997) Menopause: The men's version. *American Health*, July/Aug: 100–102.

Bonnier, P., Romain, S., Giacalone, P.L., Laffargue, F., Martin, P.M., and Piana, L. (1995) Clinical and biologic prognostic factors in breast cancer diagnosed during post-menopausal hormone replacement therapy. *Obstetrics and Gynecology*, 85: 11–17.

Bonta, B.D. (1997) Cooperation and competition in peaceful societies. *Psychological Bulletin*, 121: 299–320.

Boston Women's Health Book Collective (1984) *The New Our Bodies, Ourselves*. New York: Simon and Schuster.

Boulet, M.J., Oddens, B.J., Lehert, P., Vemer, H.M. and Visser, A. (1994) Climacteric and menopause in seven South-east Asian countries. *Maturitas*, 19: 157–176.

Bowles, C. (1990) The menopausal experience: Sociocultural influences and theoretical models. In R. Formanek (ed.) *The Meanings of Menopause: Historical, Medical, and Clinical Perspectives*. Hillsdale, NJ: the Analytic Press.

Boyden, T.W., Pamenter, R.W., Going, S.B., Lohman, T.G., Hall, M.C., Houtkooper, L.B., Bunt, J.C., Ritenbaugh, C., and Aickin, M. (1993) Resistance exercise training is associated with decreases in serum low-density lipoprotein cholesterol levels in premenopausal women. *Archives of Internal Medicine*, 153: 97–100.

Brangman, S.A. (1995) African–American elders: Implications for health care providers. *Clinics in Geriatric Medicine*, 11.

Brenner, P.F. (1988) The menopausal syndrome. *Obstetrics and Gynecology*, 72: 6S–11S.

Brett, K.M. and Madans, J.H. (1997) Use of postmenopausal hormone replacement therapy: estimates from a nationally representative cohort study. *American Journal of Epidemiology*, 145: 536–545.

Brody, J.A. and Schneider, E.L. (1986) Diseases and disorders of aging: an hypothesis. *Journal of Chronic Diseases*, 39: 871–876.

Bromberger, J.T. and Matthews, K.A. (1994) Employment status and depressive symptoms in middle-aged women: A longitudinal investigation. *American Journal of Public Health*, 84: 202–206.

—— (1996) A "feminine" model of vulnerability to depressive symptoms: A longitudinal investigation of middle-aged women. *Journal of Personality and Social Psychology*, 70: 591–598.

Brown, S. (1988) Osteoporosis: Sorting fact from fallacy. *The Network News: National Women's Health Network*, July–Aug: 1–2.

Browner, W.S., Pressman, A.R., Evitt, M.C., Cummings, S.R., and the Study of Osteoporotic Fractures Research Group (1996) Mortality following fractures in older women. *Archives of Internal Medicine*, 156: 1521–1525.

Bruce, M.L., Leaf, P.J., Rozal, G.P.M., Florio, L., and Hoff, R.A. (1994) Psychiatric status and 9-year mortality data in the New Haven Epidemiologic Catchment Area Study. *American Journal of Psychiatry*, 151: 716–721.

Brunner, E., White, I., Thorogood, M., Bristow A., Curle, D., and Marmot, M. (1997) Can dietary interventions change diet and cardiovascular risk factors? A meta-analysis of randomized controlled trials. *American Journal of Public Health*, 87: 1415–1422.

Budoff, P.W. (1980) *No More Menstrual Cramps and Other Good News*. New York: G.P. Putnam's Sons.

Bungay, G.T., Vessey, M.P., and McPherson, C.K. (1980) Study of symptoms in middle-life with special reference to the menopause. *British Medical Journal*, July: 181–183.

Burger, H.G., Dudley, E.C., Hopper, J.L., Shelley, J.M., Green, A., Smith, A., Dennerstein, L., and Morse, C. (1995) The endocrinology of the menopausal transition: A cross-sectional study of a population-based sample. *Journal of Clinical Endocrinology and Metabolism*, 80: 3537–3545.

Burnside, I. (1993) Healthy older women – in spite of it all. *Journal of Women and Aging*, 5: 9–24.

Bush, T., Barrett-Connor, E., Cowan, L., Criqui, M., Wallace, R., Suchindran, C., Tyroler, H., and Rifkind, B.M. (1987) Cardiovascular mortality and noncontraceptive use of estrogen in women: Results from the Lipid Research Clinics Program follow-up study. *Circulation*, 75: 1102–1109.

Butler, R.N. (1989) Dispelling ageism: The cross-cutting intervention. *Annals of the American Academy of Political and Social Science*, 503: 138–147.

Butler, R.N., Collins, K., Meier, D., Muller, C.F., and Pinn, V.W. (1995) Older women's health: Clinical care in the postmenopausal years. *Geriatrics*, 50: 33–41.

Caird, M. (1989 [1894]) *The Daughters of Danaus*. New York: The Feminist Press.

Calle, E.E., Miracle-McMahill, H.L., Thun, M.J., and Heath, C.W. (1995) Estrogen replacement therapy and risk of fatal colon cancer in a prospective cohort of post-menopausal women. *Journal of the National Cancer Institute*, 87: 517–523.

Campbell, B.C. and Udry, J.R. (1994) Implications of hormonal influences on sexual behavior for demographic models of reproduction. *Annals of the New York Academy of Sciences*, 709: 117–127.

Campbell, W.W., Crim, M.C., Young, V.R., and Evans, W.J. (1994) Increased energy requirements and changes in body composition with resistance training in older adults. *American Journal of Clinical Nutrition*, 60: 167–175.

Campos-Outcalt, D., Ellis, J., Aickin, M., Valencia, J., Wunsch, M., and Steele, L. (1995) Prevalence of cardiovascular disease risk factors in a southwestern Native American tribe. *Public Health Reports*, 110: 742–748.

Cann, C.E., Martin, M.C., Genant, H.K., and Jaffe, R.B. (1984) Decreased spinal mineral content in amenorrheic women. *Journal of the American Medical Association*, 251: 626–629.

Cannistra, L.B., O'Malley, C.J., and Balady, G.J. (1995) Comparison of outcome of cardiac rehabilitation in Black women and White women. *American Journal of Cardiology*, 75: 890–893.

Cantor, M.H. (1989) Social care: Family and community support systems. *Annals of the American Academy of Political and Social Science*, 503: 99–112.

Carlisle, D.M., Leake, B.D., and Shapiro, M.F. (1997) Racial and ethnic disparities in the use of cardiovascular procedures: Associations with type of health insurance. *American Journal of Public Health*, 87: 263–267.

Carroll, D., Niven, C., and Sheffield, D. (1993) Gender, social circumstances, and health. In C.A. Niven and D. Carroll (eds) *The Health Psychology of Women*. Switzerland: Harwood Academic Publishers (pp. 157–170).

Casey, D. (1994) Depression in the elderly. *Southern Medical Journal*, 87: 559–563.

Casper, R.F., Yen, S.S.C., and Wilkes, M.M. (1979) Menopausal flushes: A neuroen-docrine link with pulsatile luteinizing hormone secretion. *Science*, 205: 823–825.

Cauley, J.A., Gutai, J.P., Kuller, L.H., Scott, J., and Nevitt, M.C. (1994) Black–White differences in serum sex hormones and bone mineral density. *American Journal of Epidemiology*, 139: 1035–1046.

Cauley, J.A., Seeley, D.G., Ensrud, K., Ettinger, B., Black, D., and Cummings, S.R. (1995) Estrogen replacement therapy and fractures in older women. *Annals of Internal Medicine*, 122: 9–16.

Chang, R.J., Plouffe, L. and Schaffer, K. (1994) Physiology of menopause. In J. Lorrain, L. Plouffe, V. Ravnikar, L. Speroff, and N. Watts (eds) *Comprehensive Management of Menopause*. New York: Springer-Verlag.

Chappard, D., Plantard, B., Petitjean, M., Alexandre, C., and Riffat, G. (1991) Alcoholic cirrhosis and osteoporosis in men: A light and scanning electron microscopy study. *Journal of Studies of Alcohol*, 52: 269–274.

Chapuy, M.C., Arlot, M.E., Duboeuf, F., Brun, J., Crouzet, B., Arnaud, S., Delmas, P.D., and Meunier, P.J. (1992) Vitamin D3 and calcium to prevent hip fractures in elderly women. *New England Journal of Medicine*, 327: 1637–1642.

Charles, C., Gafni, A., and Whela, T. (1997) Shared decision-making in the medical encounter: what does it mean? (or it takes at least two to tango). *Social Science and Medicine*, 44: 681–692.

Christiansen, C. and Riis, B. (1990) Five years with continuous combined oestrogen/progestogen therapy: Effects on calcium metabolism, lipoproteins, and bleeding pattern. *British Journal of Obstetrics and Gynaecology*, 97: 1087–1092.

Clapp, J.E. and Little, K. (1995) The interaction between regular exercise and selected aspects of women's health. *American Journal of Obstetrics and Gynecology*, 173: 2–9.

Clark, D.O. (1997) US trends in disability and institutionalization among older Blacks and Whites. *American Journal of Public Health*, 87, 438–440.

Clarkson, T.B., Shivley, C.A., Morgan, T.M., Koritnik, D.R., Adams, M.R., and Kaplan, J.R. (1990) Oral contraceptives and coronary artery atherosclerosis of cynomolgus monkeys. *Obstetrics and Gynecology*, 75: 217–222.

Cline, J.M., Soderqvist, G., von Schoultz, E., Skoog, L., and von Schoultz, B. (1996) Effects of hormone replacement therapy on the mammary gland of surgically post-menopausal cynomolgus macaques. *American Journal of Obstetrics and Gynecology*, 174: 93–100.

Cobleigh, M.A., Berris, R.F., Bush, T., Davidson, N.E., Robert, J., Sparano, J.A., Tormey, D.C., and Wood, W. (1994) Estrogen replacement therapy in breast cancer survivors: A time for change. *Journal of the American Medical Association*, 272: 540–545.

Cockburn, J. and Smith, P.T. (1991) The relative influence of intelligence and age on everyday memory. *Journal of Gerontology*, 46: 31–36.

Cockerill, I.M., Wormington, J.D., and Nevill, A.A. (1994) Menstrual cycle effects on mood and perceptual-motor performance. *Journal of Psychosomatic Research*, 38: 763–771.

Cohen, D. (1994) Dementia, depression, and nutritional status. *Primary Care*, 21: 107–119.

Cohen, S., Tyrell, D.A. and Smith, A.P. (1993) Negative life events, perceived stress, negative affect and susceptibility to the common cold. *Journal of Personality and Social Psychology*, 64: 131–140.

Colditz, G. (1996) The benefits of hormone replacement therapy do not outweigh the increased risk of breast cancer. *Journal of NIH Research*, 8: 40–45.

Colditz, G., Willett, W.C., Stampfer, M., Rosner, B., Speizer, F., and Hennekens, C.H. (1987) Menopause and the risk of coronary heart disease in women. *New England Journal of Medicine*, 316: 1105–1110.

Colditz, G., Egan, K.M., and Stampfer, M.J. (1993) Hormone replacement therapy and risk of breast cancer: results from epidemiologic studies. *American Journal of Obstetrics and Gynecology*, 168: 1473–1480.

Collaborative Group on Hormonal Factors in Breast Cancer (1997) Breast cancer and hormone replacement therapy: Collaborative reanalysis of data from 51 epidemiological studies of 52,705 women with breast cancer and 108,411 women without breast cancer. *Lancet*, 350: 1047–1059.

Coney, S. (1994) *The Menopause Industry: How the medical establishment exploits women.* Alameda, CA: Hunter House.

Conrad, J., Basdevant, A., Thomas, J-L., Ochsenbein, E., Denis, C., Guyene, T.T., and Degrelle, H. (1995) Cardiovascular risk factors and combined estrogen–progestin replacement therapy: A placebo-controlled study with nomegestral acetate and estradiol. *Fertility and Sterility*, 64: 957–962.

Cooke, D.J. and Greene, J.D. (1981) Types of life events in relation to symptoms at the climacterium. *Journal of Psychosomatic Research*, 25: 5–11.

Cooper, A. and Whitehead, M. (1995) Menopause: refining benefits and risks of hormone replacement therapy. *Current Opinion in Obstetrics and Gynecology*, 7: 214–219.

Corby, N. and Azrit, J.M. (1983) Old and alone: the unmarried in later life. In R.B. Weg (ed.) *Sexuality in the Later Years: Roles and Behavior*. New York: Academic Press.

Corson, S. (1995) A practical guide to prescribing estrogen replacement therapy. *International Journal of Fertility*, 40: 229–247.

Corti, M-C., Guralnik, J.M., Salive, M.E., Harris, T., Field, T.S., Wallace, R.B., Berkman, L.F., Seeman, T.E., Glynn, R.J., Hennekens, C.H., and Havlik, R.J. (1995) HDL cholesterol predicts coronary heart disease mortality in older persons. *Journal of the American Medical Association*, 274: 539–544.

Couzi, R.J., Helzlsouer, K.J., and Fetting, J.H. (1995) Prevalence of menopausal symptoms among women with a history of breast cancer and attitudes toward estrogen replacement therapy. *Journal of Clinical Oncology*, 13: 2737–2744.

Crombez, G., Eccleston, C., Baeyens, F., and Elen, P. (1996) The disruptive nature of pain: An experimental investigation. *Behaviour Research and Therapy*, 34: 911–918.

Crouch, E.A.C. and Wilson, R. (1982) *Risk/Benefit Analysis*. Cambridge: Ballinger Publishing.

Cummings, S.R. (1985) Are patients with hip fractures more osteoporotic? Review of the evidence. *American Journal of Medicine*, 78: 487–494.

Cunningham, W.R. and Brookbank, J.W. (1988) *Gerontology: The Psychology, Biology, and Sociology of Aging*. New York: Harper & Row.

Cutler, W.B. (1988) *Hysterectomy: Before and After*. New York: Harper & Row.

Cutler, W.B. and Garcia, C-R. (1992) *Menopause: A Guide for Women and Men Who Love Them*. New York: Norton.

Dalsky, G.P., Stocke, K.S., Ehsani, A.A., Slatopolsky, E., Lee, W.C., and Birge, S.I. (1988) Weight-bearing exercise training and lumbar bone mineral content in postmenopausal women. *Annals of Internal Medicine*, 108: 824–828.

Daly, E., Vessey, M.P., Hawkins, M.M., Carson, J., Gough, P., and Marsh, S. (1996) Risk of venous thromboembolism in users of hormone replacement therapy. *Lancet*, 348: 977–980.

Daly, L. and Bonner, J. (1990) Comparative studies of 30 μg ethinyl estradiol combined with gestodene and desogestrel on blood coagulation, fibrinolysis, and platelets. *American Journal of Obstetrics and Gynecology*, 163: 430–437.

Daniel, J. (1994) Learning to love growing old. *Psychology Today*, Sept/Oct: 61–70.

Daniell, H.W. (1997) Osteoporosis after orchiectomy for prostate cancer. *Journal of Urology*, 157: 439–444.

Datan, N. and Rodeheaver, D. (1983) Beyond generativity: Toward a sensuality of later life. In R.B. Weg (ed.) *Sexuality in the Later Years: Roles and Behavior*. New York: Academic Press.

Davidson, J.M. (1980) Hormones and sexual behavior in the male. In D.T. Krieger and J.C. Hughes (eds) *Neuroendocrinology*. Sunderland, MA: Sinauer Associates.

Davis, J.W., Ross, P.D., and Wasnich, R.D. (1995) A longitudinal study of estrogen and calcium supplement use among Japanese women living in Hawaii. *Preventative Medicine*, 24: 159–165.

Davis, M.A., Moritz, D.J., Neuhaus, J.M., Barclay, J.D., and Gee, L. (1997) Living arrangements, changes in living arrangements, and survival among community dwelling older adults. *American Journal of Public Health*, 87: 371–377.

Davis, S., Winkeby, M.A., and Farquher, J.W. (1995) Increasing disparity in knowledge of cardiovascular disease risk factors and risk-reduction strategies by socioeconomic status: Implications for policy-makers. *American Journal of Preventative Medicine*, 11: 318–323.

Davis-Berman, J. (1988) Self-efficacy and depressive symptomatology in older adults: An exploratory study. *International Journal of Aging and Human Development*, 27: 32–39.

Dawson-Hughes, B. (1991) Calcium supplementation and bone loss: A review of controlled clinical trials. *American Journal of Clinical Nutrition*, 54: 274S–280S.

Dawson-Hughes, B., Dallal, G.E., Krall, E.A., Harris, S., Sokoll, L., and Falconer, G. (1991) Effect of vitamin D supplementation on wintertime and overall bone loss in healthy postmenopausal women. *Annals of Internal Medicine*, 115: 505–512.

Dawson-Hughes, B., Harris, S.S., Krall, E.A., Dallal, G.E., Falconer, G., and Green, C.L. (1995) Rates of bone loss in postmenopausal women randomly assigned to one of two dosages of vitamin D. *American Journal of Clinical Nutrition*, 61: 1140–1145.

de Bakker, I.P. and Everaerd, W. (1996) Measurement of menopausal hot flushes: Validation and cross-validation. *Maturitas*, 25: 87–98.

De Beauvoir, S. (1953) *The Second Sex*, translated by H.M. Parshley. New York: Knopf.

Denke, M.A. (1994) Individual responsiveness to a cholesterol-lowering diet in postmenopausal women with moderate hypercholesterolemia. *Archives of Internal Medicine*, 154: 1977–1982.

Denney, N. (1986) Practical problem solving. Paper presented at the meeting of the American Psychological Association, Washington, D.C.

Depner, C.E. and Ingersoll-Dayton, B. (1985) Conjugal social support: Patterns in later life. *Journal of Gerontology*, 40: 761–766.

Deptula, D., Singh, R., and Pomara, N. (1993) Aging, emotional states and memory. *American Journal of Psychiatry*, 150: 429–434.

Derby, C.A., Hume, A.L., McPhillips, J.B., Barbour, M.M., and Carleton, R.A. (1995) Prior and current health characteristics of postmenopausal estrogen replacement therapy users compared with nonusers. *American Journal of Obstetrics and Gynecology*, 173: 544–550.

Derman, R.J. (1995) Effects of sex steroids on women's health: Implications for practitioners. *American Journal of Medicine*, 98: 137S–143S.

Dinnerstein, M. and Weitz, R. (1994) Jane Fonda, Barbara Bush and other aging bodies: Femininity and the limits of resistance. *Feminist Issues*, fall: 3–24.

Doress-Worters, P.B. (1994) Adding elder care to women's multiple roles: A critical review of the caregiver stress and multiple roles literatures. *Sex Roles*, 31: 597–616.

Douketis, J.D., Ginsberg, J.S., Holbrook, A., Crowther, M., Duku, E.K., and Burrows, R.F. (1997) A reevaluation of the risk for venous thromboembolism with the use of oral contraceptives and hormone replacement therapy. *Archives of Internal Medicine*, 157: 1522–1530.

Doyle, G.J. and McLean, L. (1994) Unilateral increase in mammographic density with hormone replacement therapy. *Clinical Radiology*, 49: 50–51.

Drinkwater, B.L., Nilson, K., Chestnut, C.H., Bremner, W.J., Shainholtz, S., and Southworth, M.B. (1984) Bone mineral content of menorrheic and amenorrheic athletes. *New England Journal of Medicine*, 311: 277–281.

Dufour, M., Archer, L., and Gordis, E. (1992) Alcohol and the elderly. *Clinics in Geriatric Medicine*, 8: 127–141.

Eaton, C.B., Reynes, J., Assaf, A.R., Feldman, H., Lasater, T., and Carleton, R.A. (1993) Predicting physical activity change in men and women in two New England communities. *American Journal of Preventative Medicine*, 9: 209–219.

Ebbiary, N.A.A., Lenton, E.A. and Cooke, I.D. (1994) Hypothalamic–pituitary ageing: progressive increase in FSH and LH concentrations throughout the reproductive life in regularly menstruating women. *Clinical Endocrinology*, 41: 199–206.

Eden, J.A. and Wren, B.G. (1996) Hormone replacement therapy after breast cancer: a review. *Cancer Treatment Reviews*, 22: 335–343.

Ehrenreich, B. and English, D. (1979) *For Her Own Good: 150 Years of the Experts' Advice to Women*. Garden City NY: Anchor.

Elias, M.F., Elias, J.W., and Elias, P.K. (1990) Biological and health influences on behavior. In J.E. Birren and K.W. Schaie (eds) *Handbook of the Psychology of Aging (3rd edn)*. New York: Academic Press (pp. 79–102).

Eller, D. and Goldstein, L. (1997) Master the slender life. *Prevention*, July: 100–108.

Ellison, P. and Lager, C. (1986) Moderate recreational running is associated with lowered salivary progesterone profiles in women. *American Journal of Obstetrics and Gynecology*, 154: 1000–1003.

Emster, V.L., Grady, D., Miike, R., Black, D., Selby, J., and Kerlikowske, K. (1995) Facial wrinkling in men and women, by smoking status. *American Journal of Public Health*, 85: 78–82.

Erlik, Y., Meldrum, D.R., and Judd, H.L. (1982) Estrogen levels in postmenopausal women with hot flashes. *Obstetrics and Gynecology*, 59: 403–407.

Ettinger, B. (1988) Optimal use of postmenopausal hormone replacement. *Obstetrics and Gynecology*, 72: 31S–36S.

Ettinger, B., Selby, J.V., Citron, J.T., Ettinger, V.M., and Zhang, D. (1993) Gynecologic complications of cyclic estrogen progestin therapy. *Maturitas*, 17: 197–204.

Ettinger, B., Friedman, G.D., Bush, T., and Quesenberry, C.P. (1996) Reduced mortality associated with long-term postmenopausal estrogen therapy. *Obstetrics and Gynecology*, 87: 6–12.

Evans, W.J. (1995) Effects of exercise on body composition and functional capacity of the elderly. *Journal of Gerontology*, 30A: 147–150.

Everson, S.A., Matthews, K.A., Guzick, D.S., Wing, R., and Kuller, L.H. (1995) Effects of surgical menopause on psychological characteristics and lipid levels: the Healthy Women Study. *Health Psychology*, 14: 435–443.

Fairney, A., Kyd, P., Thomas, E., and Wilson, J. (1998) The use of cyclical etidronate in osteoporosis: Changes after completion of 3 years' treatment. *British Journal of Rheumatology*, 37: 51–56.

Farish, E., Fletcher, C.D., Hart, D.M., and Smith, M.L. (1990) Effects of bilateral oophorectomy on lipoprotein metabolism. *British Journal of Obstetrics and Gynaecology*, 97: 78–82.

Feldman, H.A., Goldstein, I., Hatzichristou, D.G., Krane, R.J., and McKinlay, J.B. (1994) Impotence and its medical and psychosocial correlates: results of the Massachusetts male aging study. *Journal of Urology*, 151: 54–61.

Felson, D.T., Zhang, Y., Hannan, M.T., Kiel, D.P., Wilson, P.W.F., and Anderson, J.J. (1993) The effect of postmenopausal estrogen therapy on bone density in elderly women. *New England Journal of Medicine*, 329: 1141–1146.

Felson, D.T., Zhang, Y., Hannan, M.T., Kannel, W.B., and Kiel, D.P. (1995) Alcohol intake and bone mineral density in elderly men and women. *American Journal of Epidemiology*, 142: 485–492.

Fentem, P.H. (1994) Benefits of exercise in health and disease. *British Journal of Medicine*, 308: 1291–1295.

Ferin, M., Jewelewicz, R., and Warren, M. (1993) *The Menstrual Cycle: Physiology, Reproductive Disorders, and Infertility*. New York: Oxford University Press.

Fessler, L. (1950) The psychopathology of climacteric depression. *Psychoanalytic Quarterly*, 19: 27–41.

Field, C.S., Ory, S.J., Wahner, H.W., Herrmann, R.R., Judd, H.L., and Riggs, B.L. (1993) Preventive effects of transdermal 17B-estradiol on osteoporotic changes after surgical menopause: A two-year placebo-controlled trial. *American Journal of Obstetrics and Gynecology*, 168: 114–121.

Findlay, I., Cunningham, D., and Dargie, H.J. (1994) Coronary heart disease, the menopause, and hormone replacement therapy. *British Heart Journal*, 71: 213–214.

Fitzgerald, C.T., Killick, S.R., and Bennett, D.A. (1994) Age related changes in the female reproductive tract. *British Journal of Obstetrics and Gynaecology*, 101: 229–233.

Flint, M. and Samil, R.S. (1990) Cultural and subcultural meanings of the menopause. *Annals of the New York Academy of Sciences*, 592: 134–148.

Foa, E., Zinbarg, R., and Rothblum, B.O. (1992) Uncontrollability and unpredictability in post-traumatic stress disorders. *Psychological Bulletin*, 112: 218–238.

Fogel, C.E. and Woods, N.F. (1995) Midlife women's health. In C.I. Fogel and N.F. Woods (eds) *Women's Health Care: A Comprehensive Handbook*. Thousand Oaks: Sage (pp. 79–100).

Fogelman, I. (1991) Oestrogen, the prevention of bone loss and osteoporosis. *British Journal of Rheumatology*, 30: 276–281.

Folsom, A.R., McGovern, P.G., Nabulsi, A.A., Shahar, E., Kahn, E.S.B., Winkhart, S.P., and White, A.D. (1996) Changes in plasma lipids and lipoproteins associated with starting or stopping postmenopausal hormone replacement therapy. *American Heart Journal*, 132: 952–958.

Formanek, R. (1990) Continuity and change and "The Change of Life": Premodern views of the menopause. In R. Formanek (ed.) *The Meanings of Menopause: Historical, Medical and Clinical Perspectives*. Hillsdale NJ: The Analytic Press.

Foucault, M. (1978) *The History of Sexuality: Volume I: An Introduction*. New York: Pantheon Books.

Franklin, S.T., Ames, B.D., and King, S. (1994) Acquiring the family elder care role. *Research on Aging*, 16: 27–42.

Freedman, R. and Woodward, S. (1992) Behavioral treatment of menopausal hot flushes: Evaluation by ambulatory monitoring. *American Journal of Obstetrics and Gynecology*, 167: 439–449.

French, M. (1992) *The War Against Women*. New York: Ballantine.

Frey, K.A. (1982) Middle-aged women's experience and perception of menopause. *Women and Health*, 6: 25–36.

Fries, J.F. (1989) The compression of morbidity: near or far? *The Millbank Quarterly*, 67: 208–232.

Fries, J., Singh, G., Morfeld, D., Hubert, H.B., Lane, N.E., and Brown B.W. (1994) Running and the development of disability with age. *Annals of Internal Medicine*, 121: 502–509.

Fry, P.S. (1989) Preconceptions of vulnerability and control in old age: A critical reconstruction. In P.S. Fry (ed.) *Psychological Perspectives of Helplessness and Control in the Elderly*. New York: North-Holland (pp. 1–39).

Fuchs, C.S., Stampfer, M.J., Colditz, G.A., Giovannucci, E.L., Manson, J.E., Kawachi, I., Hunter, D.J., Hankinson, S.E., Hennekens, C.H., Rosner, B., Speizer, F.E., and Willett, W.C. (1995) Alcohol consumption and mortality among women. *New England Journal of Medicine*, 332: 1245–1250.

Gallagher, J.C. (1996) The role of vitamin D in the pathogenesis and treatment of osteoporosis. *Journal of Rheumatology*, 23: 15–18.

Gallo, J.J., Royall, D.R., and Anthony, J.C. (1993) Risk factors for the onset of depression in middle age and later life. *Social Psychiatry and Psychiatric Epidemiology*, 28: 101–108.

Gamble, V.N. (1997) Under the shadow of Tuskegee: African Americans and health care. *American Journal of Public Health*, 57: 112–137.

Gambrell, R.D. (1990) Estrogen therapy and breast cancer. *International Journal of Fertility*, 35: 202–204.

—— (1995) Combined continuous hormone replacement therapy: A critical review. *Obstetrics and Gynecology*, 86: 869–870.

Gambrell, R.D., Massey, F.M., Castaneda, T.A., Ugenas, A.J., Ricci, C.A., and Wright, J.M. (1980) Use of progestogen challenge test to reduce the risk of endometrial cancer. *Obstetrics and Gynecology*, 55: 732–738.

Gambrell, R.D., Hillard, P., Jones, K.P., Mishell, D.R., Nachtigall, L.E., and Weinstein, L. (1993) Promoting compliance with HRT: A round table discussion. *Menopause Management*, May: 10–16, 35–38.

Gannon, L.R. (1985) *Menstrual Disorders and Menopause: Biological, Psychological, and Cultural Research*. New York: Praeger.

—— (1990) Endocrinology of menopause. In R. Formanek (ed.) *The Meanings of Menopause: Historical, Medical and Clinical Perspectives*. Hillsdale, NJ: The Analytic Press.

—— (1996) Perspectives on biological, social, and psychological phenomena in middle- and old-age women: Interference or intervention? In S. Clancy and L. DiLalla (eds) *Assessment and Intervention Issues Across the Life-span*. New York: Lawrence Erlbaum.

Gannon, L.R. and Ekstrom, B. (1993) Attitudes toward menopause: The influence of sociocultural paradigms. *Psychology of Women Quarterly*, 17: 275–288.

Gannon, L.R. and Stevens, J. (in press) Portraits of menopause in the print media. *Women and Health*.

Gannon, L.R., Hansel, S., and Goodwin, J. (1987) Correlates of menopausal hot flashes. *Journal of Behavioral Medicine*, 10: 277–285.

Gardner, A.W. and Poehlman, E.T. (1995) Predictors of the age-related increase in blood pressure in men and women. *Journal of Gerontology*, 50A: M1–M6.

Garrison, R.J., Sawin, C.T., Alexander, L.L., and Wilson, P.W.F. (1994) Plasma estradiol in premenopausal women: the Framingham offspring study. *Journal of Women's Health*, 3: 435–443.

Garton, M., Reid, D., and Rennie, E. (1994) The climacteric, osteoporosis and hormone replacement; views of women aged 45–49. *Maturitas*, 21: 7–15.

Gasperino, J.A., Wang, J., Pierson, R.N., and Heymsfield, S.B. (1995) Age-related changes in musculoskeletal mass between Black and White women. *Metabolism*, 44: 30–34.

Gatz, M., Harris, J.R., and Turk-Charles, S. (1995) The meaning of health for older women. In A.L. Stanton and S.J. Gallant (eds) *The Psychology of Women's Health: Progress and Challenges in Research and Application*. Washington DC: American Psychological Association (pp. 491–529).

Gavaler, J.S. and Van Thiel, D.H. (1992) The association between moderate alcoholic beverage consumption and serum estradiol and testosterone levels in normal postmenopausal women: Relationship to the literature. *Alcoholism: Clinical and Experimental Research*, 16: 87–91.

George, G.C.W., Utian, W.H., Beumont, P.J.V., and Beardwood, C.J. (1973) Effect of exogenous oestrogens on minor psychiatric symptoms in postmenopausal women. *South African Medical Journal*, 47: 2387–2388.

Gerber, N.J. and Rey, B. (1991) Can exercise prevent osteoporosis? *British Journal of Rheumatology*, 30: 2–3.

Gerdes, L.C., EtPhil, D.L., Sonnendecker, E.W.W., and Polakow, E.S. (1982) Psychological changes effected by estrogen–progesterone and clonidine treatment in climacteric women. *American Journal of Obstetrics and Gynecology*, 142: 98–104.

Gergen, M. (1989) Loss of control among the aging? A critical reconstruction. In P.S. Fry (ed.) *Psychological Perspectives of Helplessness and Control in the Elderly*. New York: North-Holland (pp. 261–290).

Gilligan, C. (1982) *In a Different Voice: Psychological Theory and Women's Development*. Cambridge, MA: Harvard University Press.

Gilman, C.P. (1970 [1911]) *The Man-Made World or Our Androcentric Culture*. New York: Charlton Company.

Ginsburg, E.S., Mello, N.K., Mendelson, J.H., Barbieri, R.L., Teoh, S.K., Rothman, M., Gao, X., and Sholar, J.W. (1996) Effects of alcohol ingestion on estrogens in postmenopausal women. *Journal of the American Medical Association*, 276: 1747–1751.

Ginsburg, J., Swinhow, J., and O'Reilly, B. (1981) Cardiovascular responses during the menopausal hot flush. *British Journal of Obstetrics and Gynaecology*, 88: 925–930.

Glass, A.G. and Hoover, R.N. (1990) Rising incidence of breast cancer: Relationship to stage and receptor status. *Journal of the National Cancer Institute*, 82: 693–696.

Glick, P. and Fiske, S.T. (1997) Hostile and benevolent sexism. *Psychology of Women Quarterly*, 21: 119–135.

Gloth, F.M., Gundberg, C.M., Hollis, B.W., Haddad, J.G., and Tobin, J.D. (1995) Vitamin D deficiency in homebound elderly persons. *Journal of the American Medical Association*, 274: 1683–1686.

Godsland, I.F., Wynn, V., Path, F.R.C., Crook, D., and Miller, N.E. (1987) Sex, plasma lipoproteins and atherosclerosis: Prevailing assumptions and outstanding questions. *American Heart Journal*, 114: 1467–1501.

Goff, D.C., Ramsey, D.J., Labarthe, D.R., and Nichaman, M.Z. (1994) Greater case-fatality after myocardial infarction among Mexican Americans and women than among non-Hispanic Whites and men. *American Journal of Epidemiology*, 139: 474–483.

Goldstein, M.K. and Teng, N.N.H. (1991) Gynecologic factors in sexual dysfunction of the older woman. *Clinics in Geriatric Medicine*, 7: 41–61.

Golier, J.A., Marzuk, P.M., Leon, A.C., Weiner, C., and Tardiff, K. (1995) Low serum cholesterol level and attempted suicide. *American Journal of Psychiatry*, 152: 419–423.

Gong, E.J., Garrel, D., and Calloway, D.H. (1989) Menstrual cycle and basal metabolic rate in women. *American Journal of Clinical Nutrition*, 49: 252–258.

Gordon, G.S. (1990) Prevention of bone loss and fractures in women. *Maturitas*, 6: 225–242.

Gordon, S.F., Thompson, K.A., Ruoff, G.E., Imig, J.R., Lane, P.J., Schwenker, C.E., and the Transdermal Estradiol Patch Study Group (1995) Efficacy and safety of a seven-day, transdermal estradiol drug-delivery system: Comparison with conjugated estrogens and placebo. *International Journal of Fertility*, 40: 126–134.

Gorsky, R.D., Koplan, J.P., Peterson, H.B., and Thacker, S.B. (1994) Relative risks and benefits of long-term estrogen replacement therapy: A decision analysis. *Obstetrics and Gynecology*, 83: 161–166.

Grady, D., Gebretsadik, T., Kerlikowske, K., Ernster, V., and Petitti, D. (1995) Hormone replacement therapy and endometrial cancer risk: A meta-analysis. *Obstetrics and Gynecology*, 85: 304–313.

Graeber, R.C. (1982) Alterations in performance following rapid transmeridian flight. In F.M. Brown, and R.C. Graeber (eds) *Rhythmic Aspects of Behavior*. Hillsdale NJ: Lawrence Erlbaum.

Grambs, J.D. (1989) *Women over Forty: Visions and realities*. New York: Springer.

Green, L.A. and Ruffin, M.T. (1994) A closer examination of sex bias in the treatment of ischemic cardiac disease. *Journal of Family Practice*, 39: 331–336.

Greenberg, E.R., Barnes, A.B., Resseguie, L., Barrett, J.A., Burnside, S., Lauza, L.L., Neff, R.K., Stevens, M., Young, R.H., and Colton, T. (1984) Breast cancer in mothers given diethylstilbesterol in pregnancy. *New England Journal Of Medicine*, 311: 1393–1398.

Greendale, G.A., Barrett-Connor, E., Edelstein, S., Ingles, S., and Haile, R. (1995) Life-time leisure exercise and osteoporosis. *American Journal of Epidemiology*, 141: 951–959.

Greendale, G.A. and Judd, H.L. (1993) The menopause: Health implications and clinical management. *Journal of the American Geriatric Society*, 41: 426–436.

Greendale, G.A., Bodin-Dunn, L., Ingles, S., Haile, R., and Barrett-Connor, E. (1996) Leisure, home, and occupational physical activity and cardiovascular risk factors in postmenopausal women. *Archives of Internal Medicine*, 156: 418–424.

Greene, J.G. and Cooke, D.J. (1980) Life stress and symptoms at the climacterium. *British Journal of Psychiatry*, 136: 486–491.

Gregg, E.W., Kriska, A.M., Fox, K.M., and Cauley, J.A. (1996) Self-rated health and the spectrum of physical activity and physical function in older women. *Journal of Aging and Physical Activity*, 4: 349–361.

Grimes, D.A. (1988) Prevention of cardiovascular disease in women: Role of the obstetrician–gynecologist. *American Journal of Obstetrics and Gynecology*, 158: 1662–1668.

Grodin, J.M., Siiteri, P.K., and MacDonald, P.C. (1973) Source of estrogen production in postmenopausal women. *Journal of Clinical Endocrinology and Metabolism*, 36: 207–214.

Grodstein, F. and Stampfer, M. (1995) The epidemiology of coronary heart disease and estrogen replacement in postmenopausal women. *Progress in Cardiovascular Disease*, 38: 199–210.

Grodstein, F., Stampfer, M.J., Goldhaber, S.Z., Manson, J.E., Colditz, G.A., Speizer, F.E., Willett, W.C., and Hennekens, C.H. (1996) Prospective study of exogenous hormones and risk of pulmonary embolism in women. *Lancet*, 348: 983–987.

Gronbaek, M., Deis, A., Sorensen, T.A., Becker, U., Schnohr, P., and Jensen, G. (1995) Mortality associated with moderate intakes of wine, beer, or spirits. *British Medical Journal*, 310: 1165–1169.

Gupta, K. (1990) Sexual dysfunction in elderly women. *Clinics in Geriatric Medicine*, 6: 197–203.

Guralik, J.M. and Leveille, S.G. (1997) Annotation: Race, ethnicity, and health outcomes – unraveling the mediating role of socioeconomic status. *American Journal of Public Health*, 87: 728–729.

Gutthann, S.P., Rodrigues, L.A.G., Castellsague, J., and Oliart, A.D. (1997) Hormone replacement therapy and risk of venous thromboembolism: population based case-control study. *British Medical Journal*, 314: 977–981.

Guyton, A.C. (1982) *Human Physiology and Mechanisms of Disease*. Philadelphia: W.B. Saunders.

Haber, C. (1983) *Beyond Sixty-five: The Dilemma of Old Age in America's Past*. New York: Cambridge University Press.

Haertel, U., Heiss, G., Filipiak, B., and Doering, A. (1992) Cross-sectional and longitudinal associations between high density lipoprotein cholesterol and women's employment. *American Journal of Epidemiology*, 135: 68–78.

Haffner, S., Newcomb, P.A., Marcus, P., Klein, B., and Klein, R. (1995) Relation of sex hormones and dehydroepiandrosterone sulfate (DHEA-SO4) to cardiovascular risk factors in postmenopausal women. *American Journal of Epidemiology*, 142: 925–934.

Hahn, R. (1989) Compliance considerations with estrogen replacement: Withdrawal bleeding and other factors. *American Journal of Obstetrics and Gynecology*, 161: 1854–1855.

Halbreich, U., Rojansky, N., Palter, S., Hreshchyshy, M., Kreeger, J., Bakhai, Y., and Rosan, R. (1995) Decreased bone mineral density in medicated psychiatric patients. *Psychosomatic Medicine*, 57: 485–491.

Hale, R.W., Kosasa, T., Krieger, J., and Pepper, S. (1983) Human plasma beta-endorphin through the menstrual cycle. *Psychopharmacology Bulletin*, 19: 586–587.

Hallstrom, T. and Samuelsoon, S. (1990) Changes in women's sexual desire in middle age: The longitudinal study of women in Gothenburg. *Archives of Sexual Behavior*, 19: 259–268.

Hammar, M.L., Lindgren, R., Berg, G.E., Moller, C.G., and Niklasson, M.K. (1996) Effects of hormonal replacement therapy on the postural balance among postmenopausal women. *Obstetrics and Gynecology*, 88: 955–960.

Hammond, C.B. (1996) Menopause and hormone replacement therapy: An overview. *Obstetrics and Gynecology*, 87: 2S–15S.

Han, Z-H., Palnitkar, S., Sudhaker, D., Nelson, D., and Parfitt, A.M. (1996) Effect of ethnicity and age or menopause on the structure and geometry of iliac bone. *Journal of Bone and Mineral Research*, 11: 1967–1975.

193

Hanna, E., Dufour, M., Elliott, S., Stinson, F., and Harford, T.C. (1992) Dying to be equal: Women, alcohol, and cardiovascular disease. *British Journal of Addiction*, 87: 1593–1597.

Hardy, M.A. and Hazelrigg, L.E. (1993) The gender of poverty in an aging population. *Research on Aging*, 15: 243–278.

—— (1995) Gender, race/ethnicity, and poverty in later life. *Journal of Aging Studies*, 9: 43–63.

Harlow, R.E. and Cantor, N. (1996) Still participating after all these years: A study of life task participation in later life. *Journal of Personality and Social Psychology*, 71: 1235–1249.

Harris, J., Lippman, M.E., Veronesi, U., and Willet, W. (1992) Breast cancer. *New England Journal of Medicine*, 327: 319–327.

Harris, S.S. and Dawson-Hughes, B. (1994) Caffeine and bone loss in healthy post-menopausal women. *American Journal of Clinical Nutrition*, 60: 573–578.

—— (1996) Weight, body composition, and bone density in postmenopausal women. *Calcified Tissue International*, 59: 428–432.

Hartman, B.W., Kirchengast, S., Albrecht, A.E., Soregi, G., and Huber, J.C. (1996) Altered growth hormone (GH) secretion in women gaining weight during hormone replacement therapy (HRT). *Maturitas*, 25: 29–34.

Hatch, L.R. (1991) Informal support patterns of older African–American and White women. *Research on Aging*, 13: 144–170.

Hay, A.G., Bandroft, J., and Johnstone, E.C. (1994) Affective symptoms in women attending a menopause clinic. *British Journal of Psychiatry*, 164: 513–516.

Hays, J.D., Kasl, S.V., and Jacobs, S.C. (1994) The course of psychological distress following threatened and actual conjugal bereavement. *Psychological Medicine*, 24: 917–927.

Healy, D. and Williams, J.M.G. (1988) Dysrhythmia, dysphoria, and depression: The interaction of learned helplessness and circadian dysrhythmia in pathogenesis of depression. *Psychological Bulletin*, 103: 163–178.

Heaney, R.P. (1990) Estrogen–calcium interactions in the postmenopause: A quantitative description. *Bone and Mineral*, 11: 67–84.

—— (1993) Thinking straight about calcium. *New England Journal of Medicine*, 328: 503–505.

—— (1998) Bone mass, bone loss, and osteoporosis prophylaxis. *Annals of Internal Medicine*, 128: 313–314.

Heiman, J. and Hatch, J.P. (1981) Conceptual and therapeutic contributions of psychophysiology to sexual dysfunction. In S.N. Haynes and L.R. Gannon (eds) *Psycho-somatic Disorders: A Psychophysiological Approach to Etiology and Treatment*. New York: Praeger.

Hekhausen, J. and Schulz, R. (1995) A life-span theory of control. *Psychological Review*, 102: 284–304.

Helstrom, L., Sorbom, D., and Backstron, T. (1995) Influence of partner relationship on sexuality after subtotal hysterectomy. *Acta Obstetrica Gynecologia Scandinavia*, 74: 142–146.

Helzlsouer, K.J., Alberg, M.H.S., Gordon, G.B., Longcope, C., Bush, T.L., Hoffman, S.C., and Comstock, G.W. (1995) Serum gonadotropins and steroid hormones and the development of ovarian cancer. *Journal of the American Medical Association*, 274: 1926–1929.

Hemingway, H., Nicholson, A., Stafford, M., Roberts, R., and Marmot, M. (1997) The impact of socioeconomic status on health functioning as assessed by the SF-36 questionnaire: The Whitehall II study. *American Journal of Public Health*, 87: 1484–1491.

Hemminki, E., Topo, P., Malin, M., and Kangas, I. (1993) Physicians' views on hormone therapy around and after menopause. *Maturitas*, 16: 163–173.

Hemsell, D.L., Grodin, J.M., Brenner, P.F., Siiteri, P.K., and MacDonald, P.D. (1974) Plasma precursors of estrogen. II. Correlation of extent of conversion of plasma androstenedione to estrone with age. *Journal of Clinical Endocrinology and Metabolism*, 38: 476–479.

Henderson, B.E., Paganini-Hill, A., and Ross, R.K. (1988) Estrogen replacement therapy and protection from acute myocardial infarction. *American Journal of Obstetrics and Gynecology*, 159: 312–317.

Heston, T.F. and Lewis, L.M. (1992) Gender bias in the evaluation and management of acute nontraumatic chest pain. *Family Practice Research*, 12: 383–389.

Hetherington, M.M. and Burnett, L. (1994) Ageing and the pursuit of slimness: Dietary restraint and weight satisfaction in elderly women. *British Journal of Clinical Psychology*, 33: 391–400.

Hibbard, J.H. and Pope, C.R. (1992) Women's employment, social support, and mortality. *Women and Health*, 18: 119–133.

Hillbrand, M. and Spitz, R.T. (1997) Introduction. In M. Hillbrand and R.T. Spitz (eds) *Lipids, Health, and Behavior*. Washington DC: American Psychological Association (pp. 1–11).

Hirvonen, E. and Idanpaan-Heikkila, J. (1990) Cardiovascular death among women under 40 years of age using low-estrogen oral contraceptives and intrauterine devices in Finland from 1975 to 1984. *American Journal of Obstetrics and Gynecology*, 163: 281–284.

Hite, S. (1987) *The Hite Report: Women and Love*. New York: Knopf.

Hoberman, J.M. and Yesalis, C.E. (1995) The history of synthetic testosterone. *Scientific American*, February: 76–81.

Hodsman, A., Adachi, J., and Olszynski, W. (1996) Prevention and management of osteoporosis: consensus statements from the Scientific Advisory Board of the Osteoporosis Society of Canada: 6: Use of bisphosphonates in the treatment of osteoporosis. *Canadian Medical Association Journal*, 155: 945–948.

Hogan, D.P. and Eggebeen, D.J. (1995) Sources of emergency help and routine assistance in old age. *Social Forces*, 73: 917–936.

Holbrook, T.L. and Barrett-Connor, E. (1993) A prospective study of alcohol consumption and bone mineral density. *British Medical Journal*, 306: 1506–1509.

Holcomb, W.L., Stone, L.S., Lustman, P.J., Gavard, J.A. and Mostello, D. (1996) Screening for depression in pregnancy: Characteristics of the Beck Depression Inventory. *Obstetrics and Gynecology*, 88: 1021–1025.

Holte, A. (1992) Influences of natural menopause on health complaints: A prospective study of healthy Norwegian women. *Maturitas*, 14: 127–141.

Holte, A. and Mikkelsen, A. (1991) The menopausal syndrome: A factor analytic replication. *Maturitas*, 13: 193–203.

Hopkins, M. (1996) Menopause: Who, what, where, and why's. *Canadian Pharmaceutical Journal*, October: 45–47.

Hopper, J.L. and Seeman, E. (1994) The bone density of female twins discordant for tobacco use. *New England Journal of Medicine*, 330: 387–392.

Horn, J.L. (1975) *Psychometric Studies of Aging and Intelligence*. New York: Raven Press.

Horn, J.L. and Donaldson, G. (1980) Cognitive development in adulthood. In O.G. Brim, Jr. and J. Kagan (eds) (1980) *Constancy and Change in Human Development*. Cambridge, MA: Harvard University Press (pp. 445–529).

House, J.S., Lepkowski, J.M., Kinney, A.M., Mero, R.P., Kessler, R.C., and Herzog, A.R. (1994) The social stratification of aging and health. *Journal of Health and Social Behavior*, 35: 213–234.

Howard, B.V., Lee, E.T., Cowan, L.D., Fabsitz, R.R., Howard, W.J., Oopik, A.J., Robbins, D.C., Savage, P.J., Yeh, J.L., and Welty, T.K. (1995) Coronary heart disease prevalence and its relation to risk factors in American Indians. *American Journal of Epidemiology*, 142: 254–268.

Howie, L. (1992–3) Old women and widowhood: A dying status passage. *Omega*, 26: 223–233.

Hoyer, W.J. and Pludes, D.J. (1980) Aging and the attentional components of visual information processing. Paper presented at the symposium on Aging and Human Visual Function, National Academy of Sciences, Washington, DC.

Hubbard, R. (1990) *The Politics of Women's Biology*. New Brunswick: Rutgers University Press.

Hunter, D.J.S. (1976) Oophorectomy and the surgical menopause. In R.J. Beard (ed.) *The Menopause: A Guide to Current Research and Practice*. Baltimore: University Park Press.

Hunter, M. (1990) *Your Menopause: Prepare Now for a Positive Future*. London: Pandora.

Huppert, F.A. and Whittington, J.E. (1995) Symptoms of psychological distress predict 7-year mortality. *Psychological Medicine*, 25: 1073–1086.

Hussain, K., Gould, L., Sosler, B., Bharathan, T., and Reddy, C.V.R. (1996) Clinical science review: Current aspects of thrombolytic therapy in women with acute myocardial infarction. *Angiology*, 47: 23–33.

Hutton, J.D., Jacobs, H.S., Murray, M.A.F., and James, V.H.T. (1978) Relation between plasma oestrone and oestradiol and climacteric symptoms. *Lancet*, April: 678–681.

Huyck, M.E. (1990) Gender differences in aging. In J.E.Birren and K.W. Schaie (eds) *Handbook of the Psychology of Aging* (3rd edn). New York: Academic Press.

Inhelder, B. and Piaget, J. (1958) *The growth of logical thinking from childhood to adolescence*. New York: Basic books.

Iskrant, A.P. (1968) The etiology of fractured hips in females. *American Journal of Public Health*, 58: 485–491.

Jacobs, D., Blackburn, H., Higgins, M., Reed, D., Iso, H., McMillan, G., Neaton, J., Nelson, J., Potter, J., and Rifkind, B. (1992) Report of the Conference on Low Blood Cholesterol: Mortality associations. *Circulation*, 86: 1046–1060.

Jacobs, D.M., Tang, M.-X., Stern, Y., Sano, M., Marder, K., Bell, K.L., Schofield, P., Dooneief, G., Gurland, B., and Mayeux, R. (1998) Cognitive function in nondemented older women who took estrogen after menopause. *Neurology*, 50: 368–373.

Jacobs, H.S. and Loeffler, F.E. (1992) Postmenopausal hormone replacement therapy. *British Medical Journal*, 305: 1403–1408.

James, W.P.T., Nelsen, M., Ralph, A., and Leather, S. (1997) the contribution of nutrition to inequalities in health. *British Medical Journal*, 314: 1545–1549.

Jick, H., Derby, L.E., Hyers, M.W., Vasilakis, C., and Newton, K.M. (1996) Risk for hospital admission for idiopathic venous thromboembolism among users of post-menopausal oestrogens. *Lancet*, 348: 981–983.

Johansson, C., Mellstrom, D., Lerner, U., and Osterberg, T. (1992) Coffee drinking: A minor risk factor for bone loss and fractures. *Age and Aging*, 21: 20–26.

Johnell, O. (1995) Prevention of fractures in the elderly: A review. *Acta Orthopedia Scandinavica*, 66: 90–98.

Johnson, C.L., Rifkind, B.M., Sempos, C.T., Carroll, M.D., Bachorik, P.S., Briefel, R.R., Gordon, D.J., Burt, V.L., Brown, C.D., Lippel, K., and Cleeman, J.I. (1993) Declining serum total cholesterol levels among US adults. *Journal of the American Medical Association*, 269: 3002–3008.

Jonas, H.A. and Manolio, T.A. (1996) Hormone replacement and cardiovascular disease in older women. *Journal of Women's Health*, 5: 351–361.

Judd, H.L., Judd, G.E., Lucas, W.E., and Yen, S.S.C. (1974) Endocrine function of the postmenopausal ovary: Concentration of androgens and estrogens in ovarian and peripheral vein blood. *Journal of Clinical Endocrinology and Metabolism*, 39: 1020–1024.

Judd, H.L., Lucas, W.E., and Yen, S.S.C. (1976) Serum 17B-estradiol and estrone levels in postmenopausal women with and without endometrial cancer. *Journal of Clinical Endocrinology and Metabolism*, 43: 272–278.

Judd, H.L., Davidson, B.J., Frumar, A.M., Shamonki, I.M., Logasse, L.D., and Ballon, S.C. (1980) Serum androgens and estrogens in postmenopausal women with and without endometrial cancer. *American Journal of Obstetrics and Gynecology*, 136: 859–866.

Judd, H.L., Davidson, B.J., Frumar, A.M., Shamonki, I.M., and Logasse, L.D. (1982) Origin of serum estradiol in postmenopausal women. *Obstetrics and Gynecology*, 59: 680–686.

Kahn, A. and Holt, L. (1987) *Menopause: The Best Years of Your Life?* London: Bloomsbury Press.

Kampen, D.L. and Sherwin, B.B. (1994) Estrogen use and verbal memory in healthy post-menopausal women. *Obstetrics and Gynecology*, 83: 979–983.

Kanders, B., Dempster, D.W., and Lindsay, R. (1988) Interaction of calcium nutrition and physical activity on bone mass in young women. *Journal of Bone and Mineral Research*, 3: 145–149.

Kaplan, H.S. (1993) The female androgen deficiency syndrome. *Journal of Sex and Marital Therapy*, 19: 3–23.

Kaplan, M. (1983) A women's view of DSM-III. *American Psychologist*, July: 786–792.

Karling, P., Hammar, M., and Varenhorst, E. (1994) Prevalence and duration of hot flushes after surgical or medical castration in men with prostatic carcinoma. *Journal of Urology*, 152: 1170–1173.

Katz, S. (1996) *Disciplining Old Age: The Formation of Gerontological Knowledge*. Charlottesville: University of Virginia Press.

Kaufert, P. and Gilbert, P. (1986) The context of menopause: Psychotropic drug use and menopausal status. *Social Science and Medicine*, 23: 747–755.

Kaufert, P.A., Lock, M., McKinlay, S., and Avis, M (1994) Menopause as a normal physiological event or as a disease. In J. Lorrain (ed.) *Comprehensive Management of Menopause*. New York: Springer-Verlag (pp. 59–65).

REFERENCES

Kawachi, I., Willett, W.C., Colditz, G.A., Stampfer, M.J., and Speizer, F.E. (1996) A prospective study of coffee drinking and suicide in women. *Archives of Internal Medicine*, 156: 521–525.

Keith, V. (1993) Gender, financial strain, and psychological distress among older adults. *Research on Aging*, 15: 123–147.

Kelleher, C.C. (1990) Clinical aspects of the relationship between oral contraceptives and abnormalities of the hemostatic system: Relation to the development of cardiovascular disease. *American Journal of Obstetrics and Gynecology*, 163: 392–395.

Kennedy, G.J., Kelman, H.R., and Thomas, C. (1991) Persistence and remission of depressive symptoms in late life. *American Journal of Psychiatry*, 148: 174–178.

Kerlikowske, K., Grady, D., Rubin, S.M., Sandrock, C., and Ernster, V.L. (1995) Efficacy of screening mammography: a meta-analysis. *Journal of the American Medical Association*, 273: 149–154.

Kessler, R.C. and McRae, J.A. (1982) The effect of wives' employment on the mental health of married men and women. *American Sociological Review*, 47: 216–227.

Kiel, D.P., Felson, D.T., Hannan, M.T., Anderson, J.J., and Wilson, P.W.F. (1990) Caffeine and the risk of hip fracture: The Framingham Study. *American Journal of Epidemiology*, 132: 675–683.

Kim, C.J., Ryu, W.S., Kwak, J.W., Park, C.T., and Ryoo, U.H. (1996) Changes in Lp(a) lipoprotein and lipid levels after cessation of female sex hormone production and estrogen replacement therapy. *Archives of Internal Medicine*, 156: 500–504.

King, A.C., Taylor, C.B., Haskell, W.L., and Debusk, R.F. (1988) Strategies for increasing early adherence to and long-term maintenance of home-based exercise training in healthy middle-aged men and women. *American Journal of Cardiology*, 61: 628–632.

King, A.C., Taylor, C.B., and Haskell, W. (1993) Effects of differing intensities and formats of 12 months of exercise training on psychological outcome in older adults. *Health Psychology*, 12: 292–300.

King, A.C., Haskell, W.L., Young, D.R., Oka, R.K., and Stefanick, M.L. (1995) Long-term effects of varying intensities and formats of physical activity on participation rates, fitness, and lipoproteins in men and women aged 50 to 65 years. *Circulation*, 91: 2596–2604.

Kington, R.S. and Smith, J.P. (1997) Socioeconomic status and racial and ethnic differences in functional status associated with chronic diseases. *American Journal of Public Health*, 87: 805–810.

Kington, R.S., Lillard, L., and Rogowski, J. (1997) Reproductive history, socioeconomic status, and self-reported health status of women aged 50 years or older. *American Journal of Public Health*, 87: 33–37.

Kinsey, A.C., Pomeroy, W.B., Martin, C.E., and Gebhard, P.H. (1953) *Sexual Behavior in the Human Female*. Philadelphia: W.B. Saunders.

Kirwan, J.P., Kohr, W.M., Wojta, D.M., Bourey, R.E., and Holloszy, J.O. (1993) Endurance exercise training reduces glucose-stimulated insulin levels in 60- to 70-year-old men and women. *Journal of Gerontology*, 48: M84–M90.

Klein, M., Greist, J., Gurman, A., Neimeyer, R., Lesser, D., Bushnessl, N., and Smith, R. (1984) A comparative outcome study of group psychotherapy versus exercise treatments for depression. *International Journal of Mental Health*, 13: 148–176.

Kligman, E.W., and Pepin, E. (1992) Prescribing physical activity for older patients. *Geriatrics*, 47: 33–47.

Knight, R.G., Williams, S., McGee, R., and Olaman, S. (1997) Psychometric properties of the Centre for Epidemiologic Studies Depression Scale (CES-D) in a sample of women in middle life. *Behaviour Research and Therapy*, 35: 373–380.

Koenig, H.G. and Blazer, D.G. (1992) Epidemiology of geriatric affective disorders. *Clinics in Geriatric Medicine*, 8: 235–251.

Koeske, R.K. (1982) Toward a biosocial paradigm for menopausal research: Lessons and contributions from behavioral sciences. In A. Voda, M. Dinnerstein, and S.R. O'Connell (eds) *Changing Perspectives on Menopause*. Austin: University of Texas Press.

Kokkinos, P.F., Holland, J.C., Pittaras, A.E., Narayan, P., Dotson, C.O., and Papademetriou, V. (1995) Cardiorespiratory fitness and coronary heart disease risk factor association in women. *Journal of the American College of Cardiology*, 26: 358–364.

Kon, I. (1987) A sociocultural approach. In J.H. Geer and W.T. O'Donohue (eds) *Theories of Human Sexuality*. New York: Plenum.

Konstam, V. and Houser, R. (1994) Rehabilitation of women postmyocardial infarction – a new look at old assumptions. *Rehabilitation Counseling*, 25: 46–51.

Kopera, H. (1972) Possibilities and limitations of hormone therapy between puberty and the menopause. *Munchener Medizinische Wochenschrift*, 114: 754–760.

Krall, E.A. and Dawson-Hughes, B. (1994) Walking is related to bone density and rates of bone loss. *American Journal of Medicine*, 96: 20–26.

Kramer, D.A. and Melchior, J. (1990) Gender, role conflict, and the development of relativistic and dialectical thinking. *Sex Roles*, 23: 553–575.

Kramer, D.A., Kahlbaugh, P.E., and Goldston, R.B. (1992) A measure of paradigm beliefs about the social world. *Journal of Gerontology*, 47: 180–189.

Kritz-Silverstein, D. and Barrett-Connor, E. (1993) Early menopause, number of reproductive years, and bone mineral density in postmenopausal women. *American Journal of Public Health*, 83: 983–988.

—— (1996) Long-term postmenopausal hormone use, obesity, and fat distribution in older women. *Journal of the American Medical Association*, 275: 46–49.

Kritz-Silverstein, D., Barrett-Connor, E., and Wingard, D.L. (1997) Hysterectomy, oophorectomy, and heart disease risk factors in older women. *American Journal of Public Health*, 87: 676–680.

Krummel, D., Etherton, T., Peterson, S., and Kris-Etherton, P. (1993) Effects of exercise on plasma lipids and lipoproteins of women. *Experimental Biology and Medicine*, 204: 123–137.

Krupp, M.A, Tierney, L.M., Jawetz, E., Roe, R.L., and Camargo, C.A. (1985) *23rd Edition of Physician's Handbook*. Los Altos, CA: Lange Medical Publications.

Kuller, L.H. (1995) Commentary on coronary artery disease in Blacks. *Public Health Reports*, 110: 570–572.

Kuller, L.H., Meilahn, E., Benker, C., Yong, L.C., Sutton-Tyrrell, K., and Matthews, K. (1995) Development of risk factors for cardiovascular disease among women from adolescence to older ages. *American Journal of Medical Sciences*, 310: S91–S100.

Kushi, L., Fee, R.M., Folsom, A.R., Mink, P.J., Anderson, K.E., and Sellers, T.A. (1997) Physical activity and mortality in postmenopausal women. *Journal of the American Medical Association*, 277: 1287–1292.

LaCroix, A.Z., Leveille, S.G., Hecht, J.A., Grothaus, L.C., and Wagner, E.H. (1996) Does walking decrease risk of cardiovascular disease hospitalizations and death in older adults? *Journal of the American Geriatric Society*, 44: 113–120.

Lane, N.E., Bloch, D.A., Jones, H.H., Marshall, W.H., Wood, P.O., and Fries, J.F. (1986) Long-distance running, bone density, and osteoarthritis. *Journal of the American Medical Association*, 255: 1147–1151.

Lane, N.E., Bloch, D.A., Wood, P.D., and Fries, J.F. (1987) Aging, long-distance running, and the development of musculoskeletal disability. *American Journal of Medicine*, 82: 772–780.

Langer, E. and Rodin, J. (1976) The effects of choice and enhanced personal responsibility in the aged: A field experiment in an institutional setting. *Journal of Personality and Social Psychology*, 34: 191–198.

Laukkanen, P., Kauppinen, M., and Heikkinen, E. (1998) Physical activity as a predictor of health and disability in 75- and 80-year-old men and women: A five-year longitudinal study. *Journal of Aging and Physical Activity*, 6: 141–156.

Lawrence, R.H., Tennstedt, S.L., and Assmann, S.F. (1998) Quality of the caregiver-care recipient relationship: does it offset negative consequences of caregiving for family caregivers? *Psychology and Aging*, 13: 150–158.

Laya, M.B. (1997) Changes in the breast with ovarian aging. *Menopause Management*, 6: 10–16.

Leahy, J.M. (1992–1993) A comparison of depression in women bereaved of a spouse, child, or a parent. *Omega*, 26: 207–217.

Lehman, H.C. (1964) The relationship between chronological age and high level research output in physics and chemistry. *Journal of Gerontology*, 19: 157–164.

Leiblum, S.R. and Swartzman, L.C. (1986) Women's attitudes toward the menopause: an update. *Maturitas*, 8: 47–56.

Lennon, M.C. (1987) Is menopause depressing? An investigation of the perspectives. *Sex Roles*, 17: 1–16.

Leuven, J.A.G., Dersjant-Roorda, M.C., Helmerhorst, F.M., de Baer, R., Neymeyer-Leloux, A., and Havekes, L. (1990) Estrogenic effect of gestodene- or desogestrel-containing oral contraceptives on lipoprotein metabolism. *American Journal of Obstetrics and Gynecology*, 163: 358–362.

Lewinsohn, P.M., Seeley, J.R., Roberts, R., and Allen, N.B. (1997) Center for Epidemiologic Studies Depression Scale (CES-D) as a screening instrument for depression among community-residing older adults. *Psychology and Aging*, 12: 277–287.

Lewittes, H.J. (1988) Just being friendly means a lot: women, friendship, and aging. *Women and Health*, 14: 139–159.

Lewontin, R.C. (1992) *Biology as Ideology: The Doctrine of DNA*. New York: Harper.

Liao, Y. and Cooper, R.S. (1995) Continued adverse trends in coronary heart disease mortality among Blacks. *Public Health Reports*, 110: 572–579.

Lieberman, D., Kopernik, G., Porath, A., Lazer, S., and Heimer, D. (1995) Sub-clinical worsening of bronchial asthma during estrogen replacement therapy in asthmatic postmenopausal women. *Maturitas*, 21: 153–157.

Liebman, B. (1997) The changing American diet. *Nutrition Action Healthletter*, April: 8–9.

Lindberg, G., Larsson, G., Setterlind, S., and Rastam, L. (1994) Serum lipids and mood in working men and women in Sweden. *Journal of Epidemiology and Community Health*, 48: 360–363.

Lindgren, R., Berg, G., and Hammar, M. (1993) Hormonal replacement therapy and sexuality in a population of Swedish postmenopausal women. *Acta Obstetrica Gynecologia Scandinavia*, 72: 292–297.

REFERENCES

Lindheim, S.R., Notelovitz, M., Feldman, E.B., Larsen, S., Khan, F.Y., and Lobo, R.A. (1994). The independent effects of exercise and estrogen on lipids and lipoproteins in postmenopausal women. *Obstetrics and Gynecology*, 83: 167–172.

Lindheim, S.R., Vijod, B.S., Presser, S.C., Stancyzk, F., Ditkoff, E., and Lobo, R.A. (1993) A possible bimodal effect of estrogen on insulin sensitivity in postmenopausal women and the attenuating effect of added progestin. *Fertility and Sterility*, 60: 664–667.

Lobo, R.A. (1990) Cardiovascular implications of estrogen replacement therapy. *Obstetrics and Gynecology*, 75: 18S–25S.

—— (1995a) Editorial. *American Journal of Obstetrics and Gynecology*, 173: 981.

—— (1995b) Benefits and risks of estrogen replacement therapy. *American Journal of Obstetrics and Gynecology*, 173: 982–990.

Lock, M. (1993) *Encounters with Aging: Mythologies of menopause in Japan and North America.* Berkeley: University of California Press.

Logue, B.J. (1991) Taking charge: Death control as an emergent women's issue. *Women and Health*, 17: 97–121.

Longcope, C., Hunter, R., and Franz, C. (1980) Steroid secretion by the postmenopausal ovary. *American Journal of Obstetrics and Gynecology*, 138: 564–568.

Loprinzi, C.L., Michalak, J.C., Quella, S.K., O'Fallon, J.R., Hatfield, A.K., Nelimark, R.A., Dose, A.M., Fischer, T., Johnson, C., Klatt, N.E., Bate, W.W., Rospond, R.M., and Oesterling, J.E. (1994) Megestrol acetate for the prevention of hot flashes. *New England Journal of Medicine*, 331: 347–352.

Lorber, J. (1994) *Paradoxes of Gender.* New Haven: Yale University Press.

—— (1997) *Gender and the Social Construction of Illness.* Thousand Oaks: Sage.

Love, S.M. and Lindsey, K. (1997) Comparative risks and benefits of hormone therapy. *A Friend Indeed*, 14: 1–3.

Lynch, J.W., Kaplan, G.A., and Salonen, J.T. (1997) Why do poor people behave poorly? Variation in adult health behaviours and psychosocial characteristics by stages of the socioeconomic lifecourse. *Social Science and Medicine*, 44: 809–819.

Lyness, S.A., Easton, E.M., and Schneider, L.S. (1996) Cognitive performance in older and middle-aged depressed outpatients and controls. *Journal of Gerontology*, 49: P129–P136.

McCallum, J., Shadbolt, B., and Wang, D. (1994) Self-rated health and survival: A 7-year follow-up study of Australian elderly. *American Journal of Public Health*, 84: 1100–1105.

McCann, B.S., Bovbjerg, V.E., Curry, S.J., Retzlaff, B.M., Walden, C.E., and Knopp, R.H. (1996) Predicting participation in a dietary intervention to lower cholesterol among individuals with hyperlipidemia. *Health Psychology*, 15: 61–64.

McClung, M., Clemmesen, B., Daifotis, A., Gilchrist, N.L., Eisman, J., Weinstein, R.S., Fuleihan, G., Reda, C., Yates, A.J., and Ravn, P. (1998) Alendronate prevents postmenopausal bone loss in women without osteoporosis: A double-blind, randomized, controlled trial. *Annals of Internal Medicine*, 128: 253–261.

McCrea, F.B. (1983) The politics of menopause: The "discovery" of a deficiency disease. *Social Problems*, 31: 111–125.

McDonough, P., Duncan, G.J., Williams, D., and House, J. (1997) Income dynamics and adult mortality in the United States, 1972 through 1989. *American Journal of Public Health*, 87: 1476–1483.

McEwen, B.S. (1981) Neural gonadal steroid actions. *Science*, 211: 1303–1324.

201

McGrew, K.B. (1998) Daughters' caregiving decisions: From an impulse to a balancing point of care. *Journal of Women and Aging*, 10: 49–65.

McKinlay, J.B. (1981) From "promising report" to "standard procedure": seven stages in the career of a medical innovation. *The Millbank Quarterly*, 59: 374–411.

—— (1993) The promotion of health through planned sociopolitical change: Challenges for research and policy. *Social Science and Medicine*, 36: 109–117.

McKinlay, J.B., McKinlay, S.M., and Brambilla, D. (1987) The relative contributions of endocrine changes and social circumstances to depression in mid-aged women. *Journal of Health and Social Behavior*, 28: 345–363.

McKinlay, S.M. and Jeffreys, M. (1974) The menopausal syndrome. *British Journal of Preventative and Social Medicine*, 28: 108–115.

McKinlay, S.M. and McKinlay, J.B. (1989) The impact of menopause and social factors on health. In C.B. Hammond, F.P. Haseltine, and I. Schiff (eds) *Menopause: Evaluation, Treatment, and Health Concerns*. New York: Alan Liss (pp. 111–119).

McKinlay, S.M., Triant, R.S., McKinlay, J.B., Brambilla, D.J., and Ferdock, M. (1990) Multiple roles for middle-aged women and their impact on health. In M.G. Ory and H.R. Warner (eds) *Gender, Health and Longevity*. New York: Springer.

McKinlay, S.M., Brambilla, D.J., and Posner, J.G. (1992) The normal menopause transition. *Maturitas*, 14: 103–115.

MacKinnon, C. (1987) A feminist/political approach: 'pleasure under the patriarchy'. In J.H. Geer and W.T. O'Donohue (eds) *Theories of Human Sexuality*. New York: Plenum.

McNicholas, M.M.J., Heneghan, J.P., Milner, M.H., Tunney, T., Hourihane, J.B., and MacErlaine, D.P. (1994) Pain and increased mammographic density in women receiving hormone replacement therapy: A prospective study. *American Journal of Radiology*, 163: 311–315.

Maddock, J. (1978) Gonadal and pituitary hormone profiles in perimenopausal patients. In I.D. Cooke (ed.) *The Role of Estrogen/Progesterone in the Management of the Menopause*. Baltimore: University Park Press.

Maddox, G., Clark, D.O., and Steinhauser, K. (1994) Dynamics of functional impairment in late adulthood. *Social Science and Medicine*, 38: 925–936.

Maheux, R., Naud, F., Rioux, M., Grenier, R., Lemay, A., Guy, J., and Langevin, M. (1994) A randomized, double-blind, placebo-controlled study on the effect of conjugated estrogens on skin thickness. *American Journal of Obstetrics and Gynecology*, 170: 642–649.

Maier, S.F. and Seligman, M.E.P. (1976) Learned helplessness: Theory and evidence. *Journal of Experimental Psychology: General*, 105: 3–46.

Malleson, J. (1953) An endocrine factor in certain affective disorders. *Lancet*, 265: 158–164.

Manson, J.E., Willett, W.C., Stampfer, M.J., Colditz, G.A., Hunter, D.J., Hankinson, S.E., Hennekens, C.H., and Speizer, F.E. (1995) Body weight and mortality among women. *New England Journal of Medicine*, 333: 677–685.

Marcus, B.H., Dubbert, P.M., King, A.C., and Bernardine, M.P. (1995a) Physical activity in women: Current status and future directions. In A.L. Stanton and S.J. Gallant (eds) *The Psychology of Women's Health: Progress and Challenges in Research and Application*. Washington DC: American Psychological Association (pp. 349–379).

Marcus, B.H., Rakowski, W., and Rossi, J.S. (1995b) Assessing motivational readiness and decision making for exercise. *Health Psychology*, 11: 257–261.

Marcus, R. (1995) Relationship of age-related decreases in muscle mass and strength to skeletal status. *Journal of Gerontology*, 50A: 86–87.

—— (1996) The nature of osteoporosis. *Journal of Clinical Endocrinology and Metabolism*, 81: 1–5.

Markoff, R.A., Tyan, P., and Young, T. (1982) Endorphins and mood changes in long-distance running. *Medicine and Science in Sports and Exercise*, 14: 11–15.

Marmot, M., Ryff, C.D., Bumpass, L.L., Shipley, M., and Marks, N.F. (1997) Social inequalities in health: Next questions and converging evidence. *Social Science and Medicine*, 44: 901–910.

Marsh, A.G., Sanchez, T.V., Michelsen, O., Chaffee, F.L., and Fagal, S.M. (1988) Vegetarian lifestyle and bone mineral density. *American Journal of Clinical Nutrition*, 48: 837–841.

Marsh, M.S., Crook, D., Whitdroft, S.I.J., Worthington, I., Whitehead, M.I., and Stevenson, J.C. (1994) Effect of continuous combined estrogen and desogestrel hormone replacement therapy on serum lipids and lipoproteins. *Obstetrics and Gynecology*, 83: 19–23.

Marshburn, P.B. and Carr, B.R. (1992) Hormone replacement therapy: Protection against the consequences of menopause. *Postgraduate Medicine*, 92: 145–159.

Masters, W. and Johnson, V.E. (1970) *Human Sexual Inadequacy*. Boston: Little, Brown and Company.

Matthews, K.A., Shumaker, S.A., Bowen, D.J., Langer, R.D., Hunt, J.R., Kaplan, R.M., Klesges, R.C., and Rittenbaugh, C. (1997a) Women's Health Initiative: Why now? What is it? What's new? *American Psychologist*, 52: 101–116.

Matthews, K.A., Wing, R.R., Kuller, L.H., Meilahn, E.N., and Plantinga, P. (1997b) Influence of the perimenopause on cardiovascular risk factors and symptoms of middle-aged healthy women. *Archives of Internal Medicine*, 154: 2349–2355.

Mayer, P.J. (1994) Human immune system aging: approaches, examples, and ideas. In D.E. Crews and R.M. Garruto (eds) *Biological Anthropology and Aging: Perspectives on Human Variation over the Life Span*. New York: Oxford University Press (pp. 182–213).

Meijer, G.A., Westerterp, K.R., Saris, W.H.M., and Hoor, F.T. (1992) Sleeping metabolic rate in relation to body composition and the menstrual cycle. *American Journal of Clinical Nutrition*, 55: 637–640.

Meilahn, E.N., Becker, R.C., and Corrao, J.M. (1995) Primary prevention of coronary heart disease in women. *Cardiology*, 86: 286–298.

Meldrum, D.R., Shamonki, I.M., Frumar, A.M., Tataryn, I.V., Chang, R.J., and Judd, H.L. (1979) Elevations in skin temperature of the finger as an objective index of post-menopausal hot flashes: Standardization of the technique. *American Journal of Obstetrics and Gynecology*, 135: 713–717.

Meldrum, D.R., Davidson, B.J., Tataryn, I.V., and Judd, H.L. (1981) Changes in circulating steroids with aging in postmenopausal women. *Obstetrics and Gynecology*, 57: 624–628.

Melton, L.J. and Riggs, B.L (1983) Epidemiology of age-related fractures. In A.E. Avioli (ed.) *The Osteoporotic Syndrome: Detection and Prevention*, New York: Grune and Stratton.

Meltzer, L.J. (1974) The aging female: A study of attitudes toward aging and self-concept held by pre-menopausal, menopausal, and post-menopausal women. *Dissertation Abstracts International*, 35B: 1055.

Mendelson, M.A. and Hendel, R.C. (1995) Myocardial infarction in women. *Cardiology*, 86: 272–285.

Meunier, P.J. (1993) Prevention of hip fractures. *American Journal of Medicine*, 95: 75S–78S.

Meuwissen, I. and Over, R. (1992) Sexual arousal phases of the human menstrual cycle. *Archives of Sexual Behavior*, 21: 101–120.

Miles, S.H. and August, A. (1990) Courts, gender, and "the right to die." *Law, Medicine and Health Care*, 18: 85–95.

Miller, V.T., Muesing, R.A., LaRosa, J.C., Stoy, D., Fowler, S.E., and Stillman, R.J. (1994) Quantitative and qualitative changes in lipids, lipoproteins, Apolipoprotein A-I, and sex hormone-binding globulin due to two doses of conjugated equine estrogen with and without a progestin. *Obstetrics and Gynecology*, 83: 173–179.

Mineka, S. and Kihlstrom, J.F. (1978) Unpredictable and uncontrollable events: A new perspective on experimental neurosis. *Journal of Abnormal Psychology*, 2: 256–271.

Mishell, D.R. (1989) Estrogen replacement therapy: an overview. *American Journal of Obstetrics and Gynecology*, 161: 1825–1827.

Moen, P., Robinson, J., and Fields, V. (1994) Women's work and caregiving roles: A life course approach. *Journal of Gerontology*, 49: S176–S186.

Moniz, C. (1994) Alcohol and bone. *British Medical Bulletin*, 50: 67–75.

Monk, T.H., Reynolds, C.F., Kupfer, D., Hoch, C.C., Carrier, J., and Houck, P.R. (1996) Differences over the life span in daily lifestyle regularity. *Chronobiology International*, 14: 295–306.

Moore-Ede, M.C., Czeisler, C.A., and Richardson, G.S. (1983) Circadian timekeeping in health and disease. *New England Journal of Medicine*, 309: 469–476.

Moorhead, T., Hannaford, P., and Warskyj, M. (1997) Prevalence and characteristics associated with use of hormone replacement therapy in Britain. *British Journal of Obstetrics and Gynaecology*, 104: 290–297.

Mosca, L., Manson, J.E., Sutherland, S.E., Langer, R.D., Manolio, T., and Barrett-Connor, E. (1997) Cardiovascular disease in women: A statement for healthcare professionals from the American Heart Association. *Circulation*, 96: 2468–2482.

Muldoon, M.F., Manuck, S.B., and Matthews, K.A. (1990) Lowering cholesterol concentrations and mortality: quantitative review of primary prevention trials. *British Medical Journal*, 301: 309–314.

Murkies, A.L., Lombard, C., Strauss, B.J.G., Wilcox, G., Burger, H.G., and Morton, M.S. (1995) Dietary flour supplementation decreases post-menopausal hot flushes: Effect of soy and wheat. *Maturitas*, 21: 189–195.

Murphy, S., Khaw, K-T., May, H., and Compston, J.E. (1994) Milk consumption and bone mineral density in middle-aged and elderly women. *British Medical Journal*, 308: 939–941.

Murray, T.M. and Ste-Marie, L.G. (1996) Prevention and management of osteoporosis: consensus statements from the Scientific Advisory Board of the Osteoporosis Society of Canada. 7. Fluoride therapy for osteoporosis. *Canadian Medical Association Journal*, 155: 949–954.

Mutran, E.J., Reitzes, D.C., Mossey, J., and Fernandez, M.E. (1995) Social support, depression, and recovery of walking ability following hip fracture surgery. *Journal of Gerontology*, 50B: S354–S361.

Nachtigall, L.E. (1990) Enhancing patient compliance with hormone replacement therapy at menopause. *Obstetrics and Gynecology*, 75: 77S–80S.

—— (1994) Comparative study: Replens versus local estrogen in menopausal women. *Fertility and Sterility*, 61: 178–180.

Nagata, C., Matsushita, Y., and Shimizu, H. (1996) Prevalence of hormone replacement therapy and user's characteristics: a community survey in Japan. *Maturitas*, 25: 201–207.

National Institute of Health (1995) *Menopause*. Washington DC: National Institute of Health. NIH Publication.

Natrajan, P.K., Muldoon, T.G., Greenblatt, R.B., and Mahesh, V.B. (1981) Estradiol and progesterone receptors in estrogen-primed endometrium. *American Journal of Obstetrics and Gynecology*, 140: 387–392.

Nelson, M.E., Fiatarone, M.A., Morganti, C.M., Trice, I., Greenberg, R. A., and Evans, W.J. (1994) Effects of high-intensity strength training on multiple risk factors for osteoporotic fractures. *Journal of American Medical Associations*, 272: 1909–1914.

Neugarten, B.L. (1979) Time, age, and the life cycle. *American Journal of Psychiatry*, 136: 887–894.

Newcomb, P.A. and Storer, E. (1995) Postmenopausal hormone use and risk of large-bowel cancer. *Journal of the National Cancer Institute*, 87: 1067–1071.

Newnham, H.H., and Silberberg, J. (1997) Women's hearts are hard to break. *Lancet*, 349: 3–6.

Nicol-Smith, L. (1996) Causality, menopause, and depression: a critical review of the literature. *British Medical Journal*, 313: 1229–1232.

Nolan, K.A., and Blass, J.P. (1992) Preventing cognitive decline. *Clinics In Geriatric Medicine*, 8: 19–34.

Nolen-Hoeksema, S., Parker, L.E., and Larson, J. (1994) Ruminative coping with depressed mood following loss. *Journal of Personality and Social Psychology*, 67: 92–104.

Nordin, B.E.C., Need, A.G., Chatterton, B.E., Horowitz, M., and Morris, H.A. (1990) The relative contributions of age and years since menopause to postmenopausal bone loss. *Journal of Clinical Endocrinology and Metabolism*, 70: 83–88.

Notelovitz, M. (1989) Osteoporosis: Screening and exercise. In C.B. Hammond, F.P. Haseltine, and I. Schiff (eds) *Menopause: Evaluation, Treatment, and Health Concerns*. New York: Alan Liss (pp. 225–252).

—— (1990) Exercise and health maintenance in menopausal women. *Annals of the New York Academy of Sciences*, 592: 204–219.

—— (1996) Alternatives to ERT for osteoporosis and osteoporotic fractures. *Contemporary Obstetrics and Gynecology*, November: 63–76.

Notelovitz, M., Kitchens, C., Ware, M., Hirschberg, K., and Coone, L. (1983) Combination estrogen and progestogen replacement therapy does not adversely affect coagulation. *Obstetrics and Gynecology*, 62: 596.

Oakley, A. (1993) *Essays on Women, Medicine, and Health*. Edinburgh: Edinburgh University Press.

O'Brien, M. (1996) Osteoporosis and exercise. *British Journal of Sports Medicine*, 30: 191.

O'Brien, S.J. and Vertinsky, P.A. (1991) Unfit survivors: exercise as a resource for aging women. *The Gerontologist*, 31: 347–357.

O'Donnell, D.E., Webb, K.A., and McGuire, M.A. (1993) Older patients with COPD: Benefits of exercise training. *Geriatrics*, 48: 59–66.

Okonofua, F.E. (1996) the case against new reproductive technologies in developing countries. *British Journal of Obstetrics and Gynaecology*, 103: 957–962.

O'Leary-Cobb, J. (1992) The Tamoxifen Trials. *A Friend Indeed*, 9: 1–3.

—— (1993) Why women choose not to take hormone therapy. *A Friend Indeed*, 10: 1–3.

Ooms, M.E., Roos, J.C., Bezemer, P.D., van der Vijgh, J.F., Bouter, L.M., and Lips, P. (1995) Prevention of bone loss by vitamin D supplementation in elderly women: A randomized double-blind trial. *Journal of Clinical Endocrinology Metabolism*, 80: 1052–1058.

Orlander, J.D., Jick, S.S., Dean, A.D., and Jick, H. (1992) Urinary tract infections and estrogen use in older women. *Journal of American Geriatric Society*, 40: 817–820.

Orr-Walker, B., Wattie, D.J., Evans, M.C., and Reid, I.R. (1997) Effects of prolonged bisphosphonate therapy and its discontinuation on bone mineral density in post-menopausal osteoporosis. *Clinical Endocrinology*, 46: 87–92.

Pagley, P. and Goldberg, R.J. (1995) Coronary artery disease in women: A population-based perspective. *Cardiology*, 86: 265–269.

Parazzini, F., Braga, C., La Vecchia, C., Negri, E., Acerboni, S., and Franceschi, S. (1997) Hysterectomy, oophorectomy in premenopause, and risk of breast cancer. *Obstetrics and Gynecology*, 90: 453–456.

Pasquali, R., Casimirri, F., Pascal, G., Tortelli, O., Labate, A.M.M., Bertazzo, D., Vicennati, V., Gaddi, A., and the Virgilio Menopause Health Group (1997) Influence of menopause on blood cholesterol levels in women: the role of body composition, fat distribution and hormonal milieu. *Journal of International Medicine*, 241: 195–203.

Pearce, J., Hawton, K., and Blake, F. (1995) Psychological and sexual symptoms associated with menopause and the effects of hormone replacement therapy. *British Journal of Psychiatry*, 167: 163–173.

Pearlin, L. (1975) Sex roles and depression. In N. Datan (ed.) *Life-span Developmental Psychology: Normative Life Crises*. New York: Academic Press.

Pennig, M.J. and Strain, L.A. (1994) Gender differences in disability, assistance, and subjective well-being in later life. *Journal of Gerontology*, 49: 5202–5208.

Peris, P. and Guanabens, N. (1996) Male osteoporosis. *Current Opinion in Rheumatology*, 8: 357–364.

Perlman, J., Wolf, P., Finucane, F., and Madans, J. (1989) Menopause and the epidemiology of cardiovascular disease in women. In C.B. Hammond, F.P. Haseltine, and I. Schiff (eds) *Menopause: Evaluation, Treatment, and Health Concerns*. New York: Alan Liss (pp. 283–312).

Perri, M.G., Martin, D., Notelovitz, M., Leermakers, E.A., and Sears, S.F. (1997) Effects of group- versus home-based exercise in the treatment of obesity. *Journal of Consulting and Clinical Psychology*, 65: 278–285.

Persson, I., Yuen, J., Bergkvist, L., and Schairer, C. (1996) Cancer incidence and mortality in women receiving estrogen and estrogen–progestin replacement therapy – long-term follow-up of a Swedish cohort. *International Journal of Cancer*, 29: 327–332.

Persson, I., Bergkvist, L., Lindgren, C., and Yuen, J. (1997) Hormone replacement therapy and major risk factors for reproductive cancers, osteoporosis, and cardiovascular diseases: Evidence of confounding by exposure characteristics. *Journal of Clinical Epidemiology*, 50: 611–618.

Peterson, M. (1994) Physical aspects of aging: is there such a thing as "normal"? *Geriatrics*, 49: 45–49.

Pfeiffer, E. (1978) Sexuality in the aging individual. In R.L. Solnick (ed.) *Sexuality and Aging*. Los Angeles: Southern California Press.

Phillips, S. and Sherwin, S. (1992) Effects of estrogen on memory function in surgically menopausal women. *Psychoneuroendocrinology*, 17: 485–495.

Pike, M.C., Ross, R.K., and Spicer, D.V. (1998) Problems involved in including women with simple hysterectomy in epidemiologic studies measuring the effects of hormone replacement therapy on breast cancer risk. *American Journal of Epidemiology*, 147: 718–721.

Poehlman, E.T., Toth, M.J., Bunyard, L.B., Gardner, A.W., Donaldson, K.E., Colman, E., Fonong, T., and Ades, P.A. (1995) Physiological predictors of increasing total and central adiposity in aging men and women. *Archives of Internal Medicine*, 155: 2443–2448.

Poller, L., Thomson, J.M., and Coope, J. (1980) A double-blind cross-over study of piperazine oestrone sulphate and placebo with coagulation studies. *British Journal of Obstetrics and Gynaecology*, 87: 718–725.

Polo-Kantola, P., Portin, R., Polo, O., Helenius, H., Irjala, K., and Erkkola, R. (1998) The effect of short-term estrogen replacement therapy on cognition: A randomized, double-blind, cross-over trial in postmenopausal women. *Obstetrics and Gynecology*, 91: 459–466.

Popay, J., Bartley, M., and Owen, C. (1993) Gender inequalities in health: Social position, affective disorders and minor physical morbidity. *Social Science and Medicine*, 36: 21–32.

Porter, M., Penny, G.C., Russell, D., Russell, E., and Templeton, A. (1996) A population based survey of women's experience of the menopause. *British Journal of Obstetrics and Gynaecology*, 103: 1025–1028.

Posner, B.M., Franz, M.M., Quatromoni, P.A., Gagnon, D.R., Sytkowski, P.A., D'Agostino, R.B., and Cupples, L.A. (1995) Secular trends in diet and risk factors for cardiovascular disease: The Framingham Study. *Journal of the American Dietetics Association*, 95: 171–179.

Posner, J.D., McCully, K.K., Landsberg, L.A., Sands, L.P., Tycenski, P., Hofmann, M.T., Wetterholt, K.L., and Shaw, C.E. (1995) Physical determinants of independence in mature women. *Archives of Physical Medicine and Rehabilitation*, 76: 373–380.

Potter, J.D., Bostick, R.M., Grandits, G.A., Fosdick, L., Elmer, P., Wood, J., Grambsch, P., and Louis, T.A. (1996) Hormone replacement therapy is associated with lower risk of adenomatous polyps of the large bowel: The Minnesota Cancer Prevention Research Unit Case-Control Study. *Cancer Epidemiology, Biomarkers, and Prevention*, 5: 779–784.

Powell, D.H. (1994) *Profiles in Cognitive Aging*. Cambridge: Harvard University Press.

Powers, B.A. (1996) Relationships among older women living in a nursing home. *Journal of Women and Aging*, 8: 179–198.

Preisinger, E., Alacamlioglu, Y., Pils, K., Saradeth, T., and Schneider, B. (1995) Therapeutic exercise in the prevention of bone loss. *American Journal of Physical Medicine and Rehabilitation*, 74: 120–123.

Preisinger, E., Alacamlioglu, Y., Pils, K., Bosina, E., Metka, M., Schneider, B., and Ernst, E. (1996) Exercise therapy for osteoporosis: results of a randomised controlled trial. *British Journal of Sports Medicine*, 30: 209–212.

Preskorn, S. (1993) Recent pharmacologic advances in antidepressant therapy for the elderly. *American Journal of Medicine*, 94: 2S–12S

Price, E.H., Little, H.K., Grant, E., and Steel, C.M. (1997) Women need to be warned about the dangers of hormone replacement therapy. *British Medical Journal*, 314: 376–377.

Prigerson, P., Monk, T.H., Reynolds, C.F., Begley, A., Houd, P., Bierhals, A., and Kupfer, D. (1995–1996) Lifestyles regularity and activity levels as protective factors against bereavement-related depression in late-life. *Depression*, 3: 297–302.

Primomo, J. (1995) Chronic illnesses and women. In C.I. Fogel and N.F. Woods (eds) *Women's Health Care: A Comprehensive Handbook*. Thousand Oaks: Sage (pp. 651–671).

Rabbitt, P., Donla, C., Watson, P., McInnes, L., and Bent, N. (1995) Unique and interactive effects of depression, age, socioeconomic advantage, and gender on cognitive performance of normal healthy older people. *Psychology and Aging*, 10: 307–313.

Radloff, I. (1975) Sex differences in depression: The effects of occupation and marital status. *Sex Roles*, 1: 249–265.

Raffle, A.E. (1993) Postmenopausal hormone replacement therapy. *British Medical Journal*, 306: 654.

Rakoff, A.E. (1975) Female climacteric: Premenopause, menopause, postmenopause. In J.J. Gold (ed.) *Gynecologic Endocrinology* (2nd edn). New York: Harper and Row.

Rankin, S.H. (1990) Differences in recovery from cardiac surgery: A profile of male and female patients. *Heart Lung*, 19: 481–485.

Rauramaa, R. (1984) Relationship of physical activity, glucose tolerance, and weight management. *Preventive Medicine*, 13: 37–46.

Ravinkar, V.A. (1987) Compliance with hormone therapy. *American Journal of Obstetrics and Gynecology*, 156: 1332–1334.

Reeves, J.B. and Darville, R.L. (1994) Social contact pattern and satisfaction with retirement of women in dual-career earner families. *International Journal of Aging and Human Development*, 39: 163–175.

Reid, I.R., Ames, R.W., Evans, M.C., Gamble, G.D., and Sharpe, S.J. (1995) Long-term effects of calcium supplementation on bone loss and fractures in postmenopausal women: A randomized controlled trial. *American Journal of Medicine*, 98: 331–335.

Reissman, C.K. (1983) Women and medicalization: A new perspective. *Social Policy*, 14: 3–18.

Reitz, R. (1977) *Menopause: A Positive Approach*. Radnor, PA: Chilton.

Reubinoff, B.E., Wurtman, J., Rojansky, N., Adler, D., Stein, P., Schenker, J.G., Brzezinski, A. (1995) Effects of hormone replacement therapy on weight, body composition, fat distribution, and food intake in early postmenopausal women: a prospective study. *Fertility and Sterility*, 64: 963–968.

Reyes, F.I., Winter, J.S.D., and Faiman, C. (1977) Pituitary–ovarian relationships preceding the menopause. I. A cross-sectional study of serum follicle-stimulating hormone, luteinizing hormone, prolactin, estradiol, and progesterone levels. *American Journal of Obstetrics and Gynecology*, 129: 557–564.

Richardson, S.J., Senikas, V., and Nelson, J.F. (1987) Follicular depletion during the menopausal transition: Evidence for accelerated loss and ultimate exhaustion. *Journal of Clinical Endocrinology and Metabolism*, 65: 1231–1237.

Richgels, P.B. (1992) Hypoactive sexual desire in heterosexual women: A feminist analysis. *Women and Therapy*, 12: 123–135.

Rikli, R. and McManis, B. (1990) Effects of exercise on bone mineral content in postmenopausal women. *Research Quarterly for Exercise and Sport*, 61: 243–249.

Rizzoli, R. and Bonjour, J-P. (1997) Hormones and bones. *Lancet*, 349: 20–23.

Roberts, R.E., Kaplan, G.A., Shema, S.J., and Strawbridge, W.J. (1997) Does growing old increase the risk for depression? *American Journal of Psychiatry*, 154: 1384–1390.

Robinson, D., Friedman, L., Marcus, R., Tinklenberg, J., and Yesavage, J. (1994) Estrogen replacement therapy and memory in older women. *Journal of the American Geriatric Society*, 42: 919–922.

Rodin, J. (1989) Sense of control: Potentials for intervention. *Annals of the American Academy of Political and Social Sciences*, 503: 29–42.

Rodin, J. and Langer, E.J. (1977) Long-term effects of a control-relevant intervention with institutionalized aged. *Journal of Personality and Social Psychology*, 35: 897–902.

Rodriquez, C., Calle, E.E., Coates, R.J., Miracle-McMahill, H.L., Thun, M.J., and Heath, C.W. (1995) Estrogen replacement therapy and fatal ovarian cancer. *American Journal of Epidemiology*, 141: 828–835.

Rosenberg, L., Palmer, J.R., and Adams-Campbell, L.L. (1997) Postmenopausal female hormone use and venous thromboembolic disease in black women. *American Journal of Obstetrics and Gynecology*, 177: 1275.

Rosenberg, L., Palmer, J.R., Rao, R.S., and Adams-Campbell, L.L. (1998) Correlates of postmenopausal female hormone use among Black women in the United States. *Obstetrics and Gynecology*, 91: 454–458.

Rosenwaks, Z., Wentz, A.C., Jones, G.S., Urban, M.D., Lee, P.A., Migeon, C.J., Parmley, T.H., and Woodruff, J.D. (1979) Plasma levels of norepinephrine (NE) during the periovulatory period and after LH–RH stimulation in women. *American Journal of Obstetrics and Gynecology*, 53: 403–410.

Rossman, I. (1978) Sexuality and aging: An internist's perspective. In R.L. Solnick (ed.) *Sexuality and Aging*. Los Angeles: Southern California Press.

Rotter, J.B. (1966) Generalized expectancies for internal versus external control of reinforcement. *Psychological Monographs*, 80.

Rousseau, M.E. and McCool, W.F. (1996) The menopausal experience of African American women: overview and suggestions for research. *Health Care for Women International*, 18: 233–250.

Runciman, I. (1978) Sexual problems in the senior world. In R.L. Solnick (ed.) *Sexuality and Aging*. Los Angeles: Southern California Press.

Russell, J.B., Mitchell, D., Musey, P.E., and Collins, D.C. (1984) The role of B–endorphins and catechol estrogens on the hypothalmic–pituitary axis in female athletes. *Fertility and Sterility*, 42: 690–695.

Ryan, P.J., Harrison, R., Blake, G.M., and Fogelman, I. (1992) Compliance with hormone replacement therapy (HRT) after screening for postmenopausal osteoporosis. *British Journal of Obstetrics and Gynaecology*, 99: 325–328.

Ryan, A.S., Nicklas, B.J., and Dariush, E. (1996) A cross-sectional study on body composition and energy expenditure in women athletes during aging. *American Journal of Physiology*, 271: E916–E921.

Sackville-West, V. (1984 [1931]) *All Passion Spent*. Garden City, NY: Doubleday.

Samsioe, G. and Mattsson, L.-A. (1990) Some aspects of the relationship between oral contraceptives, lipid abnormalites, and cardiovascular disease. *American Journal of Obstetrics and Gynecology*, 163: 354–358.

Samuelsson, G., Hagberg, B., Dehlin, O., and Lindberg, O. (1994) Medical, social and psychological factors as predictors of survival – a follow-up from 67 to 87 years of age. *Archives of Gerontology and Geriatrics*, 18: 25–41.

Sanchez-Guerrero, J., Liang, M.H., Karlson, E.W., Hunter, D.J., and Colditz, G.A. (1995) Postmenopausal estrogen therapy and the risk for developing systemic lupus erythematosus. *Annals of Internal Medicine*, 122: 430–433.

Sands, R. and Studd, J. (1995) Exogenous androgens in postmenopausal women. *American Journal of Medicine*, 98: 76S–79S.

Santrock, J.W. (1992) *Life-Span Development* (4th edn). Dubuque, Iowa: Wm. C. Brown.

Sarrel, P.M. (1990) Sexuality and menopause. *Obstetrics and Gynecology*, 75: 26S–35S.

Sazy, J.A., and Horstmann, H.M. (1991) Exercise participation after menopause. *Clinics in Sports Medicine*, 10: 359–369.

Schaefer, E., Lichtenstein, A., Lamon-Fava, S., McNamara, J., Ordovas, J.M. (1995) Lipoproteins, nutrition, aging, and atherosclerosis. *American Journal of Clinical Nutrition*, 61: 726S–740S.

Schairer, C., Adami, H-O., Hoover, R., and Persson, I. (1997) Cause-specific mortality in women receiving hormone replacement therapy. *Epidemiology*, 8: 59–65.

Schapira, D.V., Kumar, N.B., and Lyman, G.H. (1991) Estimate of breast cancer risk reduction with weight loss. *Cancer*, 67: 2622–2625.

Schlossberg, N.K. (1980) A model for analyzing human adaptation to transition. *The Counseling Psychologist*, 9: 2–18.

Schmid, A.H. (1991) The deficiency model: An exploration of current approaches to late-life disorders. *Psychiatry*, 54: 358–367.

Schmidt, P.J. and Rubinow, D.R. (1991) Menopause-related affective disorders: A justification for further study. *American Journal of Psychiatry*, 148: 844–852.

Schreiner-Engel, P., Schiani, R.C., Smith, H., and White, D. (1981) Sexual arousability and the menstrual cycle. *Psychosomatic Medicine*, 43: 199–213.

Schrott, H.G., Legault, C., Stefanick, M.L., Miller, V.T., Larosa, J., Wood, P.D., and Lippel, K. (1994) Lipids in postmenopausal women: Baseline findings of the Postmenopausal Estrogen/Progestin Interventions Trial. *Journal of Women's Health*, 3: 155–164.

Schrott, H.G., Bittner, V., Vittinghoff, E., Herrington, D.M., and Hulley, S. (1997) Adherence to National Cholesterol Education Program treatment goals in postmenopausal women with heart disease. *Journal of the American Medical Association*, 277: 1281–1286.

Schulz, J.H. (1997) Ask older women: Are the elderly better off? *Journal of Aging and Social Policy*, 9: 7–12.

Schulz, R. and Hanusa, B.H. (1978) Long-term effects of control and predictability-enhancing interventions: Findings and ethical issues. *Journal of Personality and Social Psychology*, 36: 1194–1201.

Schwartz, J., Freeman, R., and Frishman, W. (1995) Clinical pharmacology of estrogens: Cardiovascular actions and cardioprotective benefits of replacement therapy in postmenopausal women. *Journal of Clinical Pharmacology*, 35: 1–16.

Schwingl, P.J., Hulka, B.S., and Harlow, S.D. (1994) Risk factors for menopausal hot flashes. *Obstetrics and Gynecology*, 84: 29–34.

Seaman, B. and Seaman, G. (1977) *Women and the Crisis in Sex Hormones*. New York: Rawson Associates.

Seeman, E. (1993) Osteoporosis in men: Epidemiology, pathophysiology, and treatment possibilities. *American Journal of Medicine*, 95: 22S–28S.

Seeman, T.E. and McEwen, B.S. (1996) Impact of social environment characteristics on neuroendocrine regulation. *Psychosomatic Medicine*, 58: 459–471.

Seligman, M.E.P. (1975) *Helplessness*. San Francisco: Freeman.

Sener, A.B., Seckin, N.C., Ozmen, S., Gokmen, O., Dogu, N., and Ekici, E. (1996) The effects of hormone replacement therapy on uterine fibroids in postmenopausal women. *Fertility and Sterility*, 65: 354–357.

Shangold, M.M., Gatz, M.L., and Thysen, B. (1981) Acute effects of exercise on plasma concentrations of prolactin and testosterone in recreational women runners. *Fertility and Sterility*, 35: 699–702.

Sheehy, G. (1982) *Menopause: The Silent Passage*. New York: Random House.

Shephard, R.J. (1993) Exercise and aging: Extending independence in older adults. *Geriatrics*, 48: 61–64.

Sherwin, B.B.(1993) Menopause: myths and realities. In D.E. Stewart and N.L. Stotland (eds) *Psychological aspects of women's health care: The Interface between Psychiatry and Obstetrics and Gynecology*. Washington DC: American Psychatric Press (pp. 227–248).

Shock, N.W., Greulich, R.C., Andres, R., Arenberg, D., Costa, P.T., Lakatta, E.G., and Tobin, J.D. (1984) *Normal Human Aging: The Baltimore Longitudinal Study of Aging*. Washington DC: U.S. Government Printing Office.

Shumaker, S.A. and Smith, T.R. (1995) Women and coronary heart disease: A psychological perspective. In A.L. Stanton and S.J. Gallant (eds) *The Psychology of Women's Health: Progress and Challenges in Research and Application*. Washington DC: American Psychological Association (pp. 25–50).

Sidney, K.J., Shephard, R.J., and Harrison, J.E. (1977) Endurance training and body composition of the elderly. *American Journal of Clinical Nutrition*, 30: 326–333.

Silberstein, S.D. (1995) Migraine and women. *Postgraduate Medicine*, 97: 147–153.

Silver, J.J. and Einhorn, T.A. (1995) Osteoporosis and aging. *Clinical Orthopaedics and Related Research*, 316: 10–20.

Silverstein, M.D., Heit, J.A., Mohr, D.N., Petterson, T.M., O'Fallon, W.M., and Melton, L.J. (1998) Trends in the incidence of deep vein thrombosis and pulmonary embolism. *Archives of Internal Medicine*, 158: 585–593.

Siminoski, K. and Josse, R.G. (1996) Prevention and management of osteoporosis: consensus statements from the Scientific Advisory Board of the Osteoporosis Society of Canada. 9. Calcitonin in the treatment of osteoporosis. *Canadian Medical Association Journal*, 155: 962–965.

Simon, D., Senan, C., Garnier, P., Saint-Paul, M., Garat, E., Thibult, N., and Papoz, L. (1990) Effects of oral contraceptives on carbohydrate and lipid metabolism in a health population: The Telecom Study. *American Journal of Obstetrics and Gynecology*, 163: 382–387.

Simon, G., Gater, R., Kisely, S., and Piccinelli, M. (1996) Somatic symptoms of distress: An international primary care study. *Psychosomatic Medicine*, 58: 481–488.

Simoneau, G.G. and Leibowitz, H.W. (1996) Posture, gait, and falls. In J.E. Birren and K.W. Schaie (eds) *Handbook of the Psychology of Aging* (4th edn). New York: Academic Press (pp. 204–217).

Skolnick, A.A. (1992) Is "male menopause" real or just an excuse? *Journal of the American Medical Association*, 64: 762–769.

Slaven, L. and Lee, C. (1997) Mood and symptom reporting among middle-aged women: The relationship between menopausal status, hormone replacement therapy, and exercise participation. *Health Psychology*, 16: 203–208.

Smith, D.C., Prentice, R., Thompson, D.J., and Herrmann, W.L. (1975) Association of exogenous estrogen and endometrial carcinoma. *New England Journal of Medicine*, 293: 1164–1167.

Smith, R.N.J. and Studd, J.W.W. (1993) Recent advances in hormone replacement therapy. *British Journal of Hospital Medicine*, 49: 799–808.

Smith-Rosenberg, C. (1985) Puberty to menopause: The cycle of femininity in nineteenth-century America. In C. Smith-Rosenberg (ed.) *Disorderly Conduct*. New York: Knopf.

Sojka, J.E. (1995) Magnesium supplementation and osteoporosis. *Nutrition Reviews*, 53: 71–80.

Solomon, S.J., Kurzer, M.S. and Calloway, D.H. (1982) Menstrual cycle and basal metabolic rate in women. *American Journal of Clinical Nutrition*, 36: 611–616.

Somer, E. (1997) Managing menopause with diet. *Better Homes and Gardens*, March: 102–104.

Sommer, B. (1973) The effect of menstruation on cognitive and perceptual motor behavior: A review. *Psychosomatic Medicine*, 35: 515–534.

Soroko, S., Holbrook, T.L., Edelstein, S., and Barrett-Connor, E. (1994) Lifetime milk consumption and bone mineral density in older women. *American Journal of Public Health*, 84: 1319–1322.

Sowers, J.R. (1998) Diabetes mellitus and cardiovascular disease in women. *Archives of Internal Medicine*, 158: 617–621.

Stafford, R.S., Saglam, D., Causino, N., and Blumenthal, D. (1997) Low rates of hormone replacement in visits to United States primary care physicians. *American Journal of Obstetrics and Gynecology*, 177: 381–387.

Stanford, J.L (1996) The benefits of hormone replacement therapy outweigh the breast-cancer risks for some women. *Journal of NIH Research*, 8: 40–45.

Stanley, H.L., Schmitt, B.P., Poses, R.M., and Deiss, W.P. (1991) Does hypogonadism contribute to the occurrence of a minimal trauma hip fracture in elderly men? *Journal of the American Geriatric Society*, 39: 766–771.

Staudinger, U.M., Cornelius, S.W., and Baltes, P.B. (1989) The aging of intelligence: Potential and limits. *Annals of the American Academy of Political and Social Sciences*, 503: 43–59.

Stavraky, K.M., Collins, J.A., Donner, A., and Wells, G.A. (1981) A comparison of estrogen use by women with endometrial cancer, gynecological disorders, and other illnesses. *American Journal of Obstetrics and Gynecology*, 1141: 547–555.

Steiner, D. and Marcopulos, B. (1991) Depression in the elderly. *Nursing Clinics of North America*, 26: 585–600.

Stellato, R.K., Crawford, S.L., McKinlay, S.M., and Longcope, C. (1995) Is FSH a marker of menopause? Paper presented at the North American Menopause Society Meeting, San Francisco.

Stepan, J.J., Lachman, M., Zverina, J., Pacovsky, V., and Baylink, D.J. (1989) Castrated men exhibit bone loss: effect of calcitonin treatment on biochemical indices of bone remodeling. *Journal of Clinical Endocrinology and Metabolism*, 69: 523–530.

Stevens, J. (1994) Relationship between personality traits and level of cognitive structural organization. Unpublished Master's Thesis, Southern Illinois University, Carbondale, Illinois.

Stevens, J., Kumanyika, S.K., and Keil, J.E. (1994) Attitudes toward body size and dieting: differences between elderly Black and White women. *American Journal of Public Health*, 84: 1322–1325.

Stevenson, J.C., Crook, D., and Godsland, I. (1993) Influence of age and menopause on serum lipids and lipoproteins in healthy women. *Atherosclerosis*, 98: 83–90.

Stewart, A., King, A.C., and Haskell, W.L. (1993) Endurance exercise and health-related quality of life in 50–60 year old adults. *Gerontologist*, 33: 782–789.

Stini, W.A. (1995) Osteoporosis in biocultural perspective. *Annual Review of Anthropology*, 24: 397–421.

Stock, J.L., Bell, N.H., Chestnut, C.H., Ensrud, K.E., Genant, H.K., Harris, S.T., McClung, M.R., Singer, F.R., Yood, R.A., Prior-Tillotson, S., Wei, L., and Santora, A.D. (1997) Increments in bone mineral density of the lumbar spine and hip and suppression of bone turnover are maintained after discontinuation of alendronate in postmenopausal women. *American Journal of Medicine*, 103: 291–297.

Stones, M.J. and Kozma, A. (1996) Activity, exercise, and behavior. In J.E. Birren and K.W. Schaie (eds) *Handbook of the Psychology of Aging* (4th edn). New York: Academic Press (pp. 338–352).

Strassman, B.I. (1997) Energy economy in the evolution of menstruation. *Evolutionary Anthropology*, 5: 157–164.

Strause, L.A., Saltman, P., Smith, K.T., Bracker, M., and Andon, M.B. (1994) Spinal bone loss in postmenopausal women supplemented with calcium and trace minerals. *Journal of Nutrition*, 124: 1060–1064.

Strickland, B. (1988) Sex-related differences in health and illness. *Psychology of Women Quarterly*, 12: 381–399.

Strong, P.M. (1979) Sociological imperialism and the progression of medicine. *Social Science and Medicine*, 13A: 199–215.

Studd, J. (1989) Prophylactic oophorectomy. *British Journal of Obstetrics and Gynaecology*, 96: 506–509.

—— (1997) Letter. *British Medical Journal*, 313: 1229.

Studd, J.W.W., Chakravarti, S., and Oram, D. (1977) The climacteric. In R.B. Greenblatt and J. Studd (eds) *The Menopause: Clinics in Obstetrics and Gynaecology* vol. 4. London: Saunders.

Sturdee, D.W., Wade-Evans, T., Paterson, M.E.L., Thom, M., and Studd, J.W.W. (1978) Relations between bleeding pattern, endometrial histology, and oestrogen treatment in menopausal women. *British Medical Journal*, 1: 1575–1577.

Sviland, M.A. (1978) A program of sexual liberation and growth in the elderly. In R.L. Solnick (ed.) *Sexuality and Aging*. Los Angeles: Southern California Press.

Swinburn, B.A., Walter, L.G., Arroll, B., Tilyard, M.W., and Russell, D.G. (1998) The green prescription study: A randomized, controlled trial of written exercise advice provided by general practitioners. *American Journal of Public Health*, 88: 288–291.

Szasz, T. (1980) *Sex by Prescription*. New York: Anchor Press/Doubleday.

Tang, M., Jacobs, D., Stern, Y., Marder, K., Schofield, P., Gurland, B., Andrews, H., and Mayeux, R. (1996) Effects of oestrogen during menopause on risk and age at onset of Alzheimer's disease. *Lancet*, 348: 429–432.

Tataryn, I.V., Lomax, P., Meldrum, D.R., Bajorek, J.G., Chesarek, W., and Judd, H.L. (1981) Objective techniques for the assessment of postmenopausal hot flashes. *Obstetrics and Gynecology*, 57: 340–344.

Thaul, S. and Hotra, D. (1993) *An Assessment of the NIH Women's Health Initiative*. Washington DC: National Academy Press.

Thomson, J. and Oswald, I. (1977) Effect of oestrogen on the sleep, mood, and anxiety of menopausal women. *British Medical Journal*, 1: 1575–1577.

Thompson, L.W., Gallagher-Thompson, D., Futterman, A., Gilewski, M.J., and Peterson, J. (1991) The effects of late-life spousal bereavement over a 30-month interval. *Psychology and Aging*, 6: 434–441.

Thompson, W. (1995) Estrogen replacement therapy in practice: Trends and issues. *American Journal of Obstetrics and Gynecology*, 173: 990–993.

Thorneycroft, I. (1995) Practical aspects of hormone replacement therapy. *Progress in Cardiology*, 38: 243–255.

Thorngren, K-G. (1995) Fractures in the elderly. *Acta Orthopedia Scandinavica*, 66: 208–210.

Thune, I., Brenn, T., Lund, E., and Gaard, M. (1997) Physical activity and the risk of breast cancer. *New England Journal of Medicine*, 336: 1269–1275.

Tolley, G., Kenkel, D., Fabian, R. and Webster, D. (1994) The use of health values in policy. In G. Tolley, D. Kenkel, and R. Fabian (eds) *Valuing health for policy: An economic approach*. Chicago: University of Chicago Press.

Tortiola, A.L. and Mathur, D.N. (1986) Menstrual dysfunction in Nigerian athletes. *British Journal of Obstetrics and Gynaecology*, 93: 979–985.

Travis, C.B., Gressley, D.L., and Phillippi, R.H. (1993) Medical decision making, gender, and coronary heart disease. *Journal of Women's Health*, 2: 269–279.

Travis, C.B., Gressley, D.L. and Adams, P.L. (1995) Health care policy and practice for women's health. In A.L. Stanton and S.J. Gallant (eds) *The Psychology of Women's Health: Progress and Challenges in Research and Application*. Washington DC: American Psychological Association (pp. 531–565).

Tremollieres, F.A., Pouilles, J-M., and Ribot, C. (1993) Vertebral postmenopausal bone loss is reduced in overweight women: A longitudinal study in 155 early postmenopausal women. *Journal of Clinical Endocrinology and Metabolism*, 77: 683–686.

Tremollieres, F.A., Pouilles, J-M., and Ribot, C.A. (1996) Relative influence of age and menopause on total and regional body composition changes in postmenopausal women. *American Journal of Obstetrics and Gynecology*, 175: 1594–1600.

Troisi, R.J., Speizer, F.E., Willett, W.C., Trichopoulos, D., and Rosner, B. (1995) Menopause, postmenopausal estrogen preparations, and the risk of adult-onset asthma. *American Journal of Respiratory Critical Care*, 152: 1183–1188.

Tucci, J.R., Tonino, R.P., Emkey, R.D., Peverly, C.A., Kher, U., and Santora, A.C. (1996) Effect of three years of oral Alendronate treatment in postmenopausal women with osteoporosis. *American Journal of Medicine*, 101: 488–501.

Tuppurainen, M., Kroger, H., Honkanen, R., Puntila, E., Huopio, J., Saarikoski, S., and Alhava, E. (1995) Risks of perimenopausal fractures – a prospective population-based study. *Acta Obstetrica Gynecologia Scandinavia*, 74: 624–628.

Unger, R. and Crawford, M. (1992) *Women and Gender*. New York: McGraw-Hill.

Utian, W.H. (1972) The mental tonic effect of oestrogens administered to ooporectomized females. *South African Medical Journal*, 46: 1079–1082.

—— (1990) Moderator for panel discussion I. *Obstetrics and Gynecology*, 75: 15S–17S.

Van de Mheen, H., Stronks, K., Van den Bos, J., and MacKenbach, J.P. (1997) The contribution of childhood environment to the explanation of socio-economic inequalities in health in adult life: A retrospective study. *Social Science and Medicine*, 44: 13–24.

Vandenbroucke, J.P. and Helmerhorst, F.M. (1996) Risk of venous thrombosis with hormone replacement therapy. *Lancet*, 348: 976.

van der Mooren, M.J., Demacker, P.N.M., Blom, H.J., de Rijke, Y.B., and Rolland, R. (1997) The effect of sequential three-monthly hormone replacement therapy on several cardiovascular risk estimators in postmenopausal women. *Fertility and Sterility*, 67: 67–73.

Varas-Lorenzo, C., Garcia-Rodriguez, L.A., Cattaruzzi, C., Troncon, M.G., Agostinis, L., and Perez-Gutthann, S. (1998) Hormone replacement therapy and the risk of hospitalization for venous thromboembolism: A population-based study in Southern Europe. *American Journal of Epidemiology*, 147: 387–390.

Vaux, A. (1988) *Social Support: Theory, Research and Intervention*. New York: Praeger.

Voda, A. (1982) Menopausal hot flash. In A. Voda, M. Dinnerstein, and S.R. O'Connell (eds) *Changing perspectives on Menopause*. Austin: University of Texas Press.

—— (1993) A journey to the center of the cell: Understanding the physiology and endocrinology of menopause. In J.C. Callahan (ed.) *Menopause*. Bloomington: Indiana University Press (pp. 160–193).

Wallhagen, M.I., Strawbridge, W.J., Kaplan, G.A., and Cohen, R.D. (1994) Impact of internal health locus of control on health outcomes for older men and women: A longitudinal perspective. *The Gerontologist*, 34: 299–306.

Walling, M., Andersen, B.L., Johnson, S.R. (1990) Hormonal replacement therapy for postmenopausal women: A review of sexual outcomes and related gynecologic effects. *Archives of Sexual Behavior*, 19: 119–137.

Wallston, B. and Wallston, K. (1978) Locus of control and health: A review of the literature. *Health Education Monographs*, 6: 107–117.

Walsh, B.W. (1992) Estrogen replacement and heart disease. *Clinical Obstetrics and Gynecology*, 35: 894–900.

Walsh, B. and Schiff, I. (1990) Vasomotor flushes. *Annals of the New York Academy of Sciences*, 592: 346–356.

Walsh, M. (1997) Women's behavior: Do mothers harm their children when they work outside the home? In M. Walsh (ed.) *Women, Men and Gender: Ongoing Debates*. New Haven: Yale University Press.

Watts, N.B., Notelovitz, M., Timmons, M.C., Addison, W.A., Wiita, B., and Downey, L.J. (1995) Comparison of oral estrogens and estrogens plus androgen on bone mineral density, menopausal symptoms, and lipid–lipoprotein profiles in surgical menopause. *Obstetrics and Gynecology*, 85: 529–537.

Weaver, C.M. and Plawecki, K.L. (1994) Dietary calcium: adequacy of a vegetarian diet. *American Journal of Clinical Nutrition*, 59: 1238S–1241S.

Wechsler, D. (1958) *The Measurement and Appraisal of Adult Intelligence*. Baltimore: Williams & Wilkins.

Weg, R.B. (1983) The physiological perspective. In R.B. Weg (ed.) *Sexuality in the Later Years: Roles and Behavior*. New York: Academic Press.

Weideger, P. (1977) *Menstruation and Menopause*. New York: Knopf.

Weiner, B. (1972) *Theories of Motivation: From Mechanism to Cognition*. Chicago: Rand McNally.

Weinstein, L., Bewtra, C., and Gallagher, J.C. (1990) Evaluation of a continuous combined low-dose regimen of estrogen–progestin for treatment of the menopausal patient. *American Journal of Obstetrics and Gynecology*, 162: 1534–1542.

215

Weiss, K.M. (1981) Evolutionary perspectives on human aging. In P.T. Amoss and S. Harrell (eds) *Other Ways of Growing Old*. Stanford: Stanford University Press (pp. 25–58).

Weksler, M.E. (1995) Hormone replacement therapy for men: Has the time come? *Geriatrics*, 50: 52–55.

Wever, R.A. (1982) Behavioral aspects of circadian rhythmicity. In F.M. Brown and R.C. Graeber (eds) *Rhythmic Aspects of Behavior*. Hillsdale NJ: Lawrence Erlbaum.

Whitehead, M.I. (1988) Effects of hormone replacement therapy on cardiovascular disease: An interview. *American Journal of Obstetrics and Gynecology*, 158: 1658–1659.

Whitehead, M.I. and Godfree, V. (1997) Venous thrombo-embolism and hormone replacement therapy. *Bailliere's Clinical Obstetrics and Gynecology*, 11: 587–599.

Whitehead, M.I., McQueen, J., Minardi, J., and Campbell, S. (1978) Progestogen modification of estrogen-induced proliferation in climacteric women. In I.D. Cooke (ed.) *The Role of Estrogen/Progesterone in the Management of Menopause*. Baltimore: University Park Press.

Wild, R.A. (1995) Obesity, lipids, cardiovascular risk, and androgen excess. *American Journal of Medicine*, 98: 27S–32S.

Williams, P. and Lord, S.R. (1995) Predictors of adherence to a structured exercise program for older women. *Psychology and Aging*, 10: 617–624.

Williams, P., Wood, P.D., Haskell, W.L., and Vranizan, K. (1982) The effects of running mileage and duration on plasma lipoprotein levels. *Journal of the American Medical Association*, 247: 2674–2679.

Wilson, B. (1997) *Race and heart disease*. Presented on National Public Radio, February 13, 1997. Transcript from Federal Document Clearing House, Washington, DC.

Wilson, R. (1966) *Feminine Forever*. New York: M. Evans and Company.

Wishart, J.M., Need, A.G., Horowitz, M., Morris, H.A., and Nordin, B.E.C. (1995) Effect of age on bone density and bone turnover in men. *Clinical Endocrinology*, 42: 141–146.

Wolinsky, F.D. and Johnson, R.J. (1992) Perceived health status and mortality among older men and women. *Journal of Gerontology*, 47: S304–S312.

Wolpe, J. (1958) *Psychotherapy and Reciprocal Inhibition*. Stanford: Stanford University Press.

Woolf, V. (1929/1957) *A Room of One's Own*. New York: Harcourt, Brace, & World.

Wysowski, D.K., Golden, L., and Burke, L. (1995) Use of menopausal estrogens and medroxyprogesterone in the United State, 1982–1992. *Obstetrics and Gynecology*, 85: 6–10.

Yaffe, K., Sawaya, G., Liebeburg, I., and Grady, D. (1998) Estrogen therapy in postmenopausal women: Effects on cognitive function and dementia. *Journal of the American Medical Association*, 279: 688–695.

Zita, J.N. (1993) Heresy in the female body: The rhetorics of menopause. In J.C. Callahan (ed.) *Menopause*. Bloomington: Indiana University Press (pp. 59–78).

Zweifel, J.E. and O'Brien, W.H. (1997) A meta-analysis of the effect of hormone replacement therapy upon depressed mood. *Psychoneuroendocrinology*, 22: 189–212.

AUTHOR INDEX

SUBJECT INDEX

adipose tissue 62, 63, 65, 74, 83, 134
adrenal cortex 74, 77
aerobic capacity 55, 56, 61
aerobic fitness *see* aerobic capacity
alcohol 65–6, 67, 89, 98, 128, 129, 138,
    152, 162, 163
Alzheimer's disease 69, 91, 92
amenorrhea 59, 87
androcentrism 2, 3, 4, 8, 9
androgens 62, 65, 73, 74, 76, 86, 104, 113,
    118, 121, 132, 133, 153
anger 56, 119, 120
angina pectoris 127
anterior pituitary 70, 71, 75
antidepressants 33, 38–9, 155, 178;
    selective serotonin reuptake inhibitors
    39; tricylic 39
anxiety 42, 56, 60, 80, 111, 114, 119, 121,
    143
arthritis 57
atherosclerosis 127, 131
atrophic vaginitis 79, 80, 81, 114
attention 40
autonomic nervous system 119

bereavement 25, 28, 29, 32, 38
biological determinism *see* reductionism
biological rhythms 29, 30
bisphosphonates 167
blood pressure 131, 132, 136, 140, 146,
    171
body mass index (BMI) 63
bone loss 150, 152, 153, 154, 155, 156,
    157, 159, 160, 161, 163, 164, 165, 167,
    169
bone mineral density (BMD) 54, 62, 64,
    65, 66, 90, 101, 151, 152, 153, 154,
    155, 156, 158, 159, 160, 161, 162, 163,
    165, 168

caffeine 53, 63–4, 67, 128, 158
calcitonin 150, 168
calcium 53, 54, 63, 146, 150, 152, 153,
    155, 156, 157, 158, 160, 161, 163, 168,
    172
cancer x, 37, 56, 62, 64, 86, 91, 95, 96,
    101, 104, 122, 130, 136, 167; breast 65,
    86, 90, 89, 93, 94, 95, 96, 100, 102,
    103, 146, 169; ovarian 92, 93, 103;
    uterine 88, 89, 92, 103, 136, 145, 169
cardiovascular disease 55, 56, 57, 62, 63,
    64, 65, 66, 69, 77, 86, 90, 94, 96, 98,
    99, 100, 102, 105, 106, 107, 122,
    125–48, 161, 174
cardiovascular system 24, 53, 54, 97,
    125–48; physiology 127
caregiving 26, 27, 28, 47
castration x, xi, 35, 43, 69, 71, 72, 73, 74,
    76, 78, 82, 83, 88, 93, 94, 95, 98, 99,
    100, 103, 104, 107, 112, 116, 118, 120,
    132, 134, 135, 137, 144, 145, 146, 147,
    150, 153, 154, 161, 164, 165, 167, 169
Centre for Epidemiologic Studies
    Depression Scale 32
child care 2, 28, 30, 60
cholesterol 25, 53, 54, 63, 96, 125, 126,
    127, 128, 129, 130, 131, 138, 139, 141,
    142, 147, 171; *see also* lipids
cigarette smoking 54, 64–5, 67, 84, 106,
    126, 128, 129, 131, 138, 145, 146, 153,
    162, 171, 172
circadian rhythms/desynchronization 29,
    30
climacteric *see* menopause

225